# Rudiments of Logic

George Myro
Mark Bedau
Tim Monroe

Prentice Hall, Inc.,
Englewood Cliffs, New Jersey 07632

*Library of Congress Cataloging-in-Publication Data*

Myro, George.
  Rudiments of logic.

  Includes index.
  1. Logic.  I. Bedau, Mark.  II. Monroe, Tim.
III. Title.
BC71.M96  1987      160      86-25163
  ISBN  0-13-783648-1


Editorial/production supervision: Barbara Alexander
Cover design: 20/20 Services, Inc.
Manufacturing buyer: Harry P. Baisley

*book design by r.t. monroe*

Printed in the United States of America

10  9  8  7  6  5  4  3  2  1


ISBN 0-13-783648-1   01


PRENTICE-HALL INTERNATIONAL (UK) LIMITED, *London*
PRENTICE-HALL OF AUSTRALIA PTY. LIMITED, *Sydney*
PRENTICE-HALL CANADA INC., *Toronto*
PRENTICE-HALL HISPANOAMERICANA, S.A., *Mexico*
PRENTICE-HALL OF INDIA PRIVATE LIMITED, *New Delhi*
PRENTICE-HALL OF JAPAN, INC., *Tokyo*
PRENTICE-HALL OF SOUTHEAST ASIA PTE. LTD., *Singapore*
EDITORA PRENTICE-HALL DO BRASIL, LTDA., *Rio de Janeiro*

*for*
*Aber and Paul*

# Rudiments of Logic

# Preface

This book is an introduction to formal logic. Our goal is to present logic in a way that is especially natural and easy to grasp. We want to make formal logic accessible even to those who might have had difficulty learning logic from traditional, more abstract presentations.

Accordingly, we develop logic out of a consideration of the logical features of ordinary language, and we pay special attention to the relationship between reasoning in ordinary language and in abstract symbolism. Starting with examples and intuitive ideas, we work up to precise formulations. In this way, the formal aspects of logic are developed naturally and intuitively, rather than artificially and arbitrarily.

We also strive to be especially sensitive to *philosophical* issues concerning logic. We try to indicate the philosophical importance of features of systems of logic and to identify philosophical issues concerning logic, while trying to avoid taking prejudicial stands on such issues. In the long run our aim is to promote and facilitate discussion in the philosophy of logic.

The book has five main parts. The first part introduces the notions of a line of reasoning, validity and invalidity, and logical form. The second part covers truth-functional logic, including translations, derivations, and truth-value assignments. The third part covers quantificational logic, including identity theory. In the fourth part, we look into three regions of logic that hold special interest for philosophers: functors, vacuous terms, and definite descriptions. The fifth and final part of the book is an introduction to formal metalogic, covering syntax, semantics, and derivability in the systems of logic covered earlier.

We have tried to write this book in such a way that it can be read on its own. We take special pains to tutor the reader in how to do logic. There are numerous exercises of varying degrees of difficulty, and some representative exercises are answered at the end of the book. A companion instructor's manual is available, containing more answers to exercises.

Many readers will find that they can work through most of the book in one semester, even if they have no prior knowledge of logic or mathematics. In general, one chapter covers the amount of material that an instructor can present in an hour lecture. In Part V, however, material is more compressed; a chapter might take a week of lectures to cover, and some of the exercises are quite complicated and difficult.

Introductory logic books are usually written with a keen eye on their predecessors in the field, and ours is no exception. We would especially like to acknowledge our debt to Benson Mates' *Elementary Logic*, E. J. Lemmon's *Beginning Logic*, and W.V.O. Quine's *Methods of Logic*. We have enjoyed and profited from the help of a generation of philosophy students at the University of California at Berkeley, whose advice is incorporated herein. We thank Savannah Ross, Yulia Motofuji, and Julianne Martinson for expertly typing and retyping the original class notes. We would also like to recognize the many helpful contributions of Aaron Amos and the keen editing talents of Ariana Graff and Tenli Yavneh.

Although this book is co-authored, the heart of the book comes from class handouts that George Myro developed and used for years at Berkeley. When Mark Bedau and Tim Monroe taught with him, we decided to write an introductory formal logic text based on the class handouts. Three and a half years later, this book is the result of our efforts.

| | |
|---|---|
| George Myro | Berkeley, CA |
| Mark Bedau | Hanover, NH |
| Tim Monroe | Berkeley, CA |

September 1986

# Rudiments of Logic

# PART I

## Introduction

Our first task in studying logic is to get clear on what exactly logic *is*. This involves, at least, understanding what objects logic treats, how it goes about treating them, and what we can hope to learn in studying logic. These are the topics to be covered in the following three chapters.

# Chapter 1

# Good and Bad Reasoning

**1. The Subject Matter of Logic.** Here is a little story that may or may not be true:

> At a soirée in seventeenth-century France, a somewhat worldly abbé (head of a monastery) decided to titillate the guests by telling something which his vows, strictly speaking, forbade him to tell. You know, he said (in French, of course), the first person ever to confess to me was a murderer. There was a very mild flutter of excitement. And then a well-known marquis (French nobleman) entered and, seeing the abbé, rushed to him, shook his hand, and, turning to the guests, announced: Mesdames and messieurs, I was the very first person to confess to the abbé. There was a somewhat awkward silence. The guests drew their conclusions. Madame de Burgundy, in particular, thought to herself: Aha, so the marquis is a murderer. Madame de Chablis, however, having no doubt had too much of the eponymous wine, thought: Oh, dear, so the poor abbé is a murderer.

This little story can bring to mind quite a large number of topics which are of great interest from the point of view of logic and the philosophy of logic. But let us now concentrate on what this story can illustrate about the subject matter of logic.

Apparently, according to the story, both Madame de Burgundy and Madame de Chablis inferred, concluded, or reasoned from something to something. What they reasoned *from* was the same for both of them: what the abbé said and what the marquis said. What they reasoned *to* was different for each of them: that the marquis was a murderer, and that the abbé was a murderer, respectively. We can say that we have here two *lines of reasoning*: the one that Madame de Burgundy "went through" and the one that Madame de Chablis "went through".

If so, surely it is *obvious* that Burgundy reasoned "well" and that Chablis reasoned "badly", that the line of reasoning Madame de Burgundy went through is a "good" one and the one that Madame de Chablis went through is a "bad" one.[1] We may say, tentatively, that this distinction between "good" and "bad" lines of reasoning, which our story (as conveyed to us) exemplifies, *is the main part of the subject matter of logic.*

We should note that it is lines of reasoning themselves that are "good" or "bad", independently of who goes through them or whether anyone ever does. The line of reasoning from what the abbé said and what the marquis said to what Burgundy thought would have been just as "good" even if no one had gone through it; it would have been just as "good" a line of reasoning even if what the abbé said had *not* been said (or thought) by him (or anyone else), if what the marquis said had *not* been said (or thought) by him (or anyone else), and if what Burgundy thought had *not* been thought (or said) by her (or anyone else). Similarly, the line of reasoning from what the abbé said and what the marquis said to what Chablis thought would have been a "bad" one if . . . .[2]

Evidently, we must distinguish *what* is—or can be—said, thought, surmised, assumed, supposed, etc., from someone's say*ing*, think*ing*, assum*ing*, suppos*ing*, etc., it. The latter are psychological episodes and are irrelevant to the main part of the subject matter of logic. The former make up the main part of the subject matter of logic and are not psychological episodes.[3]

Now, what is it that the abbé said? It is *that the first person ever to confess to the abbé was a murderer.*

---

[1] In fact, Chablis seems to have reasoned *so* "badly" that one may need to find an explanation of how she could have made such a mistake (the wine?) or, perhaps, even of *what kind* of mistake it might be (perhaps she misheard, or misunderstood, or misremembered what she heard?); perhaps her mistake is not the one we have described her as making. There are, of course, many different interpretations one may put on the story. For example, perhaps Chablis did not reason from what the abbé said and what the marquis said but, rather, from what the abbé said and something else she believed, namely, that any priest who reveals that someone who confessed to him was a murderer is himself "unconsciously confessing" to being a murderer, in which case she would have reasoned "well". But how to interpret the story is not the relevant issue from the point of view of logic; rather, it is something the story brings to mind.

[2] This is why it is irrelevant to logic what Chablis actually did say.

[3] It is fair to say that we have now landed in a rather controversial issue in the philosophy of logic: what *are* the items which make up the main part of the subject matter of logic? Leaving a more thorough inquiry into this issue to a later study of philosophy of logic, let us try, as much as possible, to say only what seems necessary for continuing our study of logic—hoping that, subject to possibly subtle reconstruals and changes of terminology, what we say will be agreed to by almost all serious logicians.

What is it that the marquis said? It is *that the marquis was the very first person ever to confess to the abbé.*

What is it that Burgundy thought? *That the marquis is a murderer.*

**2. Good Reasoning Defined.** We have noted that the line of reasoning *from* the first two statements *to* the third is a "good" one. But what makes the line of reasoning "good"? In what sense or way is it "good"? Well, the first two statements *imply,* or *entail,* or *have as a consequence* the third, or the third statements *is implied by,* or *is entailed by,* or *follows from* the first two. What does this mean? There is a way of thinking about it which is especially helpful for the study of logic: it is *impossible* that it should happen that the first and the second statements are *true* and the third is *false.* Or: *there is no possible situation* in which the first and the second are *true* and the third is *false.* That is, there is *no* possible situation in which

- that the first person to confess to the abbé was a murderer *is true,*

- that the first person to confess to the abbé was the marquis *is true,*

- that the marquis is a murderer *is false.*

On the other hand, there *is* a possible situation (at least one) in which

○ that the first person to confess to the abbé was a murderer *is true,*

○ that the first person to confess to the abbé was the marquis *is true,*

○ that the abbé is a murderer *is false.*

*That the first person ever to confess to the abbé was a murderer* and *that the very first person to confess to the abbé was the marquis* do *not* imply, entail, or have as a consequence *that the abbé was a murderer;* the third does *not* follow from, is *not* implied, or entailed by the first two. This is why (the sense or way in which) this line of reasoning is "bad".

There are many ways in which a line of reasoning may be "good" or "bad", at least in part depending on one's interests. But everyone wants to believe what is *true.* So one might think that those lines of reasoning which lead to what is *true* are especially "good", and those which lead to what is *false* are especially "bad". And this, no doubt, is correct. But the study of *this* distinction involves *more* than logic alone (for example, the theory of knowledge is likely to be involved). Logic concentrates on the related distinction between those lines of reasoning which are bound to lead to what is true *if* they start from what is true and those which are not like this. And, evidently, drawing this distinction does just half the job of drawing the former distinction. Nevertheless, we have so far spoken of "good" and "bad" lines of reasoning simply to enlist our intuitive beliefs and to indicate why the distinction logic studies is of interest and value. Now that we have the distinction more clearly in mind, we can kick away the scaffolding and replace our former talk about "good" and "bad" lines of reasoning with talk about the distinction between those lines of reasoning which are bound to lead to what is true *if* they start from what is true and those which are not like this.

**3. Preliminary Summary.** Let us fix more firmly in mind what we have already been talking about. We have been talking about four items:

(1)   what the abbé said,

(2)   what the marquis said,

(3)   what Burgundy thought (as a result),

(4)   what Chablis thought (as a result).

It is quite natural and informative to say that these items are:

(1)   that the first person ever to confess to the abbé was a murderer,

(2)   that the very first person to confess to the abbé was the marquis,

(3)   that the marquis was a murderer,

(4)   that the abbé was a murderer.

We see that:

(A)   there is no possible situation in which the first two are true and the third is false;

(B)   there is a possible situation in which the first two are true and the fourth is false.

This is what we mean when we say that:

(A)   the third item is implied by the first two,

(B)   the fourth item is not implied by the first two.

And we see that this is so independently of whether the items are said, thought, surmised, assumed, supposed, etc. by our personages or anyone else.

**4. Possibility and Impossibility.** We should also note the following: the fact that the first and the second items imply the third item, and the fact that the first and second items do not imply the fourth item are independent also of whether the items are *in fact* (in the *actual* possible situation) true or false. Either the abbé or the marquis (or both) may have spoken truly or falsely; the marquis may or may not be a murderer; the abbé may or may not be a murderer.[4] Regardless of all this, it remains true that there is no possible situation in which it is true that the first person ever to confess to the abbé is a murderer, it is true that the very first person to confess to the abbé is the marquis, and it is false that the marquis is a murderer. And, similarly regardless, it remains true that there is a possible situation in which the first two are true and it is false that the abbé is a murderer.

One might go so far as to say that logic is not interested in what is *in fact* true or false, but only in the *possibility* or *impossibility* of various combinations of truth and falsity. Logic is, as it were, interested in truth and falsity only once removed: in possibilities and impossibilities of truth and falsity. But of course there are truths *about* possibility and impossibility of truth and falsity, such as (A) and (B) above. So we would do better to say that logic seeks to collect—and systematize—truths about possibility and impossibility of various combinations of truth and falsity.

**Exercises**

---

1    In each group of statements listed below, can *all* the statements be true at the same time?

   (a)  Alfred is taller than Bertha.
        Bertha is not shorter than Alfred.

   (b)  Alfred is taller than Bertha.
        Bertha is at least as tall as Alfred.

   (c)  Alfred is Bertha's brother.
        Bertha is Charlie's sister.
        Alfred is not Charlie's brother.

   (d)  No two persons in this room have the same height.
        No one in this room is taller than everyone else in the room.

2    Decide whether the last statement in each group *might* be true, given the truth of the statement(s) listed.

   (a)  Given that:

          No two persons in this room have the same birthday.

        might the following statement be true?

          There are three persons in this room with the same birthday.

---

[4] Indeed, it is, after all, a *story*: the abbé and the marquis may not even have existed!

(b) Given that:

> Anyone related to Jones is related to Jones' sister.
> Anyone related to someone must be cordial to that person.
> Bert is related to Jones.

might the following statement be true?

> Bert is not cordial to Jones' sister.

3  Decide whether the last statement in each group *must* be true, given the truth of the statement(s) listed.

(a) Given that:

> Someone other than the butler killed the maid.
> The butler wore a red vest.

must the following statement be true?

> Whoever killed the maid did not wear a red vest.

(b) Given that:

> Either Smitty or Fenwick told the truth.
> Bert lied.
> Smitty lied if Bert did.

must the following statement be true?

> Fenwick told the truth.

4  Is the following line of reasoning valid?

> Buster always feels sad if the copier is broken.
> The copier is not broken.
> Therefore, Buster does not feel sad.

5  Reflect: what was the point of the story at the beginning of this chapter?

# Chapter 2

## Validity and Invalidity

**1. Terminology.** It is helpful to introduce some terminology. Items like (1)-(4) in the previous chapter are studied by logic with the aim of finding out whether it is possible or impossible for various combinations of them to be true or false. This is the crucially relevant feature of them, that they are (or at least can be) true or false in various possible situations. If we call being true and being false *truth-values*, then we can call the items which logic studies *truth-value bearers*. We can leave the study of further details of the nature of truth-value bearers to the philosophy of logic. Are they "abstract entities", or "mental entities", or "linguistic entities" (whatever these suggestions mean)? Indeed, there are three major positions in philosophy of logic, corresponding to the three suggestions. And there are three terms for the items we have been discussing that are more or less associated with the three positions, 'propositions', 'judgements', and 'sentences'. A fourth term, which is less associated with any of these three positions, is 'statement'. Each of these four terms attributes or suggests more than the neutral term 'truth-value bearers' does. Nevertheless, each of them is shorter and more familiar than the neutral term. We shall allow ourselves to use the terms more or less interchangeably, with 'statement' being used most frequently.

We can now say generally:

- A group of statements *implies* (or *entails, has as a consequence*) a statement if and only if there is *no* possible situation in which all the statements in the group are true and in which the remaining statement is false.

- A group of statements *does not imply* (or *does not entail, does not have as a consequence*) a statement if and only if there *is* a possible situation in which all the statements in the group are true and in which the remaining statement is false.

We can think of a *line of reasoning* (in one sense) as a combination of two things: a group of statements and a single statement. Let us call the statements in the group the *premises* of that line of reasoning and the single statement the *conclusion* of that line of reasoning. Then we can say:

- A line of reasoning is *valid* if and only if it is *impossible* for all its premises to be true and its conclusion false.

- A line of reasoning is *not valid* (or *invalid*) if and only if it is *possible* for all its premises to be true and its conclusion false.

**2. Possible Situations**. If we consider possible situations with respect to the truth-values of the premises and conclusion of a given line of reasoning, we see that all the possible situations are divided into four classes, and each possible situation must be in just one or another of the four classes:

Possible Situations

|                     | Class 1   | **Class 2** | Class 3        | Class 4        |
|---------------------|-----------|-------------|----------------|----------------|
| The premises are    | all *true* | all *true*  | *not* all true | *not* all true |
| The conclusion is   | *true*    | *false*     | *true*         | *false*        |

If the line of reasoning is *valid* (i.e., the premises *imply* the conclusion), then there will be *no* possible situations in Class 2. (Class 2 will be "empty".) And *vice versa*. Also, if the line of reasoning is *not* valid (i.e., the premises do *not* imply the conclusion), then there will be at least one possible situation in Class 2. And *vice versa*. Apart from this, nothing prevents the *actual* situation from being in any one of the four (kinds of) classes. From this we may expect that if we select any one of the four (kinds of) classes, then there will be a line of reasoning with respect to which the *actual* situation will fall into that (kind of) class. And, indeed, this is so. Further, there will be both a *valid* and an *invalid* line of reasoning of this sort, *with just one exception*: there will *not* be a *valid* line of reasoning in Class 2. That is to say, there are *no valid* arguments all of whose premises are true and whose conclusion is false. But there are invalid arguments like this. And there are both valid and invalid arguments of every other kind of distribution of truth-values.

A couple of observations may be made here. What we are here calling *lines of reasoning* are sometimes called *arguments* or *inferences* (and we shall ourselves sometimes use this terminology). Observe that they are *not* statements, but combinations of a group of statements with a single statement. Only statements are *true* or *false*. So lines of reasoning are *never* true and *never* false; they are always either *valid* or *invalid*. Furthermore, we have fallen into regarding a combination of *any* group of statements (the "premises") with *any* single statement (the "conclusion") as a line of reasoning, even if no one, however confused, would actually reason *from* those premises *to* that conclusion. This generalization does no harm. Finally, the group of premises may contain *any number* of statements: one, two, three, four, ..., a billion, infinitely many, or even *none at all* (as will become clear hereafter).

**3. The Obvious and Indirectly Obvious.** How shall we be studying the distinction between valid and invalid lines of reasoning? Where shall we look to make our discoveries? Well, in some cases it is *obvious* that a line of reasoning is valid, or that it is invalid. In these cases, we *already know* whether such a line of reasoning is valid or not. As soon as we attend to the line of reasoning, we are aware that it is valid or invalid, as the case may be. For example, as soon as we attend to the line of reasoning Madame de Burgundy is supposed to have gone through, we are aware that it is valid; and as soon as we attend to the line of reasoning Madame de Chablis is supposed to have gone through, we are aware that it is not valid. Unless some such cases were *obvious* to us, we couldn't even begin the study of logic (or of anything else, for that matter!). Therefore, we must *already know* certain things in order to begin the study of logic.

Do we perhaps already know not just part but *everything* which logic studies? There may be a sense in which this is true,[1] but there certainly is a sense in which this is *not* true. There are plenty of lines of reasoning that are *not at all obviously* valid or invalid. Here is a little story which illustrates a moderately complex example:

> A somewhat sadistic warden decided to have some fun with his three prisoners. All three had taken courses in logic and became proficient at infallibly recognizing as valid any line of reasoning which was in fact valid, and as invalid any line of reasoning which was in fact invalid. Two of them had perfect eyesight, but the third was blind. All three knew all of this about each other. The warden, having turned off the light in the cell, brought in five hats, two of them red and three white. He placed one hat on each of the prisoners' heads and told them what he had done. Then he turned on the lights. Each of the two sighted prisoners could see the hats on the heads of the other two prisoners, but not the hat on his own head. The blind prisoner of course could see nothing, a fact of which all three prisoners were aware. The warden then announced that he would release any prisoner who could recognize as valid any

---

[1] Work for the philosophy of logic, again!

line of reasoning from the information which that prisoner had
to a conclusion as to whether the hat on that prisoner's head
was red or white. He asked one of the sighted prisoners. The
prisoner said that there was no such line of reasoning. Then
the second sighted prisoner was asked and replied that there
was no such line of reasoning in his case either. All three prisoners could hear this interrogation. The warden thought that
the blind man, being unable to see anything, had less information than the other two prisoners and so wouldn't be able to
answer successfully. But the blind man said: There is a valid
line of reasoning from the information I have to the conclusion
that my hat is...

Now, we have all the information that the blind prisoner has. And there
are two lines of reasoning, one from that information to the conclusion
that the blind man's hat is *red*, the other from that information to the
conclusion that the blind man's hat is *white*. One of these lines of reasoning is valid, the other invalid. But it certainly is *not obvious* which is
valid and which is invalid. We would like to have a way of finding out
which is valid and which is not. More generally, we would like to have a
way or ways of finding out whether any given line of reasoning, even if it
is *not obviously valid* and *not obviously invalid*, is *in fact* valid or invalid.

How shall we find such a way or ways? Well, in a sense we *already know*.
If you try to solve the puzzle in the story, you will find yourself doing
something like the following: you will attend to certain parts of the information and then become aware that a line of reasoning from that part of
the information to a certain conclusion is *obviously* valid. For example, it
might become obvious to you that from the statement that the first prisoner could see the hats of the other two (together with some of the other
information), *it follows that* if the other two both had red hats, the first
prisoner could validly conclude that he has a white hat. It might then
become obvious to you that from the two statements:

(1)   If the other two prisoners both had red hats, the first prisoner could
      validly conclude that he had a white hat

(2)   He did not conclude that he had a white hat

together with some of the other information, *it follows that* the other two
prisoners did not both have red hats. And then if you attend to these two
lines of reasoning which (we are supposing) are obviously valid to you,
you may become aware that the line of reasoning from the information
the blind man has to the conclusion that the second prisoner and the
blind man don't both have red hats is valid. We might say this is now
*indirectly obvious* to you.

The present tentative (and vague) suggestion is that when we attend to certain things which are *obvious* to us, certain other things become *indirectly obvious* to us. And when we further attend to certain things which are either by now *indirectly obvious* or *obvious* to us, still other things become *indirectly obvious* to us. So, by our attention being directed in a certain order to various things, it becomes at length *indirectly obvious* to us how to find out whether given lines of reasoning are valid or not. Ideally, neither a teacher nor a text need give us any "new information". Ideally, all teachers and texts should need to do is direct our attention to various things in a well-ordered manner.[2]

What we have just been discussing is another topic to be more fully investigated in the philosophy of logic. But one way to see how we find ways of telling whether lines of reasoning are valid or not is to *watch* ourselves doing it. So let us study logic. But let us also watch ourselves doing it, so that we may bring these observations to bear in the philosophy of logic.

## Exercises

1 Describe a plausible case in which someone starts with things he believes and by reasoning reaches a conclusion which he disbelieves (or at least does not believe); as a result of which he rightly gives up one of the beliefs he started from.

(Hint: How do you refute a hypothesis?)

2 Describe a plausible case in which someone starts with things at least one of which he either does not yet believe or believes only weakly, and by reasoning reaches a conclusion which he already believed (perhaps has observed to be true); as a result of which he rightly either acquires or is strengthened in his belief in the one thing that was singled out above in what he started from.

(Hint: How do you confirm a hypothesis?)

3 Describe a plausible case in which someone starts with things at least one of which he does not believe and by reasoning reaches a conclusion which he also does not believe; as a result of which he is strengthened in his refusal to believe the one thing that was singled out above in what he started from.

(Hint: How do you show that there is no evidence for a particular hypothesis?)

---

[2] In practice, however, to save time (and for other reasons), "new information" *is* given. It is not excluded that something may be or seem *obvious* to us and yet be *false*. But, fortunately, by our attending to suitable things it may become *indirectly obvious* that what was or seemed obvious is *in fact* false.

4   Describe a plausible case in which someone starts with things at least one of which he so far neither believes nor disbelieves and by reasoning reaches a conclusion which he also so far neither believes nor disbelieves; as a result of which he rightly undertakes a course of action (and perhaps comes to believe the two things above which he neither believed nor disbelieved).

(Hint: How do you decide whether something should be done?)

5   Select one of the cases you have described in the preceding exercises and try to indicate in what way what the person did in the end depends (at least partly) on whether his reasoning was correct.

6   What is the color of the hat on the blind prisoner's head? Explain.

7   Suppose that the second sighted prisoner in the story above in fact had only *one* eye, so that he could see only the blind prisoner's hat and not that of the first sighted prisoner. Could the blind prisoner *still* determine the color of his own hat?

8   Can a *valid* argument have false premises and a true conclusion?

9   Can a *valid* argument have true premises and a false conclusion?

10  Can an *invalid* argument have true premises and a false conclusion?

11  *Must* an invalid argument have true premises and a false conclusion? Explain.

# Chapter 3

## Logical Form

**1. Patterns of Reasoning**. We have a very large task before us: to find a way or ways of determining which lines of reasoning are valid and which are invalid. Only some of them are obviously valid or obviously invalid. Lots are neither obviously valid nor obviously invalid. We are already equipped to deal with lines of reasoning which are initially neither obviously valid nor obviously invalid—but only in a haphazard manner. And if we reflect, we see that we have *infinitely many* lines of reasoning to deal with. We can hardly examine them one by one! It would be good to find some systematic approach.

The first step is to make it quite clear to ourselves just what a given line of reasoning is. The truth-bearers of which it consists are normally expressible in *indicative sentences* of the language which we speak. Thus we can express Madame de Burgundy's line of reasoning as follows:[1]

> The first person ever to confess to the abbé was a murderer.
> The very first person to confess to the abbé was the marquis.
>
> ___
>
> The marquis is a murderer.

The group of the first two sentences expresses the group of the *premises*, and the third sentence expresses the *conclusion*. This line of reasoning is obviously valid. Here is (the expression of) another line of reasoning which is also obviously valid:

___

[1] Clearly, we have some choice in the sentences we use to express a line of reasoning. Also, we shall generally separate the premises from the conclusion with a line, as shown.

Suzie's stuffed elephant is too large to send to Aunt Nellie.
Suzie's stuffed elephant is what Fred bought for Aunt Nellie.

---

What Fred bought for Aunt Nellie is too large to send to her.

Upon reflecting on (the expressions of) these two lines of reasoning, we come to see not only that they are both obviously valid, but that they have a *common pattern*, and that *every* line of reasoning which has this pattern is obviously valid. We can notice this pattern by paying attention to:

- the *kinds of phrases* which occur in the expression of the line of reasoning.

- the *pattern of occurrence and recurrence* of these phrases.

- the pattern of occurrence and recurrence of certain *special phrases*.

Thus, we might diagram these features in the two lines of reasoning as follows:

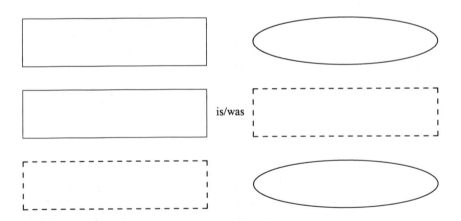

And we may discern this pattern in the two lines of reasoning, as follows:

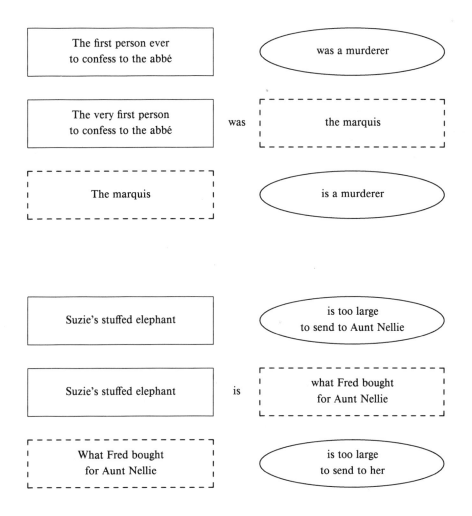

where the solid- and dashed-line rectangles represent occurrences of phrases which we shall come to call *logical subjects*. The solid-line rectangles represent occurrences of one such phrase, and the dashed-line rectangles represent occurrences of another such phrase. The ellipses represent occurrences of a phrase which we shall come to call a *logical predicate*. Finally, the 'is/was' represents a *special phrase*.

Strictly speaking, of course, *not exactly* the same phrases recur in those places. We have to use our understanding of the language to see that the two phrases:

the first person to confess to the abbé

the very first person to confess to the abbé

are mere grammatical or stylistic variants of each other, as are (in this context) the phrases

> too large to send to Aunt Nellie
>
> too large to send to her ·

Similarly, we have to see that the shift from 'is' to 'was' is to be ignored in the expression of the first line of reasoning, but not in other contexts. But then we have to use our understanding of the language to see which phrases are *logical subjects* and which are *logical predicates*—and a lot of other things about the expressions of lines of reasoning.

It may be puzzling why we chose to concentrate on just the pattern which we diagrammed above. Aren't there other patterns to be discerned in the two lines of reasoning? In particular, it may be puzzling why we treated the phrases:

> was a murderer
>
> is too large to send to Aunt Nellie

differently from the phrases:

> was the marquis
>
> is what Fred bought for Aunt Nellie

All of this will become clearer as we consider more examples and various general facts. For now, let's notice that another obviously valid line of reasoning seems to have the same pattern as the first two and fits our diagram better than other diagrams we might have chosen:

> Smith shouts.
> Smith is the mayor.
> _____
> The mayor shouts.

## Exercises

1   Draw the appropriate boxes and ellipses to show that this line of reasoning indeed has the same pattern as the two lines of reasoning discussed above.

**2. Valid Forms.** The point of the preceding discussion is that such patterns, when properly discerned, are a rather reliable clue to the validity or invalidity of very large—indeed infinitely large—classes of lines of reasoning. This is because the lines of reasoning come grouped into classes of lines of reasoning possessing *the same logical form*. And (with reservations and qualifications to be discussed later) lines of reasoning of a given logical form are either *all* of them *valid* or *all* of them *invalid*. Thus if we consider a line of reasoning and find out that it is valid and then find out what logical form it has, we will know that infinitely many lines of reasoning (viz., all those of the same logical form) are valid. So if we consider another line of reasoning and find out that it is of that same logical form, we will know that it is also valid. And the same holds (with reservations and qualifications to be discussed later) of an invalid line of reasoning.[2]

So, the second step will be to discern and somehow usefully record the logical form of a line of reasoning. This will allow us, among other things, to investigate a logical form without bothering about any of the infinitely many lines of reasoning which have that logical form. Let us say that a *logical form* is itself *valid* when *all* lines of reasoning of that logical form are valid. And let us say that a logical form is itself *invalid* when *not* all lines of reasoning of that logical form are valid. Then we will often be able to find out that a logical form is valid or invalid without considering any of the lines of reasoning of that logical form. Indeed, sometimes we can do this for an infinite class of logical forms. Here is an obvious example. We can regard the following as a suggestive diagram of infinitely many logical forms, each of which is had by infinitely many lines of reasoning:

---

[2] What exactly "logical form" is, and indeed whether there really is such a thing, is another difficult question for the philosophy of logic. In the meantime, we will fairly easily become proficient in dealing with this notion *in practice*.

PREMISES:

If [ 1 ]        then        [ 2 ]

If [ 2 ]        then        [ 3 ]

⋮

If [ $n$ ]      then        [ $n+1$ ]

CONCLUSION:

If [ 1 ]        then        [ $n+1$ ]

If, for any number $n$, we replace each numbered box by a statement, we get a line of reasoning. It should be obvious that we can do this in infinitely many ways, and that every one of the infinitely many lines of reasoning of any one of these forms is valid.

## Exercises

In each of the following twelve lines of reasoning, determine as best you can (a) whether the conclusion *follows from* the premises, and (b) for each of the premises and the conclusion, whether it is *true* or *false*. (Of course, 'I don't know' is an acceptable answer, if in fact you don't know.)

2    If there are more than fifty-three people in a group, then at least two of them have birthdays in the same week.

There are more than fifty-three people enrolled in Philosophy 14A.

There are at least two people enrolled in Philosophy 14A whose birthdays are in the same week.

3    The number of students enrolled in Philosophy 14A is not even.

If there are as many male as female students enrolled in a given course, then the number of students enrolled in that course is even.

There are not as many male as female students enrolled in Philosophy 14A.

4   On at least one occasion last month, no two people in Berkeley had the same number of coins in their pockets.

   If on any occasion no two people in Berkeley have the same number of coins in their pockets, then someone has at least 100,000 coins in his pockets on that occasion.

   ---

   On at least one occasion last month, someone in Berkeley had 100,000 coins in his pockets.

5   If Nixon is not dishonest, then he did not know in advance everything about the Watergate affair.

   Nixon did know in advance everything about the Watergate affair.

   ---

   Nixon is dishonest.

6   If Nixon knew in advance everything about the Watergate affair, then he is dishonest.

   Nixon is dishonest.

   ---

   Nixon knew in advance everything about the Watergate affair.

7   If you fry something that contains molybdenum, the result will contain molybdenum trioxide.

   Molybdenum trioxide is highly poisonous.

   Persian cucumbers contain molybdenum.

   ---

   If you fry Persian cucumbers, the result will contain a highly poisonous substance.

8   If you fry something that contains molybdenum trioxide, the result will contain molybdenum.

   Molybdenum is not at all poisonous.

   Persian pears contain molybdenum trioxide.

   ---

   If you fry Persian pears, the result will not contain any poisonous substances.

9   A body which rotates once around its axis during every revolution around another body keeps the same side directed towards that body.

   The moon rotates once during every revolution around the Earth.

   ---

   The moon keeps the same side directed towards the Earth.

10  Every body which revolves around the sun is either a planet or a comet or an asteroid.

Skylab was neither a planet nor an asteroid.

---

Skylab either did not revolve around the sun or it was a comet.

11 If Philosophy 14A meets on Mondays, Wednesdays, and Fridays only, and has forty meetings altogether, then it must either have met in August or continue to meet after November.

Philosophy 14A has forty meetings altogether and meets on Mondays, Wednesdays, and Fridays only.

Philosophy 14A will not meet after November.

---

Philosophy 14A has met in August.

12 If a substance is a potential cure for cancer, then if it is infused into cancerous cells, it will destroy them; and if it is infused into normal cells, it will leave them unharmed.

Molybdenum has been infused both into the cells in dish A and into those in dish B.

The cells in dish A are cancerous.

The cells in dish B are normal.

---

If molybdenum is a potential cure for cancer, then the cells in dish A will be destroyed and the cells in dish B will not be harmed.

13 If the present rate of pollution does not decrease drastically, life in the oceans will eventually die out.

If life in the oceans dies out and human population continues to increase at the present rate, there will be starvation.

The present rate of pollution will not decrease drastically if human population continues to increase at the present rate.

---

If human population continues to increase at the present rate, there will be starvation.

Now *reflect*: did determining whether the lines of reasoning were deductively valid help you to determine (as best you could) the truth or falsity of their conclusions, or of certain of their premises? Did it at least help you to see what *further* investigations to pursue to determine their truth or falsity?

---

# PART II

---

## Truth-Functional Logic

We shall begin our systematic study of logical form by considering a class of forms known as *truth-functional* forms. Truth-functional forms are, roughly speaking, forms possessed by statements which are compounded out of other statements using such phrases as 'not', 'and', 'or', 'if...then', and the like. Truth-functional logic, then, is the study of statements having such forms and of arguments composed out of such statements. The beauty of truth-functional logic is that the truth-value of compound statements is a function of the truth-values of their components. This fact makes it possible to develop simple and powerful techniques to demonstrate the validity or invalidity of such arguments. These techniques will be the foundation of our study of logic.

# Chapter 4

# Truth-Functional Forms

**1. Kinds of Statements.** An important way to discern the logical form of a line of reasoning is by classifying the statements of which it consists with respect to their relationships to other statements. Later we will learn how to discern a "deeper" logical form by classifying statements *also* with respect to their relationships to items which are not statements. For the moment, we may say that all statements belong to one or another of six kinds:

Negations
Conjunctions
Disjunctions
Conditionals
Biconditionals
Others[1]

All the statements of the first five kinds are *molecular*; this means that they have other statements as parts. All those Others which are naturally expressible in English are *non-molecular*: they have no parts which are statements. Negations and all those Others which are naturally expressible in English are *unary*; the rest are *binary*. Thus, at least for statements which are naturally expressible in English,[2] we have:

---

[1] It is obvious why every statement *must* belong to one or another of these six kinds. As one might expect, the further classification promised above will be a subclassification of the "Others".

[2] There are some subtle issues here. It is not unreasonable to maintain that there are kinds of statements which are not "naturally" expressible in English. Good candidates are, in technical terms, "binary truth-functions" other than the first five kinds of statement we are considering. However, all of these are *formally equivalent* (in a sense soon to be explained) to statements of one or another of the first five kinds. And this allows us to deal with them at least "indirectly". It may also be maintained that, for example, a statement expressed by 'Neither Alfred nor Bertha bowls' is *molecular*, but not of one of the first five kinds. But again, even if so, there is at least one *formally equivalent* statement of one of the first five kinds. A similar consideration may arise as to whether all Others naturally expressible in English are *unary* (even apart from this example).

|            | *unary*    | *binary*                                                      |
|------------|------------|--------------------------------------------------------------|
| *molecular*     | Negations  | Conjunctions<br>Disjunctions<br>Conditionals<br>Biconditionals |
| *non-molecular* | Others     | —                                                            |

In what sense is this a classification of statements with respect to their relationships to other statements? Well, a statement which is a negation is always the negation of some other statement. For example (the statement expressed by):

(1)  It is not the case that Alfred is friendly

is the negation of (the statement expressed by)[3] the underlined portion. Similarly,

(2) Alfred is not friendly

is the negation of the underlined portion. Every statement which is a negation is the negation of *one* other statement (hence, a negation is *unary*). The latter statement is the *negatum* of the former statement. Sometimes we have to do a bit of rephrasing to find the negatum. For example,

(3)  Bertha generates difficulties

is the negatum of:

(4)  Bertha does not generate difficulties

A statement which is a conjunction is *a conjunction of* other statements. For example:

(5) Alfred is friendly and Bertha is generous

---

[3] For the sake of economy, we shall henceforth suppress such phrases as those occurring here in parentheses, even though such suppression may be the cause of the plausibility of certain possibly false views in the philosophy of logic.

is the conjunction of the two underlined portions.  We shall insist that a conjunction is always the conjunction of exactly *two* statements, the *left conjunct* (the straight-underlined portion above) and the *right conjunct* (the dot-underlined portion above).  This is why a conjunction is *binary*.

Let us pause to note that a *negatum* or a *conjunct* (*left* or *right*) will itself be one of the six kinds of statement we have isolated.  For example, in:

(6)  Alfred does not bowl and Bertha does not ski.

we have a conjunction whose *left conjunct* is a negation, the *negatum* of which is the *non-molecular* statement:

(7)  Alfred bowls

We can now see what to do with conjunctions which have, or appear to have, more than two conjuncts.  For example:

Alfred bowls, Bertha skis, and Charlie does both.

We can regard this either as (8) the conjunction of:

Alfred bowls    (left conjunct)

Bertha skis and Charlie both bowls and skis    (right conjunct)

or as (9) the conjunction of:

Alfred bowls and Bertha skis    (left conjunct)

Charlie both bowls and skis    (right conjunct)

where, in the first case, the right conjunct is itself a conjunction; and, in the second case, the left conjunct is itself a conjunction.  Whichever of these two options we adopt is immaterial, for the two forms are *equivalent*.[4] We shall explain what this means shortly.

In parallel fashion, we shall insist that a statement which is a disjunction is the disjunction of exactly *two* statements, the *left disjunct* (straight-underlined below) and the *right disjunct* (dot-underlined below):

(10) Alfred bowls or Bertha skis

And we shall deal with disjunctions that have, or appear to have, more

---

[4] Indeed, *formally* equivalent, as will become clear below.

than two disjuncts, like:

Either Alfred skis, or Bertha bowls, or Charlies does both

in parallel fashion, (11) or (12), which are left to the reader to supply. However, we do not have this sort of freedom when we are confronted with:

(13)  Either Alfred skis and Bertha bowls or Charlie does both

which is a *disjunction* whose *left disjunct* is a *conjunction*.  Nor do we have this freedom with:

(14)  Alfred skis and either Bertha bowls or Charlie does both

which is a *conjunction* whose *right conjunct* is a *disjunction*.  For the two statements do *not* say the same thing; that is, they are *not* equivalent. A statement and any other statement are *equivalent* if and only if there is no possible situation in which they differ in truth-value.  That is, they are in every possible situation either both true or both false.  Consider a possible situation in which:

> Charlie both bowls and skis
> Alfred does not ski
> Bertha does not bowl

In this possible situation, statement (13) is true and statement (14) is false.  Hence they are *not* equivalent. You will notice then that the sentence:

Alfred skis and Bertha bowls or Charlie does both

is structurally ambiguous and must be construed either as (13) or (14).

**2. Negations, Conjunctions, and Disjunctions**. It is time to find a notation which will allow us to represent such classifications compactly and perspicuously.  Provisionally, let us represent

- a *negation* by writing the tilde '~' in front of its *negatum*

- a *conjunction* by writing the ampersand '&' between its *left conjunct* and its *right conjunct*

- a *disjunction* by writing the wedge 'v' between its *left disjunct* and its *right disjunct* and, in view of what we have just discussed, *always* enclosing a *negatum*, *conjunct*, or *disjunct* in a pair of parentheses *when and only when* it is *binary*. We may then represent the examples we have numbered above as follows:

(1)    ~ Alfred is friendly

(2)    ~ Alfred is friendly

(3)    Bertha generates difficulties

(4)    ~ Bertha generates difficulties

(5)    Alfred is friendly & Bertha is generous

(6)    ~ Alfred bowls & ~ Bertha skis

(7)    Alfred bowls

(8)    Alfred bowls & (Bertha skis & Charlie both bowls and skis)

(9)    (Alfred bowls & Bertha skis) & Charlie both bowls and skis

(10)   Alfred bowls v Bertha skis

(11)   Alfred skis v (Bertha bowls v Charlie both bowls and skis)

(12)   (Alfred skis v Bertha bowls) v Charlie both bowls and skis

(13)   (Alfred skis & Bertha bowls) v Charlie both bowls and skis

(14)   Alfred skis & (Bertha bowls v Charlie both bowls and skis)

Note that if we did not use parentheses, the two *non-equivalent* statements (13) and (14) would be indistinguishable in our representations. Note also that at this stage, we are leaving what we have classified as *non-molecular* statements in plain English, although we sometimes rephrase them so as to remove any dependence on the other non-molecular statements. For instance, we rephrased:

Charlie does both

into:

(15) Charlie both bowls and skis

since it is clear from the context that this is what is meant. But then haven't we *mis*classified statement (15) when we classified it as *non-molecular*? It is a *conjunction* of:

Charlie bowls

Charlie skis

and our previous list should be revised by replacing every occurrence of statement (15) by:

(Charlie bowls & Charlie skis)

with the parentheses being required because, in our list, (15) occurs always either as a *conjunct* or as a *disjunct*. So, for example, (12) and (14) become:

(12′)    (Alfred skis v Bertha bowls) v (Charlie bowls & Charlie  skis)

(14′)    Alfred skis & (Bertha bowls v (Charlie bowls & Charlie  skis))

It is not that (8), (9), (11), (12), (13), and (14) are "incorrect". What they represent is true enough as far as it goes. For example, (14) correctly represents that the original example (14) is a conjunction whose left con-junct is 'Alfred skis' and whose right conjunct is a disjunction, the dis-juncts of which are, respectively, 'Bertha bowls' and 'Charlie both bowls and skis'. This is *true*. But it is not the whole truth. It is *also* true that the right disjunct of the right conjunct is itself a conjunction of the state-ments 'Charlie bowls' and 'Charlie skis', respectively. Our representation (14) fails to represent this, whereas (14′) does represent it. One might say that (14) represents the logical form *in less* or *less full detail*, whereas (14′) represents it *in greater* or *fuller detail*. As we shall see, the logical form of example (14) can be represented in even greater or fuller detail than is done by (14′). (This has to do with the further subclassification of non-molecular statements hinted at above.) For some purposes it is convenient to pay attention to more detail, while for other purposes it is convenient to pay attention to less detail. At this stage, let us represent as much detail as we can.

**3. Conditionals and Biconditionals**. It is clear from our examples that *negations* are associated with the word 'not', *conjunctions* are associated with the word 'and', and *disjunctions* are associated with the word 'or'. More will be said about this later. *Conditionals* are associated with the phrase 'if...then', and *biconditionals* are associated with the phrase 'if and only if'.

A statement which is a *conditional* is the conditional of exactly *two* state-ments: the *antecedent* and the *consequent* (and hence is *binary*). The dis-tinction between the antecedent and the consequent is much more impor-tant than the relatively trivial distinction between the left conjunct or dis-junct and the right conjunct or disjunct; at the same time, it is a little harder to recognize the parts of a conditional. The *antecedent* is the statement which indicates the condition under which something (else) is true. So, the antecedent is what follows the word 'if' in an 'if...then' statement. The *consequent* is the statement which indicates what happens or is true if the antecedent holds true, so it is that part of the statement which follows the word 'then' in an 'if...then' statement.

The dependence of one statement on another indicated by the phrase 'if...then' may be indicated by a variety of other phrases as well. For instance, the phrase 'only if' is very often used in this way. Here, however, you must be careful in isolating the antecedent and consequent. It is now the consequent which follows the word 'if', and the antecedent is the statement which precedes the phrase 'only if'. Thus the straight-underlined statements below are the *antecedents* and the dot-underlined statements are the *consequents*:

If Alfred bowls, then Bertha skis

If Alfred bowls, Bertha skis

Bertha skis if Alfred bowls

Alfred bowls only if Bertha skis

Only if Bertha skis does Alfred bowl

We shall represent a *conditional* by writing the horseshoe '⊃' between the *antecedent* (to the left) and the *consequent* (to the right). Thus all five of the above examples are represented in the same way:

Alfred bowls ⊃ Bertha skis

Antecedents and consequents are enclosed in a pair of parentheses when and only when they are *binary*, like the parts of other non-molecular statements. Thus:

If Alfred bowls then either Bertha skis or Charlie does both.

If Alfred does not ski then if Bertha skis then Charlie does not do both.

are represented respectively as:

Alfred bowls ⊃ (Bertha skis v (Charlie bowls & Charlie skis))

~Alfred skis ⊃ (Bertha skis ⊃ ~(Charlie bowls & Charlie skis))

It may appear that the second of the two examples is ambiguous. For what is meant by 'Charlie does not do both'? This could mean either of the two following things:

> it is not the case that Charlie does both
> both are such that Charlie does not do them

The two are clearly *not equivalent*. We have chosen the first interpretation above. The second interpretation should be represented as:

> ~ Alfred skis ⊃ (Bertha skis ⊃ (~ Charlie bowls & ~ Charlie skis))

We see from this that the discernment and representation of logical form allows us to distinguish between different interpretations of ambiguous remarks (or different statements expressed by the same words, phrases, sentences). When confronted with a line of reasoning expressed in a way which involves such ambiguities, we can distinguish and represent clearly the different lines of reasoning which *might* be expressed and then find out which of them are valid and which invalid. We may then be able to discover which line of reasoning was *intended* by asking the author or by inferring from the context which is likely to have been intended by him (if he was sufficiently unconfused to have intended just one of them). In any case, we can determine that if he meant so-and-so, then he reasoned validly, but if he meant such-and-such, then he reasoned invalidly.

Lastly, a statement which is a *biconditional* is a biconditional of exactly *two* statements: the *left side* and the *right side*. (This distinction is as relatively trivial as that between the left conjunct or disjunct and the right conjunct or disjunct.) We represent a *biconditional* by writing the triple bar '≡' between the two sides, and, as before, enclosing the sides in a pair of parentheses when and only when they are *binary*. Thus:

> Alfred bowls if and only if Bertha skis and Charlie does both.

is represented as:

> Alfred bowls ≡ (Bertha skis & (Charlie bowls & Charlie skis))

on one interpretation. On another:

> (Alfred bowls ≡ Bertha skis) & (Charlie bowls & Charlie skis)

These are *not equivalent*.

It may occur to us that a biconditional can be regarded as a conjunction of two conditionals. The very language suggests this:

Alfred bowls if and only if Bertha skis
Alfred bowls if Bertha skis and Alfred bowls only if Bertha skis
(Bertha skis ⊃ Alfred bowls) & (Alfred bowls ⊃ Bertha skis)

But a biconditional and the conjunction of the two "corresponding" conditionals are always *formally equivalent.* So, *like* the cases of multiple conjunctions and multiple disjunctions, and *unlike* cases like (13) versus (14) and the two ambiguities lately noted, this case is one in which we get the same results (with respect to validity and invalidity) whichever alternative we choose.[5]

**4. Depth of Form.** Now, consider the line of reasoning (I):

Either Alfred bowls or Bertha skis.
Alfred does not bowl.

Bertha skis.

This line of reasoning is obviously valid. Its logical form is represented at this stage as follows:

Alfred bowls v Bertha skis
~ Alfred bowls
Bertha skis

It is obvious that every line of reasoning of this logical form is valid. *Every* line of reasoning, one of whose premises is a disjunction, the other of whose premises is the negation of the left disjunct, and the conclusion of which is the right disjunct is valid. It does not matter what statements the two disjuncts are. What matters is that the logical form exhibit the general pattern:

---

[5] There is no reason that these equivalences should be obvious to you, and it is part of our task in studying logic to determine which forms are equivalent to which others.

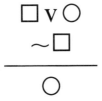

(apart from parentheses which may be required). *No more* detail of logical form is needed to guarantee that the line of reasoning is valid. Thus, in the line of reasoning (II):

> (Alfred bowls v Bertha skis) v (Charlie bowls & Charlie skis)
> ~ (Alfred bowls v Bertha skis)
> Charlie bowls & Charlie skis

the "extra" detail of logical form (which is represented inside the parentheses) is irrelevant for the validity of the line of reasoning. This is why (12) above is "good enough" for some purposes. But such extra detail *is* relevant in other lines of reasoning. For example, some (but not all) of this extra detail is relevant in the following line of reasoning (III):

> (Alfred bowls v Bertha skis) v (Charlie bowls & Charlie skis)
> ~ (Alfred bowls v Bertha skis)
> Charlie skis

This is why (12′) is a "better" representation of the logical form of the statement in question. So we must balance *representing as much* detail of logical form as we can with *paying attention to as little* of it as suffices for determining validity.[6]

**5. Paraphrasing Inward.** Let us consider how to deal with cases which may be somewhat more difficult, like:

> If either John or Mary is here, then the library is closed, and if neither is, then it's open.

We might proceed by steps which illustrate what the logician Quine calls *paraphrasing inward*: classifying and representing the larger parts first and then doing the same for smaller parts. We may decide that the whole statement is a conjunction and record this fact as follows:

---

[6] As we shall see, however, for determining *invalidity* we shall need to pay attention to *as much* logical form as we can.

If either John or Mary is here, then the library is closed
& if neither is, then it's open

Now let us focus on the left conjunct (the top line). We may then get:

(Either John or Mary is here ⊃ the library is closed)
& if neither is, then it's open

Here we have recorded that the left conjunct is a conditional and enclosed it in parentheses because it is *binary*. We may continue:

(Either John or Mary is here ⊃ the library is closed)
& (neither is ⊃ the library is open)

((John is here v Mary is here) ⊃ the library is closed)
& (neither is ⊃ the library is open)

((John is here v Mary is here) ⊃ the library is closed)
& ((Mary is not here and John is not here) ⊃ the library is open)

We have paraphrased the antecedent of the right conjunct to lessen its dependence on other parts of the sentence. (In thus paraphrasing it, we have made a choice that is discussed in a footnote in Chapter 5, Sec. 6.)

((John is here v Mary is here) ⊃ the library is closed)
& ((~ Mary is here & ~ John is here) ⊃ the library is open)

We have skipped a few steps, recognizing at once that the antecedent of the right conjunct is a conjunction of negations. Finally:

((John is here v Mary is here) ⊃ ~ the library is open)
& ((~ Mary is here & ~ John is here) ⊃ the library is open)

Inspection of what we now have shows that those segments which are statements in English containing none of the new symbols are *non-molecular*. Thus we can go no further at the present stage. Notice that we did *not* enclose the negatum of the consequent of the left conjunct (viz., 'the library is open') in parentheses because it is *unary*. We use parentheses to enclose *all and only* negata, conjuncts, disjuncts, antecedents, consequents, and sides which are *binary*.

## Exercises

---

1    Classify each of the following statements on the basis of the six-fold classification given above. If you think that a statement is ambiguous,

represent the logical form of the several different statements that might have been intended.

(a)  If Jones studies, so does Smith.

(b)  Mary and Fred are married.

(c)  Kelly finds films boring and childish, but Fenwick thinks he's wrong.

(d)  Someone is not paying attention.

(e)  If someone wins the lottery, Burns will go to the movies.

(f)  Bert's steak knife slices but will not dice.

(g)  Idris wants a new puppy if and only if he now has none.

2  Represent the logical form of each of the following statements in the manner illustrated above.

(a)  Jones and Howard are both friends of Bostwick.

(b)  Jones is a friend of Bostwick only if Howard isn't.

(c)  Kermit borrowed Miss Piggy's hammer and scissors.

(d)  If Shakespeare and Milton were outstanding poets, then either one could have written *Faust* if he knew German.

(e)  Appleby is a white Persian cat.

(f)  Appleby is an accomplished mouse catcher.

3  Represent the logical form of each of the following arguments by giving the logical form of their component statements.

(a)  Henry, when he is angry, is also vindictive.
     Only when he is vindictive is Henry argumentative.
     Therefore, Henry, when angry, is not argumentative.

(b)  If both Alfred and Bertha assent, then Charlie will assent.
     Alfred does not assent if Charlie does.
     Bertha does assent if and only if Alfred does.
     Therefore, it is not the case that both Alfred and Charlie assent.

(c)  Burns will not attach his printer unless he finds the correct slot.
     Burns is a computer wizard; he will surely find the correct slot.
     Therefore, Burns will attach his printer.

(d)  If Delilah catches the mouse, she will play with it.
     If Delilah catches the mouse and plays with it, she will get frantic.
     If Delilah gets frantic, she must not be taken to the vet.
     Therefore, if Delilah catches the mouse, she must not go to the vet.

# Chapter 5

## Formulas and Phrase-Books

**1. Abbreviating Representations.** We see from the preceding chapter that an even more compact and perspicuous (and writer's-cramp-forestalling) representation of logical form is desirable. The actual non-molecular statements occurring in a line of reasoning are at this stage irrelevant to our assessment of the validity or invalidity of the line of reasoning. Only the *kinds* of statements (negation, conjunction, disjunction, conditional, biconditional, non-molecular) which occur and the *pattern* of their occurrence and recurrence are relevant. We can separate the two bodies of information about a line of reasoning as follows.

On the one hand, we shall construct a *phrase-book* correlating capital letters of the English alphabet (allowing certain "expansions"—see below) with non-molecular statements. We shall write this as a list of items, each consisting of a capital letter, a colon, and an English sentence expressing a statement. A different letter is to be chosen for each different sentence. We are free to choose any letter to abbreviate a statement, but we may wish to choose letters in such a way that they "remind" us of that statement. For example, we might take the following phrase-book:

$$
\begin{array}{ll}
A\ :\ & \text{Alfred bowls} \\
B\ :\ & \text{Bertha skis} \\
C\ :\ & \text{Charlie bowls} \\
D\ :\ & \text{Charlie skis}
\end{array}
$$

On the other hand, we shall have a list of *formulas*, one formula for each of the premises and the conclusion of the line of reasoning, with the formula for the conclusion being written last. (The order of the premises does not matter.) We may think of a formula as simply the result of replacing in our previous representations of logical form each occurrence of a sentence expressing a non-molecular statement by the capital letter which has been paired with it in the phrase-book. Thus the list of formulas corresponding (given the above phrase-book) to the line of reasoning (I) on p. 32 is:

$$A \lor B$$
$$\sim A$$
$$B$$

And the list of formulas (given the same phrase-book) corresponding to the line of reasoning (II) on p. 33 is:

$$(A \lor B) \lor (C \ \& \ D)$$
$$\sim(A \lor B)$$
$$C \ \& \ D$$

And the list of formulas (given the same phrase-book) corresponding to the line of reasoning (III) on p. 33 is:

$$(A \lor B) \lor (C \ \& \ D)$$
$$\sim(A \lor B)$$
$$D$$

Notice that in representing a line of reasoning, the *phrase-book* and the list of *formulas* work in tandem. The line of reasoning (III) is equally well represented by:

$P$ : Alfred bowls
$Q$ : Charlie bowls
$R$ : Bertha skis
$S$ : Charlie skis

$$(P \lor R) \lor (Q \ \& \ S)$$
$$\sim(P \lor R)$$
$$S$$

And there are infinitely many variations.[1] In short, the logical form of a

---

[1] How can this be? To answer this, let us first raise another problem. What if we have a line of reasoning which has more different non-molecular statements than there are letters in the English alphabet? Since we have only 26 upper-case letters, we would not be able to represent such a line of reasoning. We shall solve this problem by creating an "expanded English alphabet", which is infinitely large, by allowing numerical subscripts: $A, B, C, \cdots,$ $X, Y, Z, A_1, B_1, C_1, \cdots, X_1, Y_1, Z_1, A_2, B_2, C_2, \cdots, X_2, Y_2, Z_2, \cdots$. Any two letters (with or without subscripts) in this sequence are to count as *different* letters. So we could also construct the phrase-book:

$D$ : Bertha skis
$D_1$ : Charlie skis
$S$ : Alfred bowls
$S_{347}$ : Charlie bowls

line of reasoning is represented by a *phrase-book* and a list of *formulas* suitably adjusted to each other in the ways illustrated.[2]

We transfer in a natural way the classificatory terminology for statements discussed in Chapter 4 to *formulas*. It is important to keep in mind the distinction between *unary* and *binary* formulas and the principle that a formula is to be enclosed in parentheses *if and only if* it is *binary* and occurs as *part* of some other formula (i.e., is a negatum, a conjunct, a disjunct, an antecedent, a consequent, or a side).

**2. Truth-Functional Forms Reconsidered.** We must now, however, return to the rather more difficult issue of classifying *statements* into the six types. In our preliminary discussion we said that negations, conjunctions, disjunctions, conditionals, and biconditionals are "associated", respectively, with the words and phrases 'not', 'and', 'or', 'if...then', and 'if and only if'. This is true enough, but it is not the whole truth. The presence of one of these words (or phrases) in a sentence expressing a statement is an important *clue* in classifying the statement into one of the six kinds. But its presence does not guarantee that the statement is best classified as of that kind, nor is its presence required for the statement to be of that kind. A number of points are relevant here.

First, we must consider what we shall call the *extent of influence of a word (or phrase)*. This is rather difficult to explain precisely, but some examples should give you the idea. The problem is that more than one of the words or phrases listed above may occur in (a sentence expressing) a statement.[3] We have already encountered several such examples; another is:

If Alfred does not bowl, Bertha does

Here both 'not' and 'if' occur. It is easy to see that 'if' takes precedence, in the sense that the entire statement is to be regarded as a conditional. This is what we mean by saying that the 'if' has the whole statement as its

---

and give another of the infinitely many possible representations of (III):

$$(S \text{ v } D) \text{ v } (D_1 \text{ \& } S_{347})$$
$$\sim(S \text{ v } D)$$
$$S_{347}$$

[2] We can and shall use this manner of representation to represent the logical form of *sets* of statements in which *no* statement is singled out as the conclusion, including sets which have just one statement as member. In effect, then, we shall be able to represent the logical form of *single statements*. But when what is represented is a *line of reasoning*, the *last* formula is to be taken as representing the conclusion.

[3] This includes words or phrases which are for present purposes "interchangeable" with these words or phrases. See below.

extent of influence. The word 'not', on the other hand, has only the contained sentence:

Alfred does not bowl

as *its* extent of influence. So the whole sentence is a *conditional*, and only the antecedent is a *negation*. On the other hand, in:

It is not the case that if Alfred bowls, Bertha does

the word 'not' has the whole sentence as its extent of influence. The word 'if' has only:

If Alfred bowls, Bertha does

So the whole statement is a *negation* whose negatum is a *conditional*.

In some cases, as we have noted, there is a "structural ambiguity". For instance,

If Alfred bowls, then so does Bertha, and Charlie admires them both.

The sentence can express either of two different statements. On one interpretation, 'if' has the whole sentence as its extent of influence, and 'and' has only the part about Bertha and Charlie. So the whole thing is a *conditional* with a *conjunction* as consequent. On another interpretation, 'and' has the whole as its extent of influence and 'if' has only the part about Alfred and Bertha. In this case, the whole is a *conjunction* whose left conjunct is a *conditional*. Even when there is no "structural ambiguity", we have to use our understanding of English as best we can to determine extents of influence. For example, does 'not' or 'or' have the larger extent of influence in the following sentence?

Alfred does not bowl or ski

Fortunately, some of our subsequent considerations will be helpful in this regard.

Second, the words we have singled out as "associated" with the different kinds of statement need not be present in a sentence expressing a statement of the corresponding kind. Any one of a number of other words, phrases, or constructions (which are, for our purposes, "interchangeable" with them) may be present instead. The *context* in which this happens often needs to be taken into account. We shall not attempt to give complete lists of "interchangeable" locutions, but here are some examples. The interchangeable words are in bold face, and the sample contexts are indicated in brackets.

*Negation-indicating* words, phrases, or constructions:

> **It is not the case** that Alfred bowls.
>
> Alfred does **not** bowl.
>
> Alfred **isn't** home.
>
> Is Alfred home? **No.**
>
> Alfred tolerates **no** opposition.
>
> Alfred **failed** to go to the market.
>
> Alfred is **in**considerate to bowl every night.
>
> Neither Alfred **nor** Bertha bowls.[4]
>
> [Alfred and Bertha don't bowl.]
> **Neither** does Charlie.
>
> [Alfred and Bertha don't bowl.]
> **Nor** does Charlie.
>
> **No** one came.

*Conjunction-indicating* words, phrases, or constructions:

> Alfred bowls **and** Bertha skis.
>
> Alfred **both** bowls **and** skis.
>
> [Alfred bowls or Bertha skis.]
> Charlie does **both**.
>
> [If Alfred bowls, Bertha skis.]
> **Both** are good athletes.
>
> Alfred bowls, **but** Bertha does not ski.
>
> Alfred bowls, **although** Bertha does not.
>
> Alfred bowls, **yet** Bertha doesn't.
>
> Alfred bowls**,** Bertha skis, (and) Charlie does **both**.
>
> [Alfred, Bertha, and Charlie bowl.]
> **Each of them** skis.
>
> [Alfred, Bertha, and Charlie bowl.]

---

[4] See below, Section 3.

**All of them** ski.

[Alfred, Bertha, and Charlie bowl.]
**Any one of them** has gloves.

[Alfred or Bertha bowls.]
**Neither** Alfred **nor** Bertha bowls.

[Alfred bowls or skis.]
Charlie does **neither**.

[Alfred or Bertha bowls.]
**Either of them** has gloves.

Alfred, **who** bowls, is a good athlete.

What should we do (for example) with the remark: 'Alfred bowls. And so does Bertha...'? In general it does not matter whether we regard this as expressing two separate statements or as a single conjunction. But if this example were a *conclusion* of a line of reasoning, it would be better to make it a conjunction. We can also distinguish a merely stylistic 'and' from a more significant one (e.g., 'Alfred smokes. And does not worry about his health').

*Disjunction-indicating* words, phrases, or constructions:

Alfred bowls **or** Bertha does.

**Either** Alfred bowls **or** Bertha does.

Alfred**,** Bertha (or) Charlie bowls.

Alfred is sleeping **unless** it is after noon.

[Alfred and Bertha bowl.]
**At least one of them** skis.

*Conditional-indicating* words, phrases, or constructions:

Alfred bowls **if** Bertha skis.

**If** Bertha skis, **then** Alfred bowls.

**Only if** Alfred bowls does Bertha ski.

Alfred bowls **in case** Bertha skis.

Bertha skis **only in case** Alfred bowls.

Alfred bowls **provided** Bertha skis.

Bertha skis **only provided** Alfred bowls.

**Given that** Bertha skis, Alfred bowls.

**Assuming that** Bertha skis, Alfred bowls.

Note that all these examples have the same antecedent and the same consequent.

*Biconditional-indicating* words, phrases, or constructions:

Alfred bowls **if and only if** Bertha skis.

Alfred bowls **just in case** Bertha skis.

**If** Alfred bowls, Bertha skis. **And vice versa.**

Third, and most important, neither the occurrence of any of the kind-of-statement indicating words nor their "extents of influence" suffice to determine what kind of statement we have before us. This is because the classification of statements that we are discussing is one that is relevant to validity and invalidity of lines of reasoning—that is, possible combinations of truth-values of statements. For example, what makes such an argument as

Alfred bowls or Bertha does.
Alfred doesn't bowl.

_____

Bertha bowls.

(and every argument of the same logical form) valid is this: in every possible situation in which the first premise is true, at least one of the statements:

Alfred bowls
Bertha bowls

is true. In every possible situation in which the second premise is true, the first of these statements is not true. So, in every possible situation in which both premises are true, the second statement is true. From this we can see that a disjunction has to be such that in every possible situation in which it is true, at least one of its disjuncts is true. And a negation has to be such that in every possible situation in which it is true, its negatum is *not* true. Consideration of other obviously valid lines of reasoning gives the following results:

● In every possible situation, a negation is true if and only if its negatum is not true.

- In every possible situation, a conjunction is true if and only if both of its conjuncts are true.

- In every possible situation, a disjunction is true if and only if at least one of its disjuncts is true.

We can summarize this graphically as:

| $P$ | $Q$ | $\sim P$ | $P \,\&\, Q$ | $P \vee Q$ |
|-----|-----|----------|--------------|-------------|
| T | T | F | T | T |
| T | F | F | F | T |
| F | T | T | F | T |
| F | F | T | F | F |

**3. Negation.** So, in order to classify a statement as a *negation*, we must not only detect a negation-indicating word or phrase whose "extent of influence" is the entire sentence, but we must also find a *candidate* negatum and then check to see whether it and the statement we are testing have *opposite truth-values in every possible situation*. For example, confronted with:

Alfred does not bowl

we find:

Alfred bowls

as an obvious *candidate* negatum. And we see that these two *do* have opposite truth-values in all possible situations.[5] Similarly for:

Neither Alfred nor Bertha bowls

an obvious *candidate* negatum is:

Either Alfred or Bertha bowls

and again these two *do* have opposite truth-values in all possible situations. By contrast,

Someone does not bowl

---

[5] Some subtle issues concerning this claim can be considered in the philosophy of logic. For instance, what happens in possible situations in which Alfred does not exist?

has as a *candidate* negatum:

Someone bowls

but these two statements do *not* have opposite truth-values in every possible situation. (Indeed, they do not have opposite truth-values even in the *actual* situation.) So 'someone does not bowl', in spite of the presence of the negation-indicating 'not', is *not* a negation (and does *not* have a *genuine* negatum).[6] And since this example is not even a plausible candidate for conjunction, disjunction, conditional, or biconditional, it must be non-molecular. The important point is this: *never* classify a statement as a *negation* unless you have found a *genuine* negatum, a statement which *does* have an opposite truth-value in every possible situation.

**4. Conjunction.** Similarly, in order to classify a statement as a *conjunction*, we must find two *candidate* conjuncts and check to see whether *in every possible situation the original statement is true if and only if both of these are true.* For instance,

Alfred bowls and skis

passes the test, but:

Someone bowls and skis

does not. For the two *candidate* conjuncts are:

Someone bowls
Someone skis

Consider a possible situation in which half of the population bowls, the other half skis, but no one does both. The two original candidate conjuncts are thus true, but the original statement is false. So it is *not* a conjunction and must be non-molecular. Another example is:

Alfred and Bertha are married

On a very natural interpretation, this could be false, even though both:

---

[6] One might argue from this that 'not' does not in this example, appearances to the contrary notwithstanding, have the whole sentence as its "extent of influence". This is perhaps made more plausible by the somewhat awkward paraphrase 'someone is such that he does not bowl'. Alternatively, one could hold that the *candidate* negatum is 'everyone bowls', and that *this* does have the opposite truth-value in every possible situation. As we shall see, there is no harm in holding this. But we shall reject this proposal because "too much paraphrasing" is involved.

Alfred is married
Bertha is married

are true. This would happen if Alfred is married (to someone) and Bertha is married (to someone), but Alfred is not married to Bertha. So on this interpretation the example is *not* a conjunction, since the truth of these two statements is not sufficient to guarantee the truth of the candidate conjunction.[7]

**5. Disjunction.** Similar remarks apply to *disjunctions*. We must be able to find two *candidate* disjuncts such that *in every possible situation the original is true if and only if at least one of these is true.* Thus,

Alfred bowls or skis

passes the test, but:

Everyone bowls or skis

does not. For the two *candidate* disjuncts are:

Everyone bowls
Everyone skis

But in the possible situation we just considered, the original is true but both of these are false. So we do *not* have a genuine disjunction but a non-molecular statement.[8]

---

[7] Notice, however, that there *is* an interpretation under which the example may be regarded as a conjunction. Consider an office party at which only office-workers, not their spouses (unless they too work at the office) are present. A new employee asks: 'which of the people here are married and which are single?' The manager replies: 'Alfred and Bertha are married, the rest are single.' Of course there is no reason to assume here that Alfred and Bertha are married to each other, or that the manager means to suggest this.

[8] These tests cannot be used unreflectively. The statement 'someone bowls or skis' passes the test (and there is no harm in regarding it as a disjunction). But by now we should be sufficiently struck by its structural similarity to 'everyone bowls or skis', which fails the test, and to 'someone bowls and skis', which fails the test for conjunction, to refuse to classify it as a disjunction. Such further complications provide matter for discussion under the heading of "logical form" in philosophy of logic. But, in any case, it is obvious that the argument:

Someone bowls or skis.
Someone does not bowl.

---

Someone skis.

is *not* valid, while the superficially similar argument:

We must now discuss a matter related to interpreting disjunctions. We have said that in every possible situation a disjunction is true if and only if *at least* one of its disjuncts is true. So it is true in all those possible situations in which *both* disjuncts are true. This is said to be an *inclusive* disjunction. It is obvious that at least some disjunctions are *inclusive*. Consider someone seeing the lights in Alfred's and Bertha's house, who then remarks: Either Alfred is home or Bertha is home. This would surely be true if Alfred were home but not Bertha, if Bertha were home but not Alfred, and if Alfred and Bertha were *both* home. But some people have held that there are also *exclusive* disjunctions: in all possible situations true if and only if *exactly* one of their disjuncts is true. So these disjunctions are false in all those possible situations in which *both* of their disjuncts are true. What makes this view plausible is that the following line of reasoning seems valid:

> Alfred is either in his bedroom or in his kitchen.
> He is in his kitchen.
> _____
> He is not in his bedroom.

If the truth of the first premise allowed both disjuncts to be true, it would be possible for the two premises to be true and the conclusion to be false—and so the argument would be invalid. It is, indeed, invalid. What makes it *seem* valid is that we tacitly assume a *further* premise. We think that Alfred's bedroom and Alfred's kitchen are two different rooms, and that he cannot be in both at once. But what about a possible situation in which Alfred is so poor that he has just one room which is both his kitchen and his bedroom? It can be plausibly held that disjunctions only *seem exclusive* because of background information (or misinformation) that the two disjuncts are not—or perhaps *cannot* be—both true. (Curiously enough, this background information may be conveyed by the assertion of the disjunction. Consider: 'You may have either cake or ice cream'.) In any case, *if* there are any *exclusive* disjunctions, they can be represented by means of *inclusive* disjunction, conjunction, and negation:[9]

$$(P \lor Q) \& \sim(P \& Q)$$

_____

> Alfred bowls or skis.
> Alfred does not bowl.
> _____
> Alfred skis.

*is* valid. Our procedure allows us to explain this by uncovering a *difference of logical form* in spite of the *superficial similarity*.

[9] Conversely, *inclusive* disjunction can be represented by means of *exclusive* disjunction

**6. Extent of Influence**. It should be obvious from our examples that although conjunctions and disjunctions are conjunctions and disjunctions of *statements*, the conjunction- or disjunction-indicating words in the sentences expressing them often occur between (or within) grammatical subjects, or predicates, or both. For example:

Alfred and Bertha bowl
Alfred or Bertha bowls
Alfred bowls and skis
Alfred bowls or skis
Alfred and Bertha bowl or ski
Alfred or Bertha bowls and skis

It will be noticed that the conjunction- or disjunction-indicating word which "goes with" the *grammatical subject(s)* has the greater extent of influence. Thus, with the phrase-book:

$$P \; : \quad \text{Alfred bowls}$$
$$Q \; : \quad \text{Bertha bowls}$$
$$R \; : \quad \text{Alfred skis}$$
$$S \; : \quad \text{Bertha skis}$$

the above examples are represented, respectively, by:

$$P \;\&\; Q$$
$$P \lor Q$$
$$P \;\&\; R$$
$$P \lor R$$
$$(P \lor R) \;\&\; (Q \lor S)$$
$$(P \;\&\; R) \lor (Q \;\&\; S)$$

We can now look further at how the preceding considerations help us to determine extents of influence. Consider the statement:

Alfred does not bowl or ski

If we take as a hypothesis that 'or' has the larger extent of influence, we must find two *candidate* disjuncts and check to see whether they are in fact *genuine* disjuncts. The two plausible candidates are

---

together with conjunction:

$$(P \mathbin{\underline{\lor}} Q) \mathbin{\underline{\lor}} (P \;\&\; Q)$$

where the symbol '$\underline{\lor}$' represents *exclusive* disjunction.

Alfred does not bowl
Alfred does not ski

But it is clear that it is *not* the case that the original statement is true in every possible situation in which *at least* one of these is true. So the hypothesis that this is a disjunction is not correct. An alternative hypothesis is that 'not' has the larger extent of influence. This time we must find a *candidate* negatum and check to see whether it is a *genuine* negatum. The plausible candidate is:

Alfred bowls or skis

and indeed, in every possible situation, this and the original statement have opposite truth-values. So the original is a negation of a disjunction. Parallel considerations lead to the conclusion that:

Neither Alfred nor Bertha bowls

is also a negation of a disjunction.[10]

If we consider:

No one came

a very natural hypothesis is that 'not' has the largest "extent of influence". (One might feel: how could there be less? Certainly there is no smaller *statement* here!) This is fine, *provided* that we can find a *genuine* negatum, which has to be:

Someone came

Matters become more complicated when we consider an example such as:

---

[10] There is a complication, however. For one reason or another (e.g., that the 'n' in 'neither' and 'nor' is "fused" too tightly with 'either' and 'or' to be *thus* separated out as a negation-indicator), one may resist our result here. Two possibilities are open. One may hold that 'neither...nor' means roughly the same as 'both not...and not...', so that the original is a conjunction of negations. (But then why do 'either' and 'or' remain at least as fragments? And why is the verb in the singular, as it is *not* in 'Both Alfred and Bertha do not bowl'?) Or, one might hold that we have here a *seventh* kind of statement not taken into account in our original classification. We might delve into this in the philosophy of logic. For now, it is enough to observe that the proposed seventh kind of statement, the conjunction of negations, and the negation of a disjunction are all *equivalent*, in the sense previously explained. The upshot is that we may represent the original either as '$\sim(A \vee B)$' or as '$\sim A \;\&\; \sim B$' (given an appropriate phrase-book). Related considerations apply to the examples discussed next.

None of the salesmen who accepted the invitation either came or phoned to cancel

But even here we can find a *genuine* negatum in:

Some of the salesmen who accepted the invitation either came or phoned to cancel

But we do run into serious difficulties with a statement such as:

No one bowls unless he skis

and with:

No one bowls if he does not ski

Here no *genuine* negata are easily found, so it is best to regard these (and similar cases) as *non-molecular* until further considerations show us a better way to handle them.

**7. Conditionals and Biconditionals.** The recognition of *conditionals* and *biconditionals* also requires considerations beyond the presence of conditional- or biconditional-indicating words and their extents of influence. However, for reasons that are complicated and not fully understood, it is *not* helpful to specify tests for these two kinds of statements in a way analogous to that for negations, conjunctions, and disjunctions (i.e., in terms of the relationships of truth-values in all possible situations). Instead, we will concentrate on a certain feature that is best introduced by means of examples.[11] First, notice that some expressions are *pronouns* or

---

[11] But our approach is still motivated by the same sorts of considerations as before. Although in every possible situation in which

Alfred bowls
Alfred skis

are both true, the statement

If Alfred bowls, then he does not ski

is false, it is *not* the case that in every possible situation in which

Someone bowls
Someone skis

are both true,

If someone bowls, then he does not ski

*pronoun-like.* Second, notice that these expressions typically "*cross-refer*" to other expressions. In the examples below, the *italic* pronouns or pronoun-like expressions cross-refer to the **bold** expressions as indicated by the arrows:

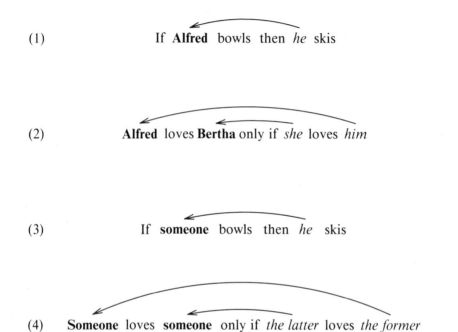

(1)                  If **Alfred** bowls then *he* skis

(2)        **Alfred** loves **Bertha** only if *she* loves *him*

(3)             If **someone** bowls then *he* skis

(4)    **Someone** loves **someone** only if *the latter* loves *the former*

Third, the expressions *to* which cross-reference is made are of two kinds: they either *purport to designate a single definite person, thing, or item,* or else they *do not.* Examples of the first kind are:

---

is false. Once again, the contrast is explained by uncovering a *difference in logical form* underneath the *superficial similarity.*

> Alfred
> the marquis
> the first person ever to confess to the abbé
> the tallest mountain
> what Fred bought for Aunt Nellie
> what the marquis said
> that man

Examples of the second kind are:

> someone
> everyone
> no one
> some marquis
> a marquis
> a person who confessed to the abbé
> a tall mountain
> any tall mountain
> something Fred bought for Aunt Nellie
> something the marquis said
> anything the marquis said
> one of those men
> a certain marquis

There may be some difficulty in deciding to which of these classes an expression belongs, and the context of utterance will often play a role.[12] Let us do the best we can.

---

[12] Notice, for instance, that according to context, expressions (like those) of the first kind may play the role of *pronoun-like* expressions:

If **a person** bowls   then   *that person*  skis

If  the abbé has absolved   **a marquis**  then *the marquis* is happy

Now when a sentence contains a pronoun or pronoun-like expression which cross-refers to an expression of the *second* kind, we shall say that an *indefinite pronomial cross-reference* is present. For example, in (3) and (4) above, there are respectively one and two indefinite pronominal cross-references present. When confronted with a sentence which, because of the presence of a conditional-indicating word or phrase and its "extent of influence", *seems* to be a conditional, we subject it to the following test: find a *candidate* antecedent and a *candidate* consequent and check to see whether an indefinite pronomial cross-reference from one to the other is present. If there is, then the statement is *not* a conditional (and is then non-molecular). If there is not, then it *is* a conditional.[13] Note that it is not the mere presence of expressions of the second kind that disqualifies a statement from being a conditional, but the presence of *indefinite pronomial cross-reference*. Thus,

If someone bowls, then someone skis

*is* a conditional, but (3) above is not.[14]

We subject a sentence which, because of the presence of a biconditional-indicating word or phrase and its "extent of influence", *seems* to be a biconditional to the same test. If there is an indefinite pronomial cross-reference from one of the *candidate* sides to the other, the statement is *not* a biconditional (and is non-molecular). If there is not, it *is* a biconditional.[15]

---

[13] Except that the statement is also *not* a conditional if the sentence expressing it is in the *subjunctive mood*; for example,

If Alfred were to bowl, he would ski.

The best we can do at this point is to classify it as non-molecular.

[14] Notice that we can use the considerations about indefinite pronominal cross-reference to reinforce our decision that the statement 'Someone either bowls or skis' is *not* a disjunction (in spite of its passing the test of possible combinations of truth-values). For, it has what appears to be a merely stylistic variant in (the admittedly rather awkward) 'Either someone bowls or he skis'. And here clearly there *is* an indefinite pronominal cross-reference from one *candidate* disjunct to the other. So these are not *genuine* disjuncts, if *genuine* disjuncts do not admit indefinite pronominal cross-reference from one to the other (just as genuine antecedents and consequents do not). A similar result will be obtained if we compare 'Everyone bowls and skis' with (the admittedly rather awkward) 'Everyone is such that he bowls and he skis'. This sort of reflection also helps us with 'who' ('which' etc.), which we characterized above as a conjunction-indicating word. The statement 'Alfred, who bowls, skis' is indeed a conjunction. But the statement 'Someone, who bowls, skis' is *not*. (And this is true quite apart from the far-from trivial distinction made by the *commas* which set off 'who bowls'; more about this later.) 'Who' is grammatically a pronoun, and in the latter example it cross-refers to 'someone'. So an indefinite pronominal cross-reference is present between the two *candidate* conjuncts. So if we reason as above, they are *not* genuine conjuncts, and the whole is *not* a conjunction. But, of course, we reach the same result by trying—and failing—to find genuine conjuncts.

[15] Unless, again, the sentence is in the *subjunctive mood*; for example,

Finally, you must not let indefinite pronomial cross-reference disqualify something from being a conditional or biconditional when that indefinite pronomial cross-reference does *not* extend from a candidate antecedent to a candidate consequent or *vice versa*, or from one side of a biconditional to the other. For example,

> If Bertha skis then someone loves her if and only if he is tolerant

*is* a conditional, though its consequent is *not* a biconditional. Similarly,

> Bertha skis if and only if someone loves her only if he is tolerant

*is* a biconditional, though its right side is *not* a conditional. However, in:

> If Bertha loves someone, then he is tolerant if she skis

having classified the whole as non-molecular, we cannot classify 'he is tolerant if she skis' as a conditional, even though there is no indefinite pronomial cross-reference *within* this *part*, because we have *not distinguished it as a statement* by finding it to be a negatum, conjunct, disjunct, antecedent, consequent, or side of some other statement. In this connection, let us remind ourselves that in difficult cases we can, and perhaps should, proceed step by step "paraphrasing inward" in the manner illustrated at the end of the previous chapter.

**8. Summary**. Very roughly speaking, and *subject to qualifications and emendations to be discussed later*, two arguments have the same logical form when their respective premises and conclusions are of the same kinds of statements, and their "components" recur in the same pattern. In doing the exercises in Chapter 4, however, you may already have been able to tell that some statements which are counted by our six-fold classification as of the same kind—namely, non-molecular—are nevertheless of different kinds (to be studied later). Thus the two arguments:

> If someone is rich, then he is happy.
> Someone is rich.
> _____
> Someone is happy.

---

Alfred would bowl if and only if he were to ski.

This is also best classified as non-molecular.

Everyone is rich.
Someone is happy.

_____

Someone is rich and happy.

are obviously of *different* forms, even though *all* the statements are non-molecular. Use your intuitions along with the clues!

**Exercises**

_____

1    Represent the logical form of the following arguments, using the phrase-book provided. (Do not try to represent the word 'therefore'.)

$D$ :    Murphy hits into a double play.
$K$ :    Kingman lays off the first pitch.
$G$ :    Murphy hits a ground ball.
$H$ :    Henderson is on first.
$R$ :    Kingman hits a home run.
$S$ :    Murphy is on second.
$N$ :    No one is on second.
$P$ :    Kingman will stride to the plate.
$U$ :    Kingman will pop up.
$L$ :    Henderson will steal second.
$M$ :    Murphy will score.
$T$ :    At least three runs will score.

(a)  Henderson will steal second if and only if he is on first and no one is on second. If Kingman hits a home run, Henderson will not steal second. Henderson will not steal second. Therefore, either Henderson is not on first, or someone is on second, or Kingman does not hit a homer.

(b)  Henderson is on first and Murphy is on second. If Kingman hits a homer and Henderson is on first and Murphy is on second, then at least three runs will score. Kingman hits a homer. Therefore, at least three runs will score.

(c)  If Murphy hits a ground ball and Henderson is on first, then Henderson will not steal second unless Murphy hits into a double-play. Murphy hits a ground ball into a double play. Therefore, Henderson, if he is on first, will not steal second.

(d)  If Murphy does not hit a double-play ball, then Kingman will stride to the plate. If Kingman strides to the plate and lays off the first pitch, he will not pop up. If Kingman pops up, Murphy will not score. But Murphy will not score. Therefore, Kingman did not stride to the plate and Murphy hit a double-play ball.

2    Provide an appropriate phrase-book and represent the logical form of the following arguments. (As above, do not try to represent the word 'therefore'.)

(a)  Unless Bertha recalibrates her digital scanner immediately, she will not pass physics. Unless Bertha passes both physics and computer science, she will not get a job at Bell Labs. But Bertha will pass computer science only if she completes her programming assignment, in which case she will not recalibrate her digital scanner immediately. Therefore, Bertha will not get a job at Bell Labs.

(b)  Bates will pass his programming assignment just in case he uses the famed "Knuth procedure" to write up the answer. If Bates does use this procedure to write up his answer, then the T.A. will not bother to read that answer, and if the T.A. does not bother to read the answer, Bates will pass the assignment. Therefore, if Bates passes the programming assignment, the T.A. will not bother to read his answer.

3    Give a representation of the logical form of each of the following sentences, using a phrase-book of your own design. Choose your phrase-book in such a way that you represent as much of the logical form as possible.

(a)  If someone commits a crime while Holmes is away, Holmes will catch him.

(b)  The crime will be solved by Holmes if the clues are elementary.

(c)  Holmes will solve the crime just in case neither Watson nor Moriarty is needed.

(d)  If the clues are elementary and Holmes is in town, then either Watson or Moriarty will be needed, but not both.

(e)  If Holmes is out of town, then anyone who commits a crime will get away with it unless he leaves too many clues while committing the crime.

# Chapter 6

## Derivations

**1. Formal Validity.** Now that we have learned how to represent the *form* of various statements and arguments, our next job is to use these representations to figure out whether a given argument is valid or not. Recall that an argument is *valid* just in case it is not possible for the premises of the argument all to be true together while the conclusion is false. Our interest in isolating the logical form of statements and arguments stems from our interest in the closely related notion of *formal validity*. An argument is said to be *formally valid* just in case it has a form such that *all* arguments of that form are valid. Similarly, an argument is said to be *formally invalid* just in case it has a form such that *not* all arguments of that form are valid. We investigate this latter notion systematically in Chapter 11.

It is clear, of course, that the notion of *formal validity* depends on our already having available the notion of a *form* of an argument. This may seem trivial, but it will have consequences that you should be forewarned about. One very important consequence of this definition is that an argument will be assessed as formally valid or not depending on *how much* of the form we are able to represent. As we shall see throughout this book, the form of an argument may be specified in greater or lesser detail, and our ability to determine whether some given argument is valid or not depends on our ability to represent more or less of the argument's form. So we may find that an argument is formally invalid when some of its form is represented, but formally valid when *more* of its form is represented. Of course, if an argument is shown to be formally valid, then it is valid. But if it is shown not to be formally valid with respect to a given way of representing its form, we cannot thereby conclude that it is invalid, for it may have a more detailed form that *is* valid.[1] Generally we can say this much: given an argument of a certain form, either every argument of that form is valid, or every argument of that form is invalid, *unless that argument has a more detailed form that is valid.*

---

[1] Recall the example at the end of the previous chapter.

Clearly, assigning forms to statements and arguments is an important business; it is also sometimes a difficult one, and many of the more controversial regions of logic and the philosophy of logic are concerned precisely with determining what logical form a certain statement or certain type of statement has.

**2. Derivation.** Our job right now is to devise a technique for determining the *formal validity* of arguments with respect to forms we have already isolated (i.e., those specifiable in terms of the classification into negations, conjunctions, disjunctions, conditionals, and biconditionals). The technique we shall employ to determine whether such an argument is formally valid is the technique of *derivation*. Let us introduce this technique by way of an example.

One *obviously* valid form is the following: from a conditional and the antecedent of that conditional, the consequent of the conditional follows. The following formulas exhibit this obviously valid form:

$$A \supset B$$
$$\underline{A \qquad\qquad}$$
$$B$$

We may then exploit the fact that this form is obviously valid to show that more complicated, less obviously valid forms are indeed valid. For instance, the following more complicated form is somewhat less obviously valid:

$$A$$
$$A \supset B$$
$$B \supset C$$
$$C \supset D$$
$$\underline{D \supset E}$$
$$E$$

We can easily "reduce" any argument of this form to a combination of smaller, simpler arguments of *obviously* valid forms (indeed, in this case, of arguments of one and the same obviously valid form, the one exhibited just above):

$$A$$
$$\underline{A \supset B}$$
$$B$$
$$\underline{B \supset C}$$
$$C$$
$$\underline{C \supset D}$$
$$D$$
$$\underline{D \supset E}$$
$$E$$

We may thus regard the more complicated form, which is valid, as a *combination* of four instances of the much simpler form isolated above.

What have we done? Let us concentrate on the first three formulas in the list above. We have taken two of the premises of the original line of reasoning (the first two formulas above) and *added a new formula* (the third formula above). This new formula is a conclusion of an *obviously* valid line of reasoning (the one exhibited earlier) from the first two formulas as premises. Now let us concentrate on the third, fourth, and fifth formulas. We have taken the new formula which we just added and another of the original premises and *added a further new formula*. This further new formula is, once again, a conclusion of an *obviously* valid line of reasoning (once again, the one exhibited earlier) from the two immediately preceding formulas: the formula we had first added and a formula which is one of the original premises. What is the role of the formula we first added? It is at once a *conclusion* of the first obviously valid argument and one of the *premises* of the second obviously valid argument (or line of reasoning). The pair of roles this formula plays can be illustrated in the diagram on the opposite page.

What does this show? It shows that the logical form whose premises are represented by the first, second, and fourth formulas, and whose conclusion is represented by the fifth formula is *valid*. Notice that the third formula, the one we first added, is *not* (i.e., does not represent) either a premise or the conclusion of *this* form. Generally, when a formula is the conclusion of one obviously valid form and one of the premises of a second obviously valid form, a third form whose premises are all those of the first form and all the *others* of the second form is also valid.[2] So we

---

[2] If this is not obvious, it can be made "indirectly obvious" by a reflection of the following sort. (We restrict ourselves to the example we are discussing.) Consider any argument whose premises are represented by the first, second, and fourth formulas, and consider any possible situation in which all three of these premises are true. Then the statement

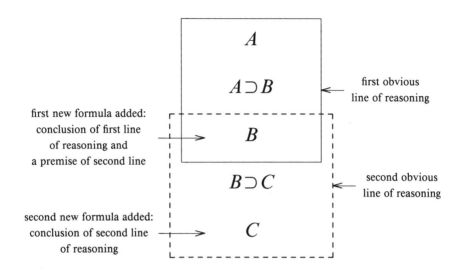

see that the first five formulas in the list show that the form whose premises are the first, second, and fourth formulas, and whose conclusion is the
fifth formula, is *valid*. Keep in mind that the third formula is *not* either a
premise or the conclusion of *this* form.[3]

Having seen this, we can by parallel reflections see that the first seven formulas on the list show that the form whose premises are the first, second,
fourth, and sixth formulas, and whose conclusion is the seventh formula,
is *valid*. Notice that neither the third nor the fifth formula is either a
premise or the conclusion of *this* form. We may continue in this vein
until we see that the entire list shows that the form whose premises are
the first, second, fourth, sixth, and eight formulas, and whose conclusion
is the ninth formula, is *valid*. But, if you will look back, this is precisely
the form with which we began as *not* obviously valid. It is now

---

represented by the third formula is true in this possible situation (since the first two are true
and the first form is obviously valid). But then the statement represented by the fifth formula (viz., the conclusion of the line of reasoning we are considering) is true in this possible situation (since the two premises of the second obvious form are true and that form is obviously valid). So in every possible situation in which the premises of the argument we are
considering are true, the conclusion is also true. That is, the argument is valid. So every
such line of reasoning is valid. That is, the *form* we are discussing is valid.

[3] Strictly speaking, we should say more cumbersomely, but more accurately: the form of
any argument whose premises are represented by the first, second, and fourth formulas, and
whose conclusion is represented by the fifth formula, is *valid*, and the statement represented
by the third formula is not either a premise or the conclusion of that argument. We shall
usually sacrifice such accuracy for ease of grasping the point.

"indirectly obvious" that it *is* valid. And it is "indirectly obvious" because we can see it as a "combination" or sequence of *obviously* valid forms linked by formulas—which we have found and written down—which are conclusions of earlier (obviously, or "indirectly obviously") valid forms and premises of later obviously valid forms. These intervening formulas (or *steps*, as we shall call them) are the third, fifth, and seventh formulas on the list. It is important to realize that they are *not* either premises or the conclusion of the form which we finally showed to be valid (though, of course, they *are* conclusions and also premises of forms which are "parts" of this form).

**3. Preliminary Summary.** We may note that such a list of formulas as the one we have been discussing corresponds rather closely to a "line of reasoning" or "argument" in a rather different sense from the one in which we have been using these terms so far. So far we have meant by 'line of reasoning' or 'argument' any combination of a set of statements (the premises) with a single statement (the conclusion). But these phrases are frequently used in ordinary discourse for a sequence consisting of the premises and the conclusion (of a "line of reasoning" in the *first* sense) *and intervening steps*, arranged in such a way as to (try to) make it indirectly obvious that a "line of reasoning" in the *first* sense is valid. You probably went through a "line of reasoning" in the *second* sense if you tried to solve the puzzle about the color of the hat on the blind man's head (Chapter 2). "Lines of reasoning" in this *second* sense we shall call *derivations*.

With certain reservations which need not concern us right now, every valid argument form is either obviously valid or is a "combination" of obviously valid forms. If we are presented with an argument form that is not obviously valid and not obviously invalid, we must try to find a sequence that begins with the premises of the argument and ends with the desired conclusion, and which consists of forms each of which is *obviously* correct. (By '*obviously* correct' we mean that it is the conclusion of an *obviously* valid form whose premises are *earlier* items in the sequence.) If we succeed, we can be assured that the conclusion really does follow from the given premises. So our job reduces to this: find a set of *obviously* correct steps of reasoning that will permit us to construct appropriate derivations of the conclusion of an argument from the premises.

Our general procedure, then, for showing that a given argument is valid is this:

(1)   Determine what the premises of the argument are and what its conclusion is.

(2)   Collect the non-molecular statements contained in the argument into a "phrase-book" and then represent the logical form of each premise and the conclusion in accordance with that phrase-book.

(3)   Show either that this form is one of the specially selected (see below) obviously valid forms or that this form is a "combination" of these obviously valid forms.

(4)   This shows that the argument is valid (indeed, formally valid) because it has a form such that all arguments of that form are valid.

**4. Rules of Derivation.** Our next task then is to adopt a preferred set of obviously valid forms of reasoning as required by step (3) above. The ones we shall adopt may seem so obvious as to be hardly worth stating, unless our goal of reducing more complicated forms to these simple ones is forgotten.[4] Ultimately, we shall have about a dozen such forms; right now we shall content ourselves with introducing six of them. We state each rule precisely and then follow it with a pair of examples:

---

DS          Given the disjunction of two formulas and the negation of one of them, infer the other.

---

Given:   $P \vee Q$              Given:   $(P \supset R) \vee \sim(Q \supset R)$

and:   $\sim Q$                    and:   $\sim(P \supset R)$

Infer:   $P$                       Infer:   $\sim(Q \supset R)$

---

MPP          Given a conditional and also the antecedent of the conditional, infer its consequent.

---

Given:   $R$                       Given:   $(P \vee Q) \supset (\sim R \supset Q)$

and:   $R \supset S$               and:   $P \vee Q$

Infer:   $S$                       Infer:   $\sim R \supset Q$

---

[4] If you have any difficulty seeing the validity of these forms, you should review what we said in Chapter 5 about recognizing "genuine" negations, conjunctions, etc.

---

| &I | Given two formulas (not necessarily distinct), infer their conjunction. |
|---|---|

---

| Given: | *P* v *Q* | | Given: | *P* & *Q* |
|---|---|---|---|---|
| and: | *S* | | and: | ~(*R* ⊃ *P*) |
| Infer: | (*P* v *Q*) & *S* | | Infer: | (*P* & *Q*) & ~(*R* ⊃ *P*) |

---

| &E | Given a conjunction, infer either conjunct. |
|---|---|

---

| Given: | *P* & *Q* | | Given: | ~(*P* & *Q*) & (*R* ⊃ *P*) |
|---|---|---|---|---|
| Infer: | *Q* | | Infer: | ~(*P* & *Q*) |

---

| DNI | Given a formula, infer its double negation. |
|---|---|

---

| Given: | *R* | | Given: | *P* ⊃ *Q* |
|---|---|---|---|---|
| Infer: | ~~*R* | | Infer: | ~~(*P* ⊃ *Q*) |

---

| DNE | Given the double negation of a formula, infer the formula. |
|---|---|

---

| Given: | ~~*P* | | Given: | ~~(~*P* v *Q*) |
|---|---|---|---|---|
| Infer: | *P* | | Infer: | ~*P* v *Q* |

Generally, rules with names ending with the letter 'E' provide a way of *eliminating* the connective in question. Thus, rules &E and DNE allow us to eliminate conjunction signs and double negation signs, respectively. Similarly, rules with names ending with the letter 'I' usually provide a way of *introducing* a formula containing the connective in question. Thus, rules &I and DNI allow us to introduce conjunction signs and double negation signs, respectively. The other names derive from the history of logic; DS represents the disjunctive syllogism and MPP represents the line of reasoning named *modus ponendo ponens*.

**5. The Need for Derivations.** We need to develop some standard way of recording the fact that a complicated argument form is indeed composed out of these simple forms. Provisionally we shall take a *derivation* to be any list of numbered lines (beginning with 1), each of which has exactly one formula written on it, and such that each formula is either one of the initial premises of the argument or may be entered on the line in accordance with one of these rules. Whenever a formula has been entered on a line in accordance with some rule, we note this by writing the line numeral(s) of the line(s) to which the rule has been applied, as well as the name of the rule itself, on the line following the formula. We can then rewrite the informal line of reasoning given above somewhat more compactly as:

| | | |
|---|---|---|
| 1 | $A$ | |
| 2 | $A \supset B$ | |
| 3 | $B \supset C$ | |
| 4 | $C \supset D$ | |
| 5 | $D \supset E$ | |
| 6 | $B$ | 1,2 MPP |
| 7 | $C$ | 6,3 MPP |
| 8 | $D$ | 7,4 MPP |
| 9 | $E$ | 8,5 MPP |

The order of the lines is immaterial, as long as each line contains a formula that is either a given premise or the result of applying one of our rules to some earlier line(s). So we could have constructed this derivation to have an even greater resemblance to the informal line of reasoning we originally gave. We have not done so because we prefer to keep our premises together at the beginning of our derivations. This is a useful convention, and we shall use it (with few if any exceptions) for the rest of this book.

Let us give two further examples of derivations. The following derivation is relatively simple, but illustrates the use of several rules in one derivation. You should make sure that you see how each line (aside from the "given" lines) can be derived from the preceding lines using the rule cited.

| | | |
|---|---|---|
| 1 | $P$ | |
| 2 | $(P \supset Q) \lor B$ | |
| 3 | $\sim B$ | |
| 4 | $P \supset Q$ | 2,3 DS |
| 5 | $Q$ | 1,4 MPP |

A slightly more complicated derivation is the following:

| 1 | $A$ | |
| 2 | $B$ | |
| 3 | $(A \mathbin{\&} B) \supset (C \mathbin{\&} D)$ | |
| 4 | $A \mathbin{\&} B$ | 1,2 &I |
| 5 | $C \mathbin{\&} D$ | 3,4 MPP |
| 6 | $D$ | 5 &E |

We can also construct relatively complicated derivations, even with just these six rules of derivation. Consider:

| 1 | $\sim Q \vee \sim\sim R$ | |
| 2 | $R \supset (S \mathbin{\&} \sim T)$ | |
| 3 | $Q \mathbin{\&} (S \supset G)$ | |
| 4 | $\sim G \vee P$ | |
| 5 | $Q$ | 3 &E |
| 6 | $\sim\sim Q$ | 5 DNI |
| 7 | $\sim\sim R$ | 1,6 DS |
| 8 | $R$ | 7 DNE |
| 9 | $S \mathbin{\&} \sim T$ | 2,8 MPP |
| 10 | $S$ | 9 &E |
| 11 | $S \supset G$ | 3 &E |
| 12 | $G$ | 10,11 MPP |
| 13 | $\sim\sim G$ | 12 DNI |
| 14 | $P$ | 4,13 DS |

**6. Strategy Hints**. The rules of derivation that we have adopted specify situations in which you may write down certain formulas, given that certain precisely specified conditions are satisfied. A derivation is, as it were, a logical bridge between given formulas (the premises of an argument) and some other formula (the conclusion of that argument). But the rules themselves do not specify how to go about building this bridge. Even if we are thoroughly familiar with *how* to apply some rule, that by itself does not tell us *when* it will be useful to do so. To develop facility at constructing derivations, we need to know when it is useful or prudent to apply some particular rule, and also when it is not. This is the province of what we will call *strategy hints* or *rules of thumb* for constructing derivations.

The most important strategy hint to keep in mind in constructing any derivation is this: *work backward*. This may sound odd, but it is really just an application of the obviously good advice that if you want to get somewhere, it helps to keep in mind where it is that you want to go and how you might get there. From a given set of formulas, one can derive an infinite number of different formulas. But typically you want to derive a single specific formula—the desired conclusion. So you are unlikely to make progress by blindly applying our rules to formulas you are given; success would depend on incredible luck. But if you keep in mind the formula you aim to derive and ask yourself how you could derive it, you will find the process of constructing a derivation to be much quicker, easier, and (potentially) more enjoyable. So remember: *work backward!*

The wisdom of this advice is dependent on the happy empirical fact that, in most cases, there is an obvious way to go about doing this. Suppose for instance that the formula we want to find a derivation of is a conjunction. To be specific, suppose that we want to find a derivation from the two formulas:

$$P \mathbin{\&} (Q \supset R)$$
$$P \supset Q$$

to the formula:

$$Q \mathbin{\&} {\sim}{\sim}R$$

We begin every derivation by writing in the given formulas at the top and the formula to be derived from them at the bottom, leaving some space to hold the intervening steps:

1  $P \mathbin{\&} (Q \supset R)$
2  $P \supset Q$


$Q \mathbin{\&} {\sim}{\sim}R$

The desired conclusion is a conjunction. How might we go about deriving a conjunction? Clearly, if we could derive one conjunct, and then the other, then by rule &I we could derive the conjunction. So our task easily splits up into two subtasks: derive one conjunct, and then the other. We indicate our new subgoals as follows (again leaving space for further developments):

1  $P \mathbin{\&} (Q \supset R)$
2  $P \supset Q$

$Q$

${\sim}{\sim}R$
$Q \mathbin{\&} {\sim}{\sim}R$             &I

Notice that we have indicated the rule by which we plan to derive the conjunction in question. Now our goal is no longer to derive '$Q$ & $\sim\sim R$', for we know how to get that if we can first derive both '$Q$' and '$\sim\sim R$'. '$Q$' of course is an atomic formula, and right now there is no way to work backward any further from it. But '$\sim\sim R$' is molecular, and obviously we could derive it from the formula '$R$', as follows:

1    $P$ & $(Q \supset R)$
2    $P \supset Q$

     $Q$

     $R$
     $\sim\sim R$                DNI
     $Q$ & $\sim\sim R$       &I

Already our (partial) derivation has a good bit of structure, even though we have not yet applied any rule to our given lines. But we have worked backward as far as we can. Now we need to work forward. Line (1) is a conjunction; generally it is a good idea to break conjunctions into their conjuncts, as allowed by rule &E. So we get:

1    $P$ & $(Q \supset R)$
2    $P \supset Q$
3    $P$             1 &E
4    $Q \supset R$     1 &E

     $Q$

     $R$
     $\sim\sim R$                DNI
     $Q$ & $\sim\sim R$       &I

Now we may apply rule MPP to lines (2) and (3) to get '$Q$', which was one of our desired goals. Also, '$Q$' and line (4) give us '$R$', our other desired goal. So we may complete the derivation:

| 1 | $P \mathbin{\&} (Q \supset R)$ | |
|---|---|---|
| 2 | $P \supset Q$ | |
| 3 | $P$ | 1 &E |
| 4 | $Q \supset R$ | 1 &E |
| 5 | $Q$ | 2,3 MPP |
| 6 | $R$ | 4,5 MPP |
| 7 | $\sim\sim R$ | 6 DNI |
| 8 | $Q \mathbin{\&} \sim\sim R$ | 5,7 &I |

Let us reconsider briefly what we have just accomplished. First we looked at the formula we were to derive and asked how we could derive it. In this case the formula to be derived was a conjunction. Then we made a hypothesis about which rule could be used to yield that formula and considered how the derivation must look if we were to use that rule. At this point—*working backward*—we actually began sketching in the derivation. We felt that it would be reasonable to hypothesize that the desired conjunction could be derived using rule &I as the last step. On this hypothesis, our attention turned to deriving each of the conjuncts separately; we then repeated the entire process, first focusing on one of the desired conjuncts and then on the other. By working backward in this way, successively altering the formula aimed for, you will (with any luck) either arrive at your initial suppositions or have reduced your goal to formulas that you can easily derive from your initial suppositions.

**7. Strategy Hints Summarized.** We can frame the following strategy hints:

☛ If the desired formula is a conjunction, try to derive each conjunct separately; then apply rule &I.

☛ If the desired formula is a double negation, try to derive the formula of which it is the double negation; then apply rule DNI.

☛ If you are given (or have already derived) a conjunction, derive each conjunct by applying rule &E.

☛ If you are given (or have already derived) a double negation, derive the formula of which it is a double negation by applying rule DNE.

☛ If you are given (or have already derived) a conditional, try to derive the antecedent; then apply rule MPP.

☛ If you are given (or have already derived) a disjunction, try to derive the negation of one side; then apply rule DS.

Remember that our primary rule of thumb in constructing derivations is to work backward as much as possible. You should therefore heed the first two strategy hints before attempting to heed the remaining four.

**Exercises**

---

1  In each of the items below, take the last formula to be the conclusion of an argument and the remaining formulas the premises of that argument. Construct a derivation using only the six rules introduced above to show that the argument represents a formally valid pattern of argument.

(a)
$$P$$
$$\sim Q$$
$$(P \text{ \& } \sim Q) \supset R$$
$$R$$

(b)
$$P \text{ v } Q$$
$$Q \supset R$$
$$((P \text{ v } Q) \text{ \& } (Q \supset R)) \supset \sim P$$
$$\sim P$$

(c)
$$P \text{ \& } \sim Q$$
$$\sim R \text{ \& } S$$
$$(\sim Q \text{ \& } \sim R) \supset T$$
$$T$$

(d)
$$P \text{ \& } \sim Q$$
$$P \supset (\sim Q \supset R)$$
$$R$$

(e)
$$P$$
$$\sim P \text{ v } (Q \text{ \& } S)$$
$$\sim (Q \text{ \& } S) \text{ v } R$$
$$R$$

(f)
$$\sim P$$
$$P \text{ v } S$$
$$(\sim P \text{ \& } S) \supset (R \text{ v } P)$$
$$R$$

(g)
$$R$$
$$\sim (P \text{ v } Q)$$
$$(P \text{ v } Q) \text{ v } \sim S$$
$$\sim S \supset (R \supset P)$$
$$P$$

(h)
$$(T \text{ \& } Q) \supset P$$
$$P \text{ \& } Q$$
$$P \supset \sim\sim(Q \text{ \& } S)$$
$$S \supset R$$
$$\sim R \text{ v } T$$
$$\sim\sim P$$

2  Do the same for each of the following groups of formulas.

(a)
$$P \text{ \& } (S \supset T)$$
$$\sim\sim Q$$
$$(\sim\sim P \text{ \& } Q) \supset S$$
$$T$$

(b)
$$\sim P$$
$$(P \text{ v } Q) \text{ v } R$$
$$\sim\sim\sim R$$
$$Q$$

(c)
$$\sim (P \text{ \& } Q)$$
$$(P \text{ \& } Q) \text{ v } R$$
$$R \supset S$$
$$S \text{ \& } R$$

(d)
$$R \supset \sim P$$
$$P \text{ v } Q$$
$$R \text{ v } \sim (P \text{ v } Q)$$
$$Q$$

---

# Chapter 7

# Complex Rules

**1. Complex Lines of Reasoning.** So far we have concentrated on rules of derivation which capture obviously valid lines of reasoning from some set of statements (the premises) to some single statement (the conclusion). Often it happens, however, that our reasoning concerns not only *statements*, but also other *lines of reasoning.* In Chapter 2 we saw an example of this in the little story about the sadistic warden and his three prisoners. Such lines of reasoning, which depend on the validity or invalidity of other lines of reasoning, are very important to logic and we shall henceforth call them *complex* lines of reasoning.

Let us consider another very simple case of this sort. Suppose, first of all, that Alfred goes through the following line of reasoning:

> It is windy.
> It is rainy.
> If it is windy and rainy, then it is stormy.
> _____
> It is stormy.

This line of reasoning is valid: if the premises are true, the conclusion must also be true. But suppose next that Bertha happens to disbelieve one of the three premises, for instance that it is rainy. So Bertha is disinclined to suppose this statement as a premise in any line of reasoning that she might go through. Still, if she reflects on the validity of Alfred's line of reasoning, Bertha can go through the following line of reasoning:

> It is windy.
> If it is windy and rainy, then it is stormy.
> _____
> If it is rainy, then it is stormy.

This second line of reasoning has some, but not all, of the premises of the first. Also, its conclusion is a conditional, whereas the conclusion of Alfred's argument was not. So clearly these are *different* lines of reasoning. Also, if the validity of Bertha's argument were not directly obvious to someone, we could probably make it indirectly obvious by appealing to the obvious validity of Alfred's line of reasoning.

**2. Supposition Numerals.** In order to handle such complex lines of reasoning systematically, we need a way to indicate precisely which premises a given conclusion depends upon. We may do this by adopting a system of bookkeeping involving what are called *supposition numerals*. Observe that when we set out lines of reasoning, we always start with certain formulas. These formulas may or may not be true, and they may or may not be believed to be true; all this is irrelevant from the point of view of logic alone. In logic, we simply *suppose* that these formulas are true in order to determine what *follows* from them—that is, what would have to be true *if* they were to be true.

Evidently, we may suppose anything we please, at any time, provided that we make it clear that we are only making a supposition. To mark this clearly, we adopt the rule:

---

S          Any formula may be written down on a line, provided that
           you take the line numeral as supposition numeral of this line.

---

We now require that each formula in a derivation must have some set of supposition numerals associated with it. These numerals are indications of which formulas that formula is viewed as following from. We indicate the supposition numerals of each formula occurring in a derivation by drawing a vertical line to the left of the line numeral and writing the supposition numerals to the left of the line.

Consider some examples. We might begin a derivation by making two suppositions (these might be the premises of an argument). In this case, we would write down:

$$1 \mid \quad 1 \quad A \qquad\qquad\qquad\qquad S$$
$$2 \mid \quad 2 \quad A \supset B \qquad\qquad\quad S$$

And in the middle of a derivation, for example at step 7, we might write:

$$7 \mid \quad 7 \quad P \,\&\, R \qquad\qquad\qquad S$$

Whenever we use any of the six rules DS, MPP, &I, &E, DNI, or DNE, we write down as the supposition numerals of the "inferred" line all those which are supposition numerals of the "given" line or lines. (We call a rule that has this feature a *simple* rule of derivation.) For example:

$$
\begin{array}{c|cll}
1 & 1 & A & \text{S} \\
2 & 2 & A \supset B & \text{S} \\
1,2 & 3 & B & \text{1,2 MPP}
\end{array}
$$

And here is another example, from the middle of a derivation:

$$
\begin{array}{c|cll}
1,2,5 & 7 & \sim P \supset (Q \supset S) & \\
1,3,5 & 8 & \sim P & \\
 & & & \\
1,2,3,5 & 14 & Q \supset S & \text{7,8 MPP}
\end{array}
$$

In this way we may distinguish between those lines which we "infer" from our suppositions and those suppositions themselves, so that we may see (in the second example) that the formula on line 14 would have to be true if our original suppositions 1, 2, 3, and 5 (whatever they are in this case) were to be true. Suppositions are, so to speak, the starting point of our reasoning.

**3. Further Discussion.** Let us try to understand this more clearly. Recall our discussion in the previous chapter of the form:

$$
\begin{array}{l}
A \\
A \supset B \\
B \supset C \\
C \supset D \\
D \supset E \\
\hline
E
\end{array}
$$

We observed that we could show it to be valid by constructing an analogue of a "line of reasoning" (in the second sense) by adding obviously correct steps. Let us recall our first attempt and concentrate on the first portion of it:

|   |       |          |
|---|-------|----------|
| 1 | $A$   |          |
| 2 | $A \supset B$ |  |
| 3 | $B$   | 1,2 MPP  |
| 4 | $B \supset C$ |  |
| 5 | $C$   | 3,4 MPP  |

—adding the convenient numbering and the specification of the *obviously* valid forms (but leaving out for the moment the citation of rule S). What was our insight then? We realized that since:

(a)   the form with (1) and (2) as premises and (3) as conclusion is *obviously* valid, and

(b)   the form with (3) and (4) as premises and (5) as conclusion is *obviously* valid,

it must be the case that:

(c)   the form with (1), (2), and (4) as premises and (5) as conclusion is *also* valid—and line (3) is neither a premise nor the conclusion of *this* form.

The system of bookkeeping using supposition numerals allows us to represent very explicitly this last observation (c):

|       |   |       |          |
|-------|---|-------|----------|
| 1     | 1 | $A$   |          |
| 2     | 2 | $A \supset B$ |  |
| 1,2   | 3 | $B$   | 1,2 MPP  |
| 4     | 4 | $B \supset C$ |  |
| 1,2,4 | 5 | $C$   | 3,4 MPP  |

The notation to the right shows the *obviously* valid forms we are relying on (observations [a] and [b] above), while the supposition numerals of line (5) reflect observation (c). We then went on to observe that as we continued:

```
  1  │  1   A
  2  │  2   A ⊃ B
 1,2 │  3   B                                    1,2 MPP
  4  │  4   B ⊃ C
1,2,4│  5   C                                    3,4 MPP
     │  6   C ⊃ D
     │  7   D                                    5,6 MPP
```

we were able to see that the form with lines (1), (2), (4), and (6) as premises and (7) as conclusion is *also* valid—and that neither (3) nor (5) is
either a premise or the conclusion of *this* form. Once again, this is very
explicitly shown by the supposition numerals of line (7):

```
    1   │  1   A
    2   │  2   A ⊃ B
   1,2  │  3   B                                 1,2 MPP
    4   │  4   B ⊃ C
  1,2,4 │  5   C                                 3,4 MPP
    6   │  6   C ⊃ D
 1,2,4,6│  7   D                                 5,6 MPP
```

Finally, we saw that the form with which we began was valid. And once
again this is very explicitly shown by the supposition numerals of line (9):

```
     1    │  1   A
     2    │  2   A ⊃ B
    1,2   │  3   B                               1,2 MPP
     4    │  4   B ⊃ C
   1,2,4  │  5   C                               3,4 MPP
     6    │  6   C ⊃ D
  1,2,4,6 │  7   D                               5,6 MPP
     8    │  8   D ⊃ E
 1,2,4,6,8│  9   E                               7,8 MPP
```

For we notice that line (9) is the *conclusion* of the form with which we
began. And if we look at its supposition numerals and then at the lines
which are numbered with the same numerals, we find on them precisely
the *premises* of the form with which we began! Of course, for this system
to work, we must not write supposition numerals at our whim, but *only in
accordance with the rules*. Only then will our derivations show that the
forms we are working on are, indeed, valid (when they are).

The arrangement of the lines which we favor, putting all the premises of the form we are working on at the beginning, makes the result even easier to see:

| | | | |
|---|---|---|---|
| 1 | 1 | $A$ | S |
| 2 | 2 | $A \supset B$ | S |
| 3 | 3 | $B \supset C$ | S |
| 4 | 4 | $C \supset D$ | S |
| 5 | 5 | $D \supset E$ | S |
| 1,2 | 6 | $B$ | 1,2 MPP |
| 1,2,3 | 7 | $C$ | 3,6 MPP |
| 1,2,3,4 | 8 | $D$ | 7,4 MPP |
| 1,2,3,4,5 | 9 | $E$ | 5,8 MPP |

The *supposition numerals* of the last line which indicate that the form with the formula on that line as conclusion and the formulas on the first five lines as premises is valid.

**4. Conditional Proof: Rule CP.** Now consider a slightly more complicated version of the line of reasoning attributed to Bertha at the beginning of this chapter. Imagine that we have made six suppositions and obtained from them some particular conclusion. This means that if all six suppositions were true, the conclusion would have to be true. Let us concentrate on just five of those suppositions and ask ourselves: what would have to be true if these *five* were true? The answer is: if these five were true, then it would have to be the case that *if* the sixth were also to be true, then the conclusion we have so far obtained would also have to be true. So, from these five suppositions, we may infer a *new* conclusion: a conditional with the sixth supposition as antecedent and our original conclusion as consequent. We have just observed that this new conclusion would have to be true if the other *five* suppositions were true. We mark this fact by *omitting* from among the supposition numerals of the new conclusion the supposition numeral of the sixth supposition (the one that we have taken to be the antecedent of our new conclusion).

It is important to note that the supposition numeral that we omit is really the supposition numeral of a *supposition* that we have put into the antecedent of the new conclusion. We may check this by seeing whether the supposition numeral we have omitted from the supposition numerals of this new conclusion is also the *line* numeral of the formula which is the antecedent of our new conclusion. Thus we have the rule:

| CP | Given two lines (not necessarily distinct), the first of which is among the suppositions of the other, infer the conditional with the formula on the first line as antecedent and the formula on the second line as consequent. As the supposition numerals of the new line, take all those of the second line with the exception of the line numeral of the first line. |
|---|---|

For example:

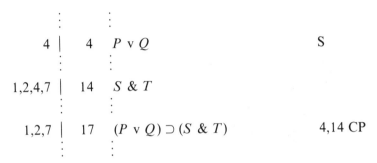

$$4 \quad | \quad 4 \quad P \vee Q \qquad\qquad\qquad\qquad S$$

$$1,2,4,7 \quad | \quad 14 \quad S \And T$$

$$1,2,7 \quad | \quad 17 \quad (P \vee Q) \supset (S \And T) \qquad\qquad 4,14 \text{ CP}$$

Rule CP is the first "complex" rule of derivation that we shall adopt. One thing that marks it as complex is that we have to do a little bit of figuring in order to get the supposition numerals of the inferred line. Above, when deriving the conditional on line (17), we had to drop '4' from the supposition numerals of line (14) in order to get those of line (17). This shows, once again, that the formula on line (4) is not a supposition of the formula on line (17): the latter formula follows from the formulas on lines (1), (2), and (7) alone, whatever they may be.

We may formalize Bertha's line of reasoning above as follows:

| | | | |
|---|---|---|---|
| 1 | 1 | $W$ | S |
| 2 | 2 | $(W \And R) \supset S$ | S |
| 3 | 3 | $R$ | S (for CP) |
| 1,3 | 4 | $W \And R$ | 1,3 &I |
| 1,2,3 | 5 | $S$ | 4,2 MPP |
| 1,2 | 6 | $R \supset S$ | 3,5 CP |

**5. Strategy Hint.** Associated with rule CP is a very useful strategy for deriving conditionals. The rule of thumb is: if you want to derive a conditional, take the antecedent of the conditional as a supposition and aim for the consequent. Then, when the consequent is reached, the conditional itself can be obtained by rule CP, and the antecedent which had been supposed for this purpose can be removed from the suppositions of the new conditional.

For example, suppose we want to show that the third formula below follows from the first two:

$$Q \supset S$$
$$S \supset (P \supset R)$$
$$P \supset (Q \supset R)$$

The desired conclusion here is a *conditional*, so applying the strategy hint, we get:

| | | | |
|---|---|---|---|
| 1 | 1 | $Q \supset S$ | S |
| 2 | 2 | $S \supset (P \supset R)$ | S |
| 3 | 3 | $P$ | S (for CP) |
| | | $Q \supset R$ | |
| | | $P \supset (Q \supset R)$ | CP |

Here also the new desired goal is a conditional, so we should apply the same strategy hint, as follows:

| | | | |
|---|---|---|---|
| 1 | 1 | $Q \supset S$ | S |
| 2 | 2 | $S \supset (P \supset R)$ | S |
| 3 | 3 | $P$ | S (for CP) |
| 4 | 4 | $Q$ | S (for CP) |
| | | $R$ | |
| | | $Q \supset R$ | CP |
| | | $P \supset (Q \supset R)$ | CP |

Now we can work backward no further, but we have managed to generate enough additional suppositions that our work is now rather straightforward. We may apply rule MPP to lines (1) and (4) to get '$S$' on line (5), then apply MPP once more to this new line and line (2). This then sets up yet a further application of MPP, and our complete derivation might look like this:

| | | | |
|---|---|---|---|
| 1 | 1 | $Q \supset S$ | S |
| 2 | 2 | $S \supset (P \supset R)$ | S |
| 3 | 3 | $P$ | S (for CP) |
| 4 | 4 | $Q$ | S (for CP) |
| 1,4 | 5 | $S$ | 1,4 MPP |
| 1,2,4 | 6 | $P \supset R$ | 2,5 MPP |
| 1,2,3,4 | 7 | $R$ | 3,6 MPP |
| 1,2,3 | 8 | $Q \supset R$ | 4,7 CP |
| 1,2 | 9 | $P \supset (Q \supset R)$ | 3,8 CP |

So remember:

☞ If you want to derive a conditional, take the antecedent of the conditional as a supposition, and try to derive the consequent; then apply CP.

**6. Rule MTT.** Let us adopt one further rule concerning conditionals. Clearly, if a conditional is true but its consequent is *false* (i.e., the negation of its consequent is true), then its antecedent must be false, since a true antecedent and a true conditional would allow us to infer the truth of the consequent (by MPP). So, if in this case the antecedent is false, its negation must be true, and that is precisely what the following rule MTT (*modus tollendo tollens*) allows us to infer:

---

MTT    Given a conditional and the negation of its consequent, infer the negation of its antecedent. As supposition numerals of the inferred formula, take all those of the two given formulas.

---

Two examples:

| | | | |
|---|---|---|---|
| 3 | 4 | $P \supset Q$ | |
| 1,2 | 10 | $\sim Q$ | |
| 1,2,3 | 13 | $\sim P$ | 4,10 MTT |

$$4 \mid \quad 6 \quad \sim(P \supset Q) \supset \sim\sim(P \vee R)$$

$$2 \mid \quad 8 \quad \sim\sim\sim(P \vee R)$$

$$2,4 \mid \quad 11 \quad \sim\sim(P \supset Q) \qquad\qquad\qquad 6,8 \text{ MTT}$$

You will find several further examples of MTT in the first derivation considered in the following section.

**7. Nevada Marriage and Divorce.** A derivation of a formula from a group of formulas is a derivation of that formula having all and only the formulas in the group as suppositions. For instance, suppose that we wish to find a derivation of the formula:

$$\sim S \ \& \sim Q$$

from the group of formulas:

$$P \supset Q$$
$$R \supset P$$
$$S \supset R$$
$$\sim Q$$

We might construct the following derivation:

| | | | |
|---|---|---|---|
| 1 | 1 | $P \supset Q$ | S |
| 2 | 2 | $R \supset P$ | S |
| 3 | 3 | $S \supset R$ | S |
| 4 | 4 | $\sim Q$ | S |
| 1,4 | 5 | $\sim P$ | 1,4 MTT |
| 1,2,4 | 6 | $\sim R$ | 2,5 MTT |
| 1,2,3,4 | 7 | $\sim S$ | 3,6 MTT |
| 1,2,3,4 | 8 | $\sim S \ \& \sim Q$ | 4,7 &I |

You should pay special attention to the fact that the last line of a derivation of some formula from a group of formulas must have *all* the formulas in that group as suppositions. It may sometimes happen that you can construct a derivation that does not actually use all of the given suppositions. For instance, suppose we want to find a derivation of the formula '$Q$' from the group of formulas:

$$P \lor S$$
$$\sim P$$
$$Q \lor \sim S$$
$$R \supset S$$

We might come up with the following derivation:

| | | | |
|---|---|---|---|
| 1 | 1 | $P \lor S$ | S |
| 2 | 2 | $\sim P$ | S |
| 3 | 3 | $Q \lor \sim S$ | S |
| 4 | 4 | $R \supset S$ | S |
| 1,2 | 5 | $S$ | 1,2 DS |
| 1,2 | 6 | $\sim\sim S$ | 5 DNI |
| 1,2,3 | 7 | $Q$ | 3,6 DS |

This sequence of lines *is* a derivation, but it is *not* a derivation of the formula '$Q$' from the four formulas listed above, since the line numeral of one of them (namely, 4) does not occur among the supposition numerals of line (7). There is, however, a simple technique for getting '4' among the supposition numerals of a line with '$Q$' on it. We need only add to this derivation the following two lines:

| | | | |
|---|---|---|---|
| ⋮ | ⋮ | | |
| 1,2,3,4 | 8 | $Q \& (R \supset S)$ | 4,7 &I |
| 1,2,3,4 | 9 | $Q$ | 8 &E |

This technique is called the *Nevada marriage and divorce*, since we first "wed" the missing supposition to the desired conclusion (with &I), and then immediately "divorce" the two (with &E). The net effect, as you can see, is to introduce the supposition numeral of the missing supposition.

☞    If you need to add a numeral to some list of supposition numerals, use the Nevada marriage and divorce: &I and then &E.

**Exercises**

---

1    In each item, derive the last formula from the other(s):

(a)           $Q \supset (P \supset R)$        (b)           $\sim\sim Q \supset P$
                      $\sim R$                                  $\sim P$
                      $Q$                                  $\sim Q$
                      $\sim P$

(c)                 $\sim P \supset \sim Q$            (d)                 $P \supset Q$
                    $Q$                                                    $Q \supset R$
                    $P$                                                    $P \supset R$

(e)                 $\sim P \supset Q$                 (f)                 $\sim P \supset \sim Q$
                    $\sim Q \supset P$                                     $Q \supset P$

(g)                 $P \supset \sim Q$                 (h)                 $P \supset (Q \supset R)$
                    $Q \supset \sim P$                                     $(P \supset Q) \supset (P \supset R)$

(i)         $P \supset (Q \supset (R \supset S))$      (j)                 $P \supset Q$
            $R \supset (P \supset (Q \supset S))$                          $(Q \supset R) \supset (P \supset R)$

(k)                 $\sim P$                           (l)                 $Q$
                    $P \supset Q$                                          $P \supset Q$

2    In each item, derive the last formula from the others:

(a)                 $P \& Q$                           (b)                 $R \& S$
                    $R \supset \sim Q$                                     $\sim P \supset \sim R$
                    $\sim R$                                               $P$

(c)                 $P \supset \sim Q$                 (d)                 $\sim P \supset \sim Q$
                    $R \vee Q$                                             $(S \supset Q) \supset Q$
                    $\sim R \supset \sim P$                                $\sim P \supset \sim (S \supset Q)$

(e)                 $P \& \sim S$                      (f)                 $P \vee T$
                    $Q \supset S$                                          $R \equiv P$
                    $(P \& \sim Q) \supset T$                              $\sim Q \supset \sim P$
                    $T$                                                    $\sim Q \supset T$

3    Which of the following statements best describes the reason that the
     Nevada marriage and divorce is an acceptable thing to do in a deriva-
     tion?

     (a) Every formula which follows from one conjunct of a given conjunc-
         tion also follows from the other conjunct.

     (b) If some formula follows from a given formula, then it also follows
         from that given formula and any other formula whatsoever.

     (c) No formula follows from *both* conjuncts of a given conjunction.

     (d) If some formula follows from one conjunct of a given conjunction,
         then it also follows from the negation of that conjunction.

     (e) If some formula follows from *both* conjuncts of a given conjunction,
         then it also follows from that conjunction.

# Chapter 8

## Derivations with Disjunction

**1. Rule vI.** We have agreed that the symbol 'v' representing disjunction is to be interpreted in the "inclusive" sense, so that a disjunction is true just in case *at least one* of its disjuncts is true. Obviously, if a given statement is true, then any disjunction having that statement as a disjunct will also be true. For example, the following argument is valid:

> Alfred owns a condo on Maui.
> _____
> Alfred owns a condo on Maui or in Alaska.

Also, given our earlier classification of 'unless' as a disjunction-indicating word, we can see that the following argument is valid:

> Clothilda enjoys skiing.
> _____
> Clothilda enjoys skiing unless she breaks her leg.

Accordingly, we may adopt the following rule:

| | |
|---|---|
| vI | Given a formula, infer a disjunction having that formula as one of the disjuncts and *any* formula whatsoever as the other disjunct. As supposition numerals of the inferred line, take all those of the given line. |

Here are three examples:

$$
\begin{array}{cccll}
1 & \mid & 1 & P & \text{S} \\
1 & \mid & 2 & Q \text{ v } P & 1 \text{ vI}
\end{array}
$$

$$1,3 \mid \quad 5 \quad P \supset Q$$

$$1,3 \mid \quad 8 \quad (P \supset Q) \lor R \qquad\qquad\qquad 5 \text{ vI}$$

$$2,4 \mid \quad 8 \quad P \equiv P$$

$$2,4 \mid \quad 12 \quad (P \equiv P) \lor (P \equiv P) \qquad\qquad 8 \text{ vI}$$

It should be clear that with respect to supposition numerals, rule vI is to behave just as any other "simple" rule (DS, MPP, MTT, &I, &E, DNI, or DNE): the supposition numerals of the inferred line are just those of the given line.

**2.  Rule vE.**  Our second rule for disjunction, on the other hand, is a "complex" rule.  It is somewhat complicated to state, but fairly easy to apply.  To see how it works, consider the following situation.  Alfred sees that from the statement that Jones is standing outside in the rain with no umbrella, *it follows that* Jones is wet.  Alfred also sees that from the statement that Jones is swimming, *it follows that* Jones is wet.  So far, Alfred is merely contemplating two lines of reasoning; he may or may not know whether Jones is in fact standing outside in the rain, or whether Jones is in fact swimming.  But now suppose that Alfred does learn that *either* Jones is standing outside in the rain with no umbrella, *or* he is swimming.  What can Alfred now conclude from all of this?  Surely it must be obvious that Jones is wet.

We have in effect the following situation: if a statement follows from each disjunct of a some disjunction, then that statement follows from the disjunction itself.  We may formalize this insight with the following rule:

| vE | Given five lines (not necessarily distinct or in this order) such that |
|---|---|

(1)  the formula on the first is a disjunction;
(2)  the second is a supposition, and the formula on it is one of the disjuncts of the first;
(3)  the third has the second among its suppositions;
(4)  the fourth is a supposition, and the formula on it is the other of the disjuncts of the first;
(5)  the fifth has the fourth among its suppositions, and the formula on it is the same formula as that on the third line.

Infer the formula that is on the third (and also the fifth) line.

As supposition numerals of the inferred line, take all those of the first line, together with all those of the third line with the exception of the line numeral of the second line, together with all those of the fifth line with the exception of the line numeral of the fourth line.

For example:

| 1 | 1 | $\sim\sim P$ v $P$ | S |
| 2 | 2 | $\sim\sim P$ | S (for vE) |
| 2 | 3 | $P$ | 2 DNE |
| 4 | 4 | $P$ | S (for vE) |
| 1 | 5 | $P$ | 1,2,3,4,4 vE |

Here line (4) counts as both the "fourth" and the "fifth" lines cited in the rule.

| 1 | 1 | $P$ v $P$ | S |
| 2 | 2 | $P$ | S (for vE) |
| 1 | 3 | $P$ | 1,2,2,2,2 vE |

Here line (2) counts as the "second", "third", "fourth", and "fifth" lines of the rule.

Note that one and the same formula will always occur on two of the five "given" lines (i.e., on the third and fifth) and also on the "inferred" line, but with different supposition numerals. Also note that one and the same line *may* count as both "second" and "third" or as both "fourth" and "fifth", or as all four of these.

A more complicated application of vE from the middle of a derivation can be illustrated thus:

$$
\begin{array}{llll}
\vdots & \vdots & & \\
1,2,6 \mid & 7 & (P \ \& \ Q) \ v \ (R \supset S) & \\
\vdots & \vdots & & \\
9 \mid & 9 & P \ \& \ Q & \text{S (for vE)} \\
\vdots & \vdots & & \\
1,4,9 \mid & 14 & (S \ \& \ T) \supset R & \\
\vdots & \vdots & & \\
17 \mid & 17 & R \supset S & \text{S (for vE)} \\
\vdots & \vdots & & \\
1,2,5,17 \mid & 22 & (S \ \& \ T) \supset R & \\
\vdots & \vdots & & \\
1,2,4,5,6 \mid & 25 & (S \ \& \ T) \supset R & \text{7,9,14,17,22 vE} \\
\vdots & \vdots & &
\end{array}
$$

The intuitive justification for this rule, once again, is that if, with the aid of certain suppositions, a conclusion follows from one of the disjuncts of a given disjunction, and if also, with the aid of certain suppositions, that same conclusion follows from the other disjunct, then the conclusion follows from the given disjunction and all those further suppositions—and, consequently, follows from all those further suppositions taken together with the suppositions from which the disjunction follows.

You must pay special attention to the method of calculating the supposition numerals when applying this rule. Notice that we are to take all those of the first line (the original disjunction in question), then those of the third line *minus* those of the second, then those of the fifth line *minus* those of the fourth. In many cases this is *not* the same as taking all those of the first, third, and fifth, then subtracting those of the second and fourth. As an illustration, consider the following **incorrect** derivation:

| 1   | 1 | $P \lor Q$ | S |
| 2   | 2 | $P$        | S (for $\lor$E) |
| 3   | 3 | $Q$        | S (for $\lor$E) |
| 2,3 | 4 | $P \& Q$   | 2,3 &I |
| 1   | 5 | $P \& Q$   | 1,2,4,3,4 $\lor$E |

In step (5), the supposition numerals have been computed using the incorrect method just mentioned: we took all those of lines (1) and (4), then subtracted those of lines (2) and (3).

**Exercises**

---

1    What would the supposition numerals of line (5) be if we had computed them correctly? Does this show that the formula on line (5) follows from that on line (1)?

---

**3. Strategy Hints.** A rule of thumb associated with rule $\lor$E is this: if you are aiming to derive a conclusion from a number of lines, one of which is a disjunction, try to derive the desired conclusion from *each* disjunct together with the other lines; then apply rule $\lor$E to obtain the desired conclusion from the disjunction and those other lines.

The following strategy is also sometimes useful: if the desired conclusion is a disjunction, try to derive one of the disjuncts; then you may obtain the desired disjunction by an application of rule $\lor$I. Very often, however, it is simply *not possible* to derive one disjunct of a desired disjunction from the given suppositions. To illustrate this, suppose that we want to derive the conclusion '$P \lor Q$' from the two suppositions

$$P \lor (R \lor Q)$$
$$\sim R$$

The conclusion is a disjunction, but, as warned, *neither* of its disjuncts follows from the two given suppositions. (We shall not develop the general technique for showing this until Chapter 11; until then, you'll just have to take our word for it. You might try to work up an informal argument to convince yourself of this claim.) So we are without an appropriate working-backward strategy. But we can apply the working-forward strategy hint just given for rule $\lor$E, since one of our suppositions is a disjunction. So we would begin as follows:

|   |   |   |   |
|---|---|---|---|
| 1 | 1 | $P$ v $(R$ v $Q)$ | S |
| 2 | 2 | $\sim R$ | S |
| 3 | 3 | $P$ | S (for vE) |
|   |   | $P$ v $Q$ |   |
|   |   | $R$ v $Q$ | S (for vE) |
|   |   | $P$ v $Q$ |   |
|   |   | $P$ v $Q$ | vE |

Our job now is to find two subderivations, as indicated. The first is an obvious application of rule vI. The second subderivation, from '$R$ v $Q$' to '$P$ v $Q$', is also quite simple, for with line (2) we may get '$Q$' and then '$P$ v $Q$', again by vI. So we have:

|   |   |   |   |
|---|---|---|---|
| 1 | 1 | $P$ v $(R$ v $Q)$ | S |
| 2 | 2 | $\sim R$ | S |
| 3 | 3 | $P$ | S (for vE) |
| 3 | 4 | $P$ v $Q$ | 3 vI |
| 5 | 5 | $R$ v $Q$ | S (for vE) |
| 2,5 | 6 | $Q$ | 2,5 DS |
| 2,5 | 7 | $P$ v $Q$ | 6 vI |
| 1,2 | 8 | $P$ v $Q$ | 1,3,4,5,7 vE |

So remember:

☛   If you want to derive a disjunction, try to derive one of the disjuncts; then apply vI.

☛   If you are given (or have already derived) a disjunction, separately suppose each disjunct and derive the desired conclusion from it; then apply vE.

## Exercises

2   In each item, derive the last formula from the other(s).

(a)                 $Q$
                    $P$ v $Q$

(b)                 $P$ & $Q$
                    $P$ v $Q$

(c)                 $P \supset R$
                    $Q \supset R$
                    $(P$ v $Q) \supset R$

(d)                 $P \supset Q$
                    $T \supset S$
                    $(P$ v $T) \supset (Q$ v $S)$

3    Do the same for each of the following items.

(a)              $P \ \& \ Q$              (b)                    $P$
          $(P \vee R) \ \& \ (Q \vee R)$                      $Q \vee R$
                                            $(P \ \& \ Q) \vee (P \ \& \ R)$

(c)           $P \vee (Q \vee R)$           (d)            $(P \vee Q) \vee R$
                 $P \supset S$                              $P \supset A$
                 $Q \supset S$                              $Q \supset B$
                 $R \supset S$                              $R \supset C$
                      $S$                               $(A \vee B) \vee C$

(e)      $(P \vee Q) \vee (R \vee S)$        (f)        $P \vee (Q \vee (R \vee S))$
          $P \vee (Q \vee (R \vee S))$                  $(P \vee Q) \vee (R \vee S)$

(g)            $P \vee (Q \vee P)$           (h)             $P \vee (P \ \& \ Q)$
                   $P \vee Q$                                    $P$

(i)        $(P \vee Q) \ \& \ (P \vee \sim Q)$   (j)     $(P \supset Q) \ \& \ (\sim P \supset Q)$
                      $P$                                        $Q$

4    Consider the following rule of "constructive dilemma":

---

CD          Given three lines (not necessarily distinct or in that order)
            such that

            (1)   the formula on the first is a disjunction;
            (2)   the formula on the second is a conditional whose
                  antecedent is the left disjunct of the formula on the
                  first line;
            (3)   the formula on the third is a conditional whose
                  antecedent is the right disjunct of the formula on the
                  first line and whose consequent is the same as the
                  consequent of the second formula;

            infer the formula that is the consequent of the conditional
            on the second (and also the third) line.

            As supposition numerals of the inferred line, take all those
            of the three given lines.

---

For example:

| 1     | 1 | $P \vee Q$   | S        |
|-------|---|--------------|----------|
| 2     | 2 | $P \supset R$ | S        |
| 3     | 3 | $Q \supset R$ | S        |
| 1,2,3 | 4 | $R$          | 1,2,3 CD |

(a) Redo Exercises 2(c) and 2(d) above using this new rule CD, but *not* using rule vE.

(b) Redo Exercises 3(c), 3(d), 3(e), and 3(f) using this new rule CD, but *not* using rule vE.

(c) Now reflect: what are the advantages of adopting rule CD *instead of* rule vE? What are the disadvantages?

(d) How would you go about showing that we do not need to adopt rule vE, if we have rule CD available?

If you wish, you may henceforth employ this rule CD in your derivations instead of (or in addition to) rule vE.

5   Suppose that we used the symbol 'v' to represent *exclusive* disjunction, so that a formula such as '$P \vee Q$' is true just in case '$P$' is true, or '$Q$' is true, *but not both*. Would the two rules of derivation vI and vE as stated above in the text still be good rules to adopt? How about DS?

# Chapter 9

## Indirect Proof and Biconditionals

**1. Indirect Proof: Rule RAA.** There is a very useful way of reasoning, often called *indirect proof* or *proof by contradiction*, that we should like to be able to capture in our derivations. To illustrate this, suppose that Alfred wants to show the validity of the following argument:

> If the library is open, then Jones is studying now.
> If Jones is studying now, he will pass logic.
> But Jones will not pass logic.
>
> ---
>
> The library is not open.

Now, if Alfred were well-versed in the application of rule MTT, he could give a derivation of the conclusion from the premises quite easily. But suppose that he does not notice that he could use MTT to good effect here. Alfred *might* still reason as follows: suppose that the library is open (contrary to the desired conclusion). Then, by two quick uses of MPP, Alfred concludes that Jones will pass logic. But that contradicts the third premise, which states that Jones will *not* pass logic. So, the additional supposition that Alfred took, that the library is open, is inconsistent with the original three premises. In other words, if the premises are all true, that supposition must be false. That is, it *follows* from the three premises that the library is closed.

Alfred has reasoned by supposing the opposite of what he ultimately wants to show and by showing that that supposition leads to a contradiction. If we agree to call a formula and its negation (and only these) *express contradictories*, we can frame the following rule RAA (for *reductio ad absurdum*):

RAA        Given three lines (not necessarily distinct or in that order)
           such that:

    (1)   the formula on the first of them is a supposition of one
         (or both) of the formulas on the other two;

    (2)   the formula on one of the remaining two lines is the ne-
         gation of the formula on the other of the remaining two
         lines.

           Infer the negation of the formula on the first given line (i.e.,
           the supposition).

           As supposition numerals of the inferred line, take all those of
           the two expressly contradictory lines, with the exception of the
           line numeral of the supposition.

For example:

| | | | |
|---|---|---|---|
| 5 | 5 | $R \vee S$ | S (for RAA) |
| 1,2,5 | 8 | $\sim(P \equiv \sim Q)$ | |
| 1,4 | 11 | $P \equiv \sim Q$ | |
| 1,2,4 | 14 | $\sim(R \vee S)$ | 5,8,11 RAA |

And the following derivation formalizes Alfred's line of reasoning above:

| | | | |
|---|---|---|---|
| 1 | 1 | $L \supset S$ | S |
| 2 | 2 | $S \supset P$ | S |
| 3 | 3 | $\sim P$ | S |
| 4 | 4 | $L$ | S (for RAA) |
| 1,4 | 5 | $S$ | 1,4 MPP |
| 1,2,4 | 6 | $P$ | 2,5 MPP |
| 1,2,3 | 7 | $\sim L$ | 4,3,6 RAA |

The justification of this rule is as follows: if a formula follows from certain
suppositions and also the negation of that formula follows from certain

suppositions, then both the formula and its negation follow from all available suppositions taken together. If all these suppositions were to be true, then everything that follows from them would have to be true. But a formula and its negation cannot *both* be true. So the suppositions cannot all be true together. It follows then that if all but one of them were true, the remaining one would have to be false. So the negation of any one of the suppositions follows from the rest of them.

**2. Strategy Hints.** Rule RAA carries with it a general strategy for approaching derivations that might appear difficult to work with using the other rules. Once we have tried more straightforward methods of doing some particular derivation and failed to succeed, we should then decide to try using rule RAA and proceed as follows: if the desired conclusion is a negation, we adopt its negatum as an additional supposition; otherwise, we adopt the negation of the desired conclusion as an additional supposition. This additional supposition will generally permit us to apply our rules in a relatively straightforward way, but now our goal is no longer to derive the original conclusion. Rule RAA stipulates that we are to arrive at an *express contradiction*, any formula on a line and its negation on some other line (with the line numeral of the additional supposition among the supposition numerals of at least one of these two lines). Once we accomplish this, we are permitted to write in the negation of the additional supposition and to drop the line numeral of that supposition.

Let us consider an example in more detail. Suppose that we are asked to find a derivation of '$Q$' from the two premises '$\sim P \supset P$' and '$P \supset Q$'. As usual, we begin by entering our premises and indicating our desired goal:

$$
\begin{array}{ll|lll}
1 & & 1 & \sim P \supset P & \quad S \\
2 & & 2 & P \supset Q & \quad S \\
& & & Q &
\end{array}
$$

Right away, however, we realize that none of the rules we have so far adopted is of much help here. Our premises are both conditionals, neither of which occurs as the antecedent of the other, or as the negated consequent of the other. So neither MPP nor MTT can be applied. And clearly none of the rules governing negation, conjunction, or disjunction can be applied (except for DNI, which is of no assistance). So we should think about applying RAA. To do this, we take the negation of the desired conclusion as an additional supposition:

$$
\begin{array}{cc|lll}
1 & & 1 & {\sim}P \supset P & \text{S} \\
2 & & 2 & P \supset Q & \text{S} \\
3 & & 3 & {\sim}Q & \text{S (for RAA)} \\
\\
& & & Q \\
\end{array}
$$

And our new goal is to get an express contradiction. Now things look better. We can apply MTT to lines (2) and (3), and then MPP to lines (1) and the new line (4), as follows:

$$
\begin{array}{cc|lll}
1 & & 1 & {\sim}P \supset P & \text{S} \\
2 & & 2 & P \supset Q & \text{S} \\
3 & & 3 & {\sim}Q & \text{S (for RAA)} \\
2,3 & & 4 & {\sim}P & \text{2,3 MTT} \\
1,2,3 & & 5 & P & \text{1,4 MPP} \\
\\
& & & Q \\
\end{array}
$$

We have now achieved our new goal, for lines (4) and (5) are expressly contradictory, and the line numeral of the additional supposition appears among the supposition numerals of at least one of them. So we may apply RAA and finish up:

$$
\begin{array}{cc|lll}
1 & & 1 & {\sim}P \supset P & \text{S} \\
2 & & 2 & P \supset Q & \text{S} \\
3 & & 3 & {\sim}Q & \text{S (for RAA)} \\
2,3 & & 4 & {\sim}P & \text{2,3 MTT} \\
1,2,3 & & 5 & P & \text{1,4 MPP} \\
1,2 & & 6 & {\sim}{\sim}Q & \text{3,4,5 RAA} \\
1,2 & & 7 & Q & \text{6 DNE} \\
\end{array}
$$

**3. Back-Burner Strategy.** Occasionally, however, we may run into problems in applying this strategy. Suppose, for instance, that we are to find a derivation of the formula '${\sim}P$' from the supposition:

$$
{\sim}({\sim}P \supset Q)
$$

Already we should suspect that this is going to present problems, since none of the rules currently available to us helps in transforming negations of conditionals. So we shall adopt the RAA strategy just discussed. Since the desired conclusion is a negation, we take its negatum as an additional supposition:

$$
\begin{array}{ll|lll}
1 & & 1 & \sim(\sim P \supset Q) & \text{S} \\
2 & & 2 & P & \text{S (for RAA)} \\
\\
& & & \sim P & \text{RAA}
\end{array}
$$

But, unlike in the previous example, this additional supposition has failed to produce any clear progress. We still cannot do anything obvious with line (1), and the new supposition, line (2), is just a sentential letter. We could perhaps apply rule DNI to it, but that does not look very promising. So we need to look elsewhere.

Remember that since we have adopted an RAA strategy, our goal is to come up with some formula on one line and its negation on some other line. We might then notice that we *already* have a negation on the first line in our partial derivation. So, since nothing else looks like it's going to work, we might adopt a new goal: try to derive the negatum of the negation that already occurs in our derivation. In other words, our new goal should now be to get the formula '$\sim P \supset Q$' on a line in our derivation. If we succeed in doing this, we can then apply rule RAA; so we may indicate our new goal by writing this formula on the second-to-last line:

$$
\begin{array}{ll|lll}
1 & & 1 & \sim(\sim P \supset Q) & \text{S} \\
2 & & 2 & P & \text{S (for RAA)} \\
\\
& & & \sim P \supset Q & \\
& & & \sim P & \text{RAA}
\end{array}
$$

Now things are beginning to look promising, since we do have a fairly standard strategy for deriving a conditional: take the antecedent as a new supposition and try to derive the consequent, for an application of CP. So we have:

$$
\begin{array}{ll|lll}
1 & & 1 & \sim(\sim P \supset Q) & \text{S} \\
2 & & 2 & P & \text{S (for RAA)} \\
3 & & 3 & \sim P & \text{S (for CP)} \\
\\
& & & Q & \\
& & & \sim P \supset Q & \text{CP} \\
& & & \sim P & \text{RAA}
\end{array}
$$

Our goal now is to derive '$Q$' from the available suppositions. Can we do this easily? We should immediately notice that lines (2) and (3) are expressly contradictory. In other words, they are exactly what we would need to apply RAA, if we had a suitable supposition for RAA. (We might think that we already have a supposition for RAA—line (2)—but we took that supposition in order to derive '~P', and we should not change our minds on that now.) So lines (2) and (3) are a sort of embarrassment of riches: they are just what we need to apply RAA, but we don't have a suitable supposition to appeal to. But of course nothing prevents us from immediately taking a new supposition so that we can apply RAA. Since our present goal is 'Q', we should take '~Q' as a new supposition, as follows:

| | | | |
|---|---|---|---|
| 1 | 1 | $\sim(\sim P \supset Q)$ | S |
| 2 | 2 | $P$ | S (for RAA) |
| 3 | 3 | $\sim P$ | S (for CP) |
| 4 | 4 | $\sim Q$ | S (for RAA) |
| | | | |
| | | $Q$ | |
| | | $\sim P \supset Q$ | CP |
| | | $\sim P$ | RAA |

We cannot just go ahead and apply RAA, since the supposition that we just took must appear as a supposition numeral of at least one of the contradictory lines. So we must insert the so-called "Nevada marriage and divorce" and finish up as follows:

| | | | |
|---|---|---|---|
| 1 | 1 | $\sim(\sim P \supset Q)$ | S |
| 2 | 2 | $P$ | S (for RAA) |
| 3 | 3 | $\sim P$ | S (for CP) |
| 4 | 4 | $\sim Q$ | S (for RAA) |
| 2,4 | 5 | $P \mathbin{\&} \sim Q$ | 2,4 &I |
| 2,4 | 6 | $P$ | 5 &E |
| 2,3 | 7 | $\sim\sim Q$ | 4,3,6 RAA |
| 2,3 | 8 | $Q$ | 7 DNE |
| 2 | 9 | $\sim P \supset Q$ | 3,8 CP |
| 1 | 10 | $\sim P$ | 2,1,9 RAA |

The strategy we employed to generate what turned out to be line (9) as our new goal is sometimes quite useful, but is in some ways the reverse of what we usually do. Usually it is of no interest to us to know that we *cannot* apply a particular rule to some line or set of lines; our interest is usually in finding rules that we *can* apply. Here, however, the key step was to realize that there was nothing that we could do with line (1). We then "put it on the back burner": we decided to do nothing with it and instead to try to derive its negatum, thus setting up the application of RAA on what turned out to be line (10).

This "back-burner" form of the RAA strategy is a useful one and one you should keep in mind if confronted with a line that none of our rules allows you to manipulate easily. If a formula is a negation of a *binary* formula, it is a sure bet to be of this sort. So remember:

☞ If you have a negation of a binary formula, take its negatum as your new goal; if you succeed in deriving that negatum, you can then apply RAA to the original negation and its negatum.

**4. Biconditional Rules**. Let us move then to our discussion of the two rules for manipulating biconditionals. The first rule is quite simple:

---

≡E Given a biconditional of two formulas, infer a conditional with either formula as antecedent and the other formula as consequent. As supposition numerals of the inferred line, take all those of the given line.

---

For example:

$$1,3 \quad | \quad 5 \quad (P \vee Q) \equiv R$$

$$1,3 \quad | \quad 9 \quad (P \vee Q) \supset R \qquad\qquad 5 \equiv E$$

Rule ≡E is very straightforward; it allows us to infer, from a given biconditional, either of the two conditionals that can be formed taking one side of the biconditional as antecedent and the other side as consequent. This is obviously a useful rule to have when working forward in a derivation and one of the available suppositions, or one of the lines we have so far derived, is a biconditional.

The second biconditional rule is slightly more complicated. It is also a "complex" rule:

≡I          Given four lines (not necessarily distinct or in that order) such that:

(1)  the first is a supposition;
(2)  the second has the first among its suppositions;
(3)  the third is a supposition;
(4)  the fourth has the third among its suppositions;
(5)  one and the same formula is on the first and fourth lines, and one and the same formula is on the second and third lines.

Infer a biconditional of the two formulas.

As supposition numerals of the inferred line, take all those of the second line with the exception of the line numeral of the first line, and also all those of the fourth line with the exception of the line numeral of the third line.

For example:

$$3 \mid \quad 3 \quad P \qquad\qquad\qquad\qquad S \text{ (for } \equiv I)$$

$$1,3 \mid \quad 5 \quad {\sim}S$$

$$8 \mid \quad 8 \quad {\sim}S \qquad\qquad\qquad\qquad S \text{ (for } \equiv I)$$

$$4,8 \mid \quad 13 \quad P$$

$$1,4 \mid \quad 15 \quad P \equiv {\sim}S \qquad\qquad\qquad 3,5,8,13 \equiv I$$

Let us make sure that we see clearly how the rule is applied here. Line (3) is entered as a supposition and occurs as one of the suppositions of line (5). Similarly, line (8) is entered as a supposition and occurs as one of the suppositions of line (13). Since each formula has been shown to follow *from the other* (and any other available suppositions), we may then derive the *biconditional* of those two formulas, discarding the additional suppositions that we took in order to show that each follows from the other.

Another example of the application of $\equiv$I:

$$3 \mid \qquad 3 \quad P \vee Q \qquad\qquad\qquad\qquad \text{S (for } \equiv\text{I)}$$

$$1,3 \mid \qquad 8 \quad {\sim}(S \vee Q)$$

$$10 \mid \qquad 10 \quad {\sim}(S \vee Q) \qquad\qquad\qquad\qquad \text{S (for } \equiv\text{I)}$$

$$1,4,10 \mid \qquad 13 \quad P \vee Q$$

$$1,4 \mid \qquad 15 \quad (P \vee Q) \equiv {\sim}(S \vee Q) \qquad\qquad 3,8,10,13 \equiv\text{I}$$

Rule $\equiv$I is somewhat more complicated than rule $\equiv$E, but in effect it really boils down to the reverse of rule $\equiv$E. If for instance we could derive some conditional, say '$P \supset Q$', and its converse '$Q \supset P$', then it seems fitting that we should be allowed to write in the biconditional '$P \equiv Q$'. This is *almost* what the rule $\equiv$I allows us to do. According to rule $\equiv$I, you do not actually have to have these two conditionals written into the derivation; it is sufficient (and also necessary) to have '$P$' written in, having '$Q$' as one of its suppositions, and also '$Q$' written in, with '$P$' as one of its suppositions. Of course we *could*, if we wanted, write in the two conditionals, for rule CP would allow us to write in '$P \supset Q$' if we have '$Q$' with '$P$' as one of its suppositions, and also '$Q \supset P$' if we have '$P$' with '$Q$' as one of its suppositions. But note carefully that rule $\equiv$I does *not* require that we in fact have both of these conditionals entered into our derivation. In effect, it saves us having to write in these two extra lines. Once we have shown that one formula may be derived from some second formula (and perhaps others), *and* that that second can be derived from the first (and perhaps others still), then we may enter the biconditional of those two formulas and cite $\equiv$I as the rule justifying the step.

**5. Strategy Hints.** Associated with rule $\equiv$I is the following strategy hint:

☛ If the desired conclusion is a biconditional, first assume the left side and derive the right side from it and other available suppositions, and then assume the right side and derive the left side from it and those other suppositions; then apply rule $\equiv$I to derive the desired biconditional.

Suppose, for example, that we are to derive the formula '$(P \ \& \ Q) \equiv Q$' from the single supposition '$P$'. Since the desired conclusion is a biconditional, our first step is to write in the given supposition, the desired conclusion, and the two *new* desired goals as specified by this strategy hint, as follows:

| | | | |
|---|---|---|---|
| 1 | 1 | $P$ | S |
| 2 | 2 | $P \ \& \ Q$ | S (for $\equiv$I) |
| | | | |
| | | $Q$ | |
| | | $Q$ | S (for $\equiv$I) |
| | | | |
| | | $P \ \& \ Q$ | |
| 1 | | $(P \ \& \ Q) \equiv Q$ | $\equiv$I |

The gaps here indicate our immediate goals: we must first get from '$P \ \& \ Q$' to '$Q$', and then from '$Q$' to '$P \ \& \ Q$'. The first part can be accomplished very simply using rule &E, and the second part is almost as simple, when we realize that '$P$' already occurs in our derivation as a supposition. So the complete derivation is:

| | | | |
|---|---|---|---|
| 1 | 1 | $P$ | S |
| 2 | 2 | $P \ \& \ Q$ | S (for $\equiv$I) |
| 2 | 3 | $Q$ | 2 &E |
| 4 | 4 | $Q$ | S (for $\equiv$I) |
| 1,4 | 5 | $P \ \& \ Q$ | 1,4 &I |
| 1 | 6 | $(P \ \& \ Q) \equiv Q$ | 2,3,4,5 $\equiv$I |

Make sure that you see clearly just how the rule $\equiv$I is applied here.

We may also frame the following strategy hint for rule $\equiv$E:

☞   If you are given (or have already derived) a biconditional, derive each of the two associated conditionals by rule $\equiv$E.

It is usually more useful to have conditionals in a derivation than biconditionals, since you might then be able to apply MPP or MTT. Note also that it is not always necessary to derive *both* conditionals; sometimes only one is needed to let you get to where you're going.

## Exercises

1   In each item, derive the last formula from the other(s).

(a)
$$P \supset \sim P$$
$$\sim P$$

(b)
$$\sim P \supset P$$
$$P$$

(c)
$$Q$$
$$P \equiv Q$$
$$P$$

(d)
$$P \supset Q$$
$$Q \supset P$$
$$P \equiv Q$$

(e)
$$P \equiv Q$$
$$\sim P \equiv \sim Q$$

(f)
$$\sim P \equiv \sim Q$$
$$P \equiv Q$$

(g)
$$\sim P$$
$$\sim Q$$
$$\sim (P \lor Q)$$

(h)
$$P \equiv \sim Q$$
$$Q \equiv \sim R$$
$$P \equiv R$$

(i)
$$(P \lor Q) \equiv P$$
$$Q \supset P$$

(j)
$$P \& (Q \lor R)$$
$$(P \& Q) \lor (P \& R)$$

(k)
$$(P \& Q) \lor (P \& R)$$
$$P \& (Q \lor R)$$

(l)
$$P \lor (Q \& R)$$
$$(P \lor Q) \& (P \lor R)$$

(m)
$$(P \lor Q) \& (P \lor R)$$
$$P \lor (Q \& R)$$

(n)
$$P \& Q$$
$$\sim (P \supset \sim Q)$$

(o)
$$\sim (P \supset \sim Q)$$
$$P \& Q$$

(p)
$$\sim (P \lor Q)$$
$$\sim P \& \sim Q$$

(q)
$$\sim P \& \sim Q$$
$$\sim (P \lor Q)$$

(r)
$$P \& Q$$
$$\sim (\sim P \lor \sim Q)$$

(s)
$$\sim (\sim P \lor \sim Q)$$
$$P \& Q$$

(t)
$$P \supset Q$$
$$\sim P \lor Q$$

(u)
$$\sim P \lor Q$$
$$P \supset Q$$

(v)
$$\sim P \supset Q$$
$$P \lor Q$$

(w)
$$P \lor Q$$
$$\sim P \supset Q$$

(x)
$$\sim (P \supset Q)$$
$$P$$

(y)
$$\sim (P \supset Q)$$
$$\sim Q$$

(z)
$$P \supset Q$$
$$(Q \supset P) \supset P$$
$$Q$$

2   In each item, derive the last formula from the other.

(a)
$$P \equiv Q$$
$$(S \equiv P) \equiv (S \equiv Q)$$

(b)
$$P$$
$$(P \equiv Q) \equiv Q$$

(c)
$$P$$
$$(P \supset Q) \equiv Q$$

(d)
$$\sim P$$
$$\sim(P \equiv Q) \equiv Q$$

(e)
$$(P \equiv Q) \equiv P$$
$$Q$$

(f)
$$P \supset Q$$
$$P \equiv (P \ \& \ Q)$$

3   Consider the following simplified version of the rule ≡I (which we shall label '≡I*' to distinguish it from the original version introduced above):

---

≡I*          Given two conditionals (not necessarily distinct or in this order) such that the antecedent of the first is the consequent of the second and the consequent of the first is the antecedent of the second, infer the biconditional whose left side is the antecedent of the first formula and whose right side is the consequent of the first formula. As supposition numerals of the inferred line, take all those of the two given lines.

---

For example:

$$
\begin{array}{lll}
1   & 1 \quad P \supset Q & \text{S} \\
2   & 2 \quad Q \supset P & \text{S} \\
1,2 & 3 \quad P \equiv Q & 1,2 \equiv \text{I*}
\end{array}
$$

(a) Redo every derivation in Exercise 1 above which has a biconditional as conclusion, using ≡I* but not ≡I.

(b) Redo every derivation in Exercise 2 above which has a biconditional as conclusion, using ≡I* but not ≡I.

(c) Now reflect: what are the advantages to adopting ≡I* instead of ≡I? What are the disadvantages?

(d) Can you figure out how to show that rule ≡I is not needed if we have rule ≡I* available?

You may henceforth use this rule ≡I* in any derivations you are asked to construct, instead of (or in addition to) ≡I.

# Chapter 10

## Theorems and Derived Rules

**1. Theorems**. It may have already occurred to some of you that by means of the rule CP (or also rules RAA and ≡I), one may wind up with a line which has *no* supposition numerals at all. Consider, for example, the following simple derivation:

| 1 | 1 | $P$ | S |
| Λ | 2 | $P \supset P$ | 1,1 CP |

We indicate the fact that in accordance with the statement of rule CP we are to enter no supposition numerals by writing the symbol 'Λ', which we take to stand for the empty set. What does it mean to say that this line has no supposition numerals? Recall that a derivation gives us a guarantee that a formula follows from its suppositions—that is, the formula would have to be true *if* all of its suppositions were true. The formula *might* very well be false if one or more of its suppositions were not true. But it can be false *only* in case at least one of its suppositions is false. So a formula derived without any supposition numerals at all can be false *only* in case at least one of its suppositions is false. But it does not have any suppositions that could be false—because it does not have any suppositions at all! So it itself *cannot be false!*

We see that a derived formula with no supposition numerals is bound to be true. We prove that it's bound to be true since we have an argument in which we infer it without basing our inference on any suppositions (assumptions or premises). In effect, we have this situation: no matter what is or were to be true, this formula is bound to be true.

Here is a rather more complicated example of deriving a formula having no suppositions:

| | | | |
|---:|---:|:---|:---|
| 1 | 1 | $\sim(P \equiv Q)$ | S (for CP) |
| 2 | 2 | $P$ | S (for $\equiv$I) |
| 3 | 3 | $Q$ | S (for RAA) |
| 2,3 | 4 | $P$ & $Q$ | 2,3 &I |
| 2,3 | 5 | $Q$ | 4 &E |
| 2,3 | 6 | $P$ | 4 &E |
| 2,3 | 7 | $P \equiv Q$ | 2,5,3,6 $\equiv$I |
| 1,2 | 8 | $\sim Q$ | 3,1,7 RAA |
| 9 | 9 | $\sim Q$ | S (for $\equiv$I) |
| 10 | 10 | $\sim P$ | S (for RAA) |
| 11 | 11 | $P$ | S (for $\equiv$I) |
| 12 | 12 | $\sim Q$ | S (for RAA) |
| 11,12 | 13 | $P$ & $\sim Q$ | 11,12 &I |
| 11,12 | 14 | $P$ | 13 &E |
| 10,11 | 15 | $\sim\sim Q$ | 12,10,14 RAA |
| 10,11 | 16 | $Q$ | 15 DNE |
| 17 | 17 | $Q$ | S (for $\equiv$I) |
| 18 | 18 | $\sim P$ | S (for RAA) |
| 17,18 | 19 | $Q$ & $\sim P$ | 17,18 &I |
| 17,18 | 20 | $Q$ | 19 &E |
| 9,17 | 21 | $\sim\sim P$ | 18,9,20 RAA |
| 9,17 | 22 | $P$ | 21 DNE |
| 9,10 | 23 | $P \equiv Q$ | 11,16,17,22 $\equiv$I |
| 1,9 | 24 | $\sim\sim P$ | 10,1,23 RAA |
| 1,9 | 25 | $P$ | 24 DNE |
| 1 | 26 | $P \equiv \sim Q$ | 2,8,9,25 $\equiv$I |
| $\Lambda$ | 27 | $\sim(P \equiv Q) \supset (P \equiv \sim Q)$ | 1,26 CP |

Formulas derivable from no suppositions at all are called *logical truths* or *theorems* of the system. They obviously have a great philosophical interest.[1] But they also have a purely logical interest as well, which we must now consider.

**2. Using Theorems.** Once we have established that certain formulas are bound to be true, we might want to find a way to use them in later lines of reasoning. For example, we might want to add them to our derivation— without thereby adding further *suppositions*—to make our arguments shorter. Since the formula:

$$\sim(P \text{ v } Q) \supset (\sim P \text{ \& } \sim Q)$$

---

[1] So eventually we shall have to discuss them. Philosophical question: what can it mean to say that '$P \supset P$' is "bound to be true", since is has no particular meaning without an accompanying phrase-book?

is a theorem, we might want to insert it into a derivation in which one of the lines is '~$(P \lor Q)$'. With the aid of this theorem and rule MPP, we can derive other formulas like '~$P$' and '~$Q$'.

How could we *justify* adding such a line to a derivation? We might contemplate adopting a rather general rule to the effect that at any time a theorem may be written down, without any supposition numerals. Two questions would arise about this: (1) How can we recognize a theorem? (2) What is the justification for such a rule? So far, our only means of recognizing a theorem is by constructing a derivation of the formula in question without any supposition numerals. So we would have to keep a running record of theorems we have already derived, and in applying the suggested rule, check to see whether the formula in question is among the theorems so far derived.

The justification for the suggested rule is that, although useful, it is not really needed. For instead of writing down a theorem in accordance with this proposed rule, we could insert at that point the entire derivation of the theorem. The result would be a (longer) derivation employing only our original rules. Similarly, instead of writing down a substitution-instance[2] of a theorem in accordance with this rule, we could insert at that point a substitution-instance of the derivation of the theorem. It is easy to see that if we performed a suitable replacement throughout a derivation of a theorem, we would get a derivation of the substitution-instance. (To convince yourself of this, go through our rules, one by one, and see that every instance of the application of a rule remains correct if such a replacement is made.) That is, we could transform in a very straightforward manner *any* derivation employing the suggested rule into one not employing it.

It doesn't seem very practical to keep a running record of theorems already derived. So we shall prove only a few theorems and employ this result to frame a few more auxiliary or derived rules to facilitate our derivations. To say that a rule is *derived* is to say that we have a straightforward means of transforming every derivation in which it is used into one in which it is not used. The most straightforward means of performing this transformation is to *replace* an application of the rule by a derivation not employing it (or, ultimately, any other derived rule). And once we have a derivation of the corresponding theorem, we know how to perform this replacement in each case.

---

[2] A *substitution-instance* of a formula is the result of replacing every occurrence of some (or all) of the sentential letters occurring in that formula by any formula whatsoever. (Each occurrence of any given letter must, however, be replaced by the same formula.)

**3. Derived Rules.** So far we have introduced thirteen rules of derivation, all of which we hereby classify as "basic" rules. Now we shall adopt five additional derived rules. These are:

---

~⊃         Given a negation of a conditional, infer either the antecedent of the conditional, or the negation of the consequent. As supposition numerals of the inferred line, take all those of the given line.

---

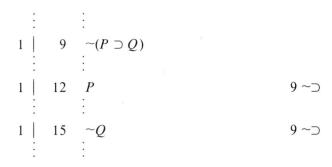

$$1 \mid \quad 9 \quad \sim(P \supset Q)$$

$$1 \mid \quad 12 \quad P \qquad\qquad\qquad\qquad\qquad\qquad 9 \; {\sim}\!\supset$$

$$1 \mid \quad 15 \quad \sim Q \qquad\qquad\qquad\qquad\qquad\qquad 9 \; {\sim}\!\supset$$

---

~≡         Given a negation of a biconditional, infer the biconditional whose left side is the left side of the negated biconditional and whose right side is the negation of the right side of the negated biconditional. As supposition numerals of the inferred line, take all those of the given line.

---

$$3 \mid \quad 7 \quad \sim(M \equiv W)$$

$$3 \mid \quad 12 \quad M \equiv \sim W \qquad\qquad\qquad\qquad\qquad 7 \; {\sim}\!\equiv$$

---

v⊃         Given a disjunction, infer the conditional whose antecedent is the negation of the left disjunct and whose consequent is the right disjunct. As supposition numerals of the inferred line, take all those of the given line.

---

$$
\begin{array}{c}
\vdots \qquad \vdots \\
2 \mid \quad 4 \quad T \vee Y \\
\vdots \qquad \vdots \\
2 \mid \quad 9 \quad {\sim}T \supset Y \qquad\qquad\qquad 4\ \vee\supset \\
\vdots \qquad \vdots
\end{array}
$$

---

⊃v      Given a conditional, infer the disjunction whose left disjunct is the negation of the antecedent and whose right disjunct is the consequent. As supposition numerals of the inferred line, take all those of the given line.

---

$$
\begin{array}{c}
\vdots \qquad \vdots \\
1 \mid \quad 9 \quad T \supset M \\
\vdots \qquad \vdots \\
1 \mid \quad 12 \quad {\sim}T \vee M \qquad\qquad\qquad 9\ \supset\mathrm{v} \\
\vdots \qquad \vdots
\end{array}
$$

---

DeM      Given a negation of a conjunction, infer the disjunction whose left disjunct is the negation of the left conjunct and whose right disjunct is the negation of the right conjunct. As supposition numerals of the inferred line, take all those of the given line.

Given a negation of a disjunction, infer the conjunction whose left conjunct is the negation of the left disjunct and whose right conjunct is the negation of the right disjunct. As supposition numerals of the inferred line, take all those of the given line.

Given a conjunction of two negations, infer the negation of the disjunction whose left disjunct is the negatum of the left conjunct and whose right disjunct is the negatum of the right conjunct. As supposition numerals of the inferred line, take all those of the given line.

Given a disjunction of two negations, infer the negation of the conjunction whose left conjunct is the negatum of the left disjunct and whose right conjunct is the negatum of the right disjunct. As supposition numerals of the inferred line, take all those of the given line.

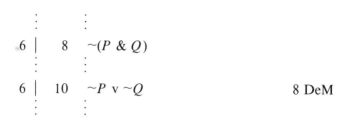

$$\begin{array}{ccll}
6 \mid & 8 & \sim(P \And Q) & \\
\\
6 \mid & 10 & \sim P \vee \sim Q & \qquad\qquad 8 \text{ DeM}
\end{array}$$

We have already provided a justification of rule $\sim\!\equiv$ with the long derivation in the first section. The derivations necessary to justify the remaining derived rules are left to the reader as exercises. See Exercise 1.

You will notice that rule DeM (for "DeMorgan's laws") has *four* parts. These correspond to important equivalences involving disjunctions, conjunctions, and negations. The second form, for instance, tells us that if the formula '$\sim(P \vee Q)$' occurs on a line in a derivation, then we may write down the formula '$\sim P \And \sim Q$' on a later line, taking the same supposition numerals. This is precisely the transformation we discussed earlier in connection with the theorem:

$$\sim(P \vee Q) \supset (\sim P \And \sim Q)$$

Of course, as we have already pointed out, we never *need* to use a derived rule. But using them judiciously can often save us a good deal of work. For instance, in Chapter 9 it took us ten steps to get from '$\sim(\sim P \supset Q)$' to '$\sim P$'. Now that we have rule $\sim\!\supset$ at our disposal, we can give a much shorter derivation:

$$\begin{array}{ccll}
1 \mid & 1 & \sim(\sim P \supset Q) & \qquad S \\
1 \mid & 2 & \sim P & \qquad 1 \sim\!\supset
\end{array}$$

As a somewhat more interesting example, let us reconsider Exercise 1(t) of Chapter 9. Having only the basic rules at your disposal, this is a rather tricky derivation; if you succeeded in constructing a derivation from '$P \supset Q$' to '$\sim P \vee Q$', you probably did it by including a series of steps very similar to your derivation of Exercise 1(s). And that makes for a rather lengthy derivation. With rule DeM available, however, we can give a much shorter derivation. We may begin by adopting an RAA strategy:

$$\begin{array}{ccll}
1 \mid & 1 & P \supset Q & \qquad S \\
2 \mid & 2 & \sim(\sim P \vee Q) & \qquad S \text{ (for RAA)} \\
\\
\mid & & \sim P \vee Q &
\end{array}$$

Now, line (2) is a negation of a disjunction; thus we may apply DeM as follows:

| | | | |
|---|---|---|---|
| 1 | 1 | $P \supset Q$ | S |
| 2 | 2 | $\sim(\sim P \vee Q)$ | S (for RAA) |
| 2 | 3 | $\sim\sim P \mathbin{\&} \sim Q$ | 2 DeM |
| | | $\sim P \vee Q$ | |

The derivation can then be completed quite simply:

| | | | |
|---|---|---|---|
| 1 | 1 | $P \supset Q$ | S |
| 2 | 2 | $\sim(\sim P \vee Q)$ | S (for RAA) |
| 2 | 3 | $\sim\sim P \mathbin{\&} \sim Q$ | 2 DeM |
| 2 | 4 | $\sim\sim P$ | 3 &E |
| 2 | 5 | $\sim Q$ | 3 &E |
| 1,2 | 6 | $\sim P$ | 1,5 MTT |
| 1 | 7 | $\sim\sim(\sim P \vee Q)$ | 2,4,6 RAA |
| 1 | 8 | $\sim P \vee Q$ | 7 DNE |

Clearly, the effort you spend learning the derived rules thoroughly will not be wasted.

**4. Complete Systems of Rules.** The system of *basic* rules that we have adopted so far (S, DS, MPP, MTT, DNI, DNE, &I, &E, vI, vE, ≡I, ≡E, CP, and RAA) is a *complete* system of rules for truth-functional logic, although it is somewhat complicated to prove this. To say that a system of rules is *complete* is to say that if some formula follows from a set of premises, then there is a derivation of that formula from those premises as suppositions, using only those rules. More compactly, if a formula *follows from* some set of formulas, then it is *derivable from* those formulas using just the basic rules.

It is rather difficult to prove this fact, but we can at least show that certain rules of derivation are not needed if certain other ones are at hand. For instance, although we have decided to count DS as a *basic* rule of derivation, it is not actually needed, since we can always find a way to do without it, if we are so inclined. It can also be shown that RAA is not needed. We have adopted it, like DS, because it is very useful and convenient. So there is some arbitrariness in our selection of basic rules (as you have already gathered from several of the exercises in preceding chapters).

**Exercises**

---

1    Using only the basic rules, prove the following theorems:

(a)         $\sim\!\dot{P} \supset ((P \vee Q) \supset Q)$         (b)         $(\sim\!P \vee Q) \equiv (P \supset Q)$

(c)         $\sim\!(P \mathbin{\&} Q) \equiv (\sim\!P \vee \sim\!Q)$         (d)         $(P \supset Q) \vee (P \supset \sim\!Q)$

(e)         $\sim\!(P \vee Q) \equiv (\sim\!P \mathbin{\&} \sim\!Q)$         (f)         $\sim\!(P \mathbin{\&} \sim\!P)$

(g)         $\sim\!(P \supset Q) \supset P$         (h)         $P \vee \sim\!P$

(i)         $\sim\!(P \supset Q) \supset \sim\!Q$         (j)         $P \supset ((P \supset Q) \supset Q)$

(k)         $(P \vee Q) \equiv (\sim\!P \supset Q)$         (l)         $P \equiv P$

2    Explain as clearly as you can why the rule v⊃ is a derived rule in rela-
     tion to the basic rules.

3    Using only the basic rules, but *not* DS, give a derivation of the third
     formula below from the first two.

$$P$$
$$\sim\!P$$
$$Q$$

4    Give a derivation of the second formula below from the first. You may
     use any of the basic rules introduced so far, as well as DS (but no
     derived rules).

$$Q \supset R$$
$$(Q \mathbin{\&} S) \supset (R \mathbin{\&} S)$$

5    Give a derivation of the last formula below from the others. You may
     use any of the basic rules introduced so far, but no derived rules.

$$S \supset R$$
$$P \equiv Q$$
$$((Q \mathbin{\&} R) \vee S) \vee \sim\!(P \equiv Q)$$
$$R$$

6    Find a derivation, using only the *basic* rules, of the formula '$Q$' from
     the two formulas '$\sim\!P$' and '$P \vee Q$'. Do not, however, use rule DS.
     What does this indicate about the necessity of adopting DS as a rule of
     derivation?

7   We have claimed that the rule RAA is not needed if we have the other rules—i.e., that anything that can be derived from some given premises using RAA (and perhaps other basic rules) can also be derived from those same premises without using RAA. Sketch a proof of this claim. (Hint: reread Section 1 of Chapter 9.)

8   Rule $\sim\equiv$ allows you to move a negation sign from the front of a biconditional onto its *right* side. You will notice that it does *not* allow you to move the negation sign onto the *left* side. Show that you can nevertheless find a derivation of the formula '$\sim P \equiv Q$' from the supposition '$\sim(P \equiv Q)$'.

9   Using any rules introduced in or before this chapter (i.e. any basic or derived rules), construct derivations of the following theorems:

(a)  $(P \equiv Q) \equiv ((P \& Q) \vee (\sim P \& \sim Q))$

(b)  $(P \supset Q) \vee (Q \supset R)$

(c)  $\sim P \supset (\sim(Q \equiv P) \equiv Q)$

(d)  $((P \& \sim Q) \supset R) \equiv (P \supset (Q \vee R))$

10  In theory, you never *need* to suppose the same formula more than once in any given derivation. In practice, however, you can make the structure of a derivation much easier to understand by taking a supposition at an appropriate time, whether or not that formula is already supposed earlier in the derivation. Abandon good style for the moment and rewrite the long derivation in Section 1 above in such a way that you never suppose the same formula more than once.

# Chapter 11

# Truth-Value Assignments

**1. Counterexamples**. Recall that a valid argument is one such that there is no possible case in which its premises (if any) would be true and its conclusion would be false. So an invalid argument is one for which there is such a possible case. A formally valid argument is one which has a form such that all arguments of that form are valid.

Our standard way of determining that an argument is formally valid is to produce a *derivation* of its conclusion from its premises (if any). One way of determining that an argument is not formally valid is to produce a *counterexample*, an argument sharing the same form while having *obviously* true premises and an *obviously* false conclusion. For instance, the following argument is not formally valid, though this may not be directly obvious:

> If Snowflake wallows in the mud, she will develop hives.
> If Snowflake develops hives, she will need the vet.
> Snowflake does not wallow in the mud.
> ―――――――――――――――――――――――――――――――
> Snowflake will not need the vet.

We can show the lack of formal validity here by offering the following counterexample:

> If Nixon is an aardvark, he has feet.
> If Nixon has feet, he also has toes.
> Nixon is not an aardvark.
> ―――――――――――――――――――――――――――
> Nixon has no toes.

The premises here are all *obviously* true, while the conclusion is *obviously* false. So the argument is not valid. Since the latter argument is not valid, the former is *not formally valid*, unless it either has a more detailed form such that all arguments of that form are valid, or it is "informally valid" (look again at our brief remarks at the beginning of Chapter 6).

**2. Problems with Counterexamples.** But this procedure is unsatisfactory for at least three reasons:

- If the argument under investigation is of a high degree of complexity, it may be extremely difficult to think up a counterexample, even though there is one.

- This procedure imports an impurity into logic; in determining that an argument is *not formally valid* (which is a logical matter), we have to rely on what (we think) is "obviously true" and what is "obviously false" (which is a matter of what we know or think about the actual world).

- It might happen that although there are arguments of a certain form having true premises and a false conclusion, it is *not known* (and certainly not obvious) that the premises are true and their conclusion false—and indeed it might happen that these arguments are not even expressible in a given language, say English, but perhaps only in another language (or, perhaps, not at all).

So it is desirable to find an alternative and preferably more general method for determining that an argument is *not formally valid*. We still want to do this by showing that there is an argument which is of a certain form and which is not valid. But we no longer try to do this by producing an actual argument with an obviously false conclusion but obviously true premises. Rather, we try to show that it is possible for some argument or other of that form (but which is otherwise unspecified) to have true premises and a false conclusion. For, if it is possible to do this, then that argument is invalid.

How shall we go about showing that there is such an argument? We do this by specifying conditions under which the premises of an argument of that form would be true and its conclusion false. In doing this, we rely on the fact that the truth-value of statements of certain forms depends on the truth-values of their components.

**3. Truth-Value Assignments.** We can see that:

- the negation of any statement is true just in case that statement is false;

- the conjunction of any two statements is true just in case both of those two statements are true;

- the disjunction of any two statements is true just in case one or both of those two statements are true.

So, for statements of a form which involves only negation, conjunction, and disjunction, we can specify conditions under which such a statement is true, and conditions under which such a statement is false, in terms of the truth-values of its component statements. For example, consider a statement of the form that we would symbolize as:

$$P \ \& \ (\sim Q \lor R)$$

It is easy to see that if the statement corresponding to '*P*' is true, the statement corresponding to '*Q*' is false, and the statement corresponding to '*R*' is false, then the original statement is true. We can summarize this in what we shall call a "truth-value assignment":

$$
\begin{array}{ccc}
P & - & T \\
Q & - & F \\
R & - & T
\end{array}
$$

This is a truth-value assignment under which the formula above is assigned the value 'T'. (There are of course others.) Similarly, the truth-value assignment:

$$
\begin{array}{ccc}
P & - & T \\
Q & - & T \\
R & - & F
\end{array}
$$

is one which would make the original statement false, so this truth-value assignment assigns that same formula 'F'. (There are also others.)

Now that we can specify conditions under which *statements* of certain forms would be true or would be false, we also can specify, for *arguments* involving just those forms, conditions under which their premises would be true and their conclusion false (if this is possible, of course). This then shows that these arguments are invalid arguments. For example, suppose that the first two formulas below represent the premises of some argument, and the third the conclusion.

$$
\begin{array}{c}
P \ \& \ (\sim Q \lor R) \\
\sim Q \ \& \ R \\
\sim P
\end{array}
$$

Then the truth-value assignment:

$$P \quad - \quad T$$
$$Q \quad - \quad F$$
$$R \quad - \quad T$$

assigns 'T' to each of the premises and 'F' to the conclusion. This shows that there are arguments of this form which are not valid. So the argument is not formally valid.

## Exercises

1  For each of the following formulas, find a truth-value assignment which assigns 'T' to the formula; then find a truth-value assignment which assigns 'F' to the formula.

(a)  $(P \lor Q) \mathbin{\&} (R \lor \mathord{\sim}Q)$

(b)  $\mathord{\sim}(P \mathbin{\&} Q)$

(c)  $\mathord{\sim}(P \lor R)$

(d)  $\mathord{\sim}(P \mathbin{\&} Q) \mathbin{\&} \mathord{\sim}(P \lor R)$

(e)  $\mathord{\sim}(P \mathbin{\&} Q) \lor \mathord{\sim}(P \lor R)$

(f)  $\mathord{\sim}(\mathord{\sim}(P \mathbin{\&} Q) \mathbin{\&} \mathord{\sim}(P \lor R))$

(g)  $(P \mathbin{\&} \mathord{\sim}Q) \mathbin{\&} \mathord{\sim}(\mathord{\sim}P \lor Q)$

2  Show that the following argument forms are not valid by providing a truth-value assignment in which the last formula in each case is false, and the others are true.

(a)    $\mathord{\sim}P \lor Q$          (b)        $Q \lor R$
       $P \lor R$                      $(\mathord{\sim}Q \lor P) \mathbin{\&} R$
       $Q \lor \mathord{\sim}R$                      $Q \mathbin{\&} R$
       $\mathord{\sim}Q$

(c)    $(\mathord{\sim}P \lor Q) \lor R$      (d)        $\mathord{\sim}P \lor Q$
       $\mathord{\sim}S \lor \mathord{\sim}P$                  $\mathord{\sim}R \lor \mathord{\sim}S$
       $T$                            $\mathord{\sim}S \lor P$
       $\mathord{\sim}(\mathord{\sim}S \mathbin{\&} T) \lor R$              $\mathord{\sim}Q \lor R$
       $T \mathbin{\&} \mathord{\sim}P$

(e)    $\mathord{\sim}(P \lor Q) \lor R$      (f)        $\mathord{\sim}P \lor R$
       $\mathord{\sim}R$                          $\mathord{\sim}Q \lor S$
       $Q \lor R$                      $\mathord{\sim}R \lor Q$
                                      $P \lor \mathord{\sim}S$

(g)              ~(P & Q) v R          (h)      ~(P & ~Q) v ~(~S & ~T)
                   ~R v S                             ~(T v Q)
                   Q & ~S                         ~U v (T v (~S & P))
                    P & Q                              T v Q

(i)          (P & ~Q) v (P & R)        (j)      ~M v (~(Q & ~A) v ~G)
                  Q v ~P                              Q & ~A
               (~P v ~R) v ~Q                         G & ~M

3   Find *all* truth-value assignments under which the formula
    'P & (~Q v R)' is assigned the value 'F'.

4   Find *all* truth-value assignments under which the formula
    '(P & Q) v (R & ~P)' is assigned the value 'T'.

# Chapter 12

# Conditionals

**1. Conditionals in Ordinary Discourse.** We have found a very general and convenient method for determining that an argument is *not formally valid*: we specify conditions under which an argument of the same form would have all of its premises true and its conclusion false. This method rests on the fact that the truth-value of statements of certain forms depends on the truth-value of their components. By assigning truth-values to components, we specify (where possible) conditions under which a given statement would be true or would be false. So far, however, we have considered doing this only for statements whose forms involved only negation, conjunction, and disjunction. It is desirable to extend this method.

It seems clear that we can extend the method in a straightforward manner only if the truth-values of conditionals and biconditionals *also* depends on the truth-values of their components. Is this so? Does, for example, the truth-value of a conditional depend solely on the truth-values of its antecedent and its consequent? At first blush, the answer seems to be discouragingly negative. To be sure, a conditional having a true antecedent and a false consequent is clearly false. (For the force of a conditional is precisely to exclude falsity of the consequent in case the antecedent is true.) But it seems that when the antecedent and consequent have some *other* combination of truth-values, the conditional may be true or it may be false—depending, apparently, on other factors. Consider the two conditionals:

If there is no food in the world, everyone will live forever.

If there is no food in the world, everyone will starve.

The antecedent of each conditional is true and the consequent of each is false. So the parts have the same truth-values. But the first conditional *seems* false, while the second *seems* true.

**Exercises**

---

1   Find three pairs of conditionals in English such that in each pair one of the conditionals seems pretty clearly true and the other seems pretty clearly false, *and*:

   (a) in each conditional of the first pair, both the antecedent and the consequent are obviously true.

   (b) in each conditional of the second pair, both the antecedent and the consequent are obviously false.

   (c) in each conditional of the third pair, the antecedent is obviously false and the consequent is obviously true.

---

**2. Conditionals and Rules of Derivation.** But further reflection seems to lead to the opposite result. For instance, using our rules we can derive the conditional '$P \supset Q$' from '$Q$'; we can also derive this conditional from '$\sim P$', as we saw in Exercises 1(k) and (l) of Chapter 7. Similarly, we can derive *any* conditional from its consequent, or from the negation of its antecedent. This means that—provided our rules are correct—a conditional is true if either its consequent is true or its antecedent is false, or both. But aren't our rules *obviously* correct? If they are, then we must conclude that a conditional is true when any one of three possible combinations of truth-values of its antecedent and consequent obtain, and that it is false only when the fourth obtains. Thus we have:

| $A$ | $C$ | $A \supset C$ |
|:---:|:---:|:---:|
| T | T | T |
| T | F | F |
| F | T | T |
| F | F | T |

And since a biconditional is, roughly speaking, "the conjunction of conditionals in both directions", we have the following truth-table for the biconditional:

| $A$ | $C$ | $A \equiv C$ |
|:---:|:---:|:---:|
| T | T | T |
| T | F | F |
| F | T | F |
| F | F | T |

So it looks as if the truth-value of certain forms involving conditionals and biconditionals *does*, after all, depend solely on the truth-values of their components.

It must be admitted that we have on our hands a certain conflict of intuitions. On the one hand, when we consider statements one by one, we are inclined to think that the truth-value of conditionals (or biconditionals) does *not* depend in a simple manner on the truth-values of their components. When, on the other hand, we consider certain obviously correct forms of inference (such as our rules), we are inclined to think that the truth-value of conditionals and biconditionals *does* depend, after all, in a simple manner on the truth-values of their components.

**Exercises**

---

    2    Explain as clearly as you can where you think our rules go wrong, or might go wrong, to yield a result which conflicts with our convictions based on considering individual conditional statements. Or, make some suggestions about how to explain this conflict.

---

**3. Resolving the Conflict.** This conflict is an example of one sort of problem in the domain of the philosophy of logic and will require further consideration at some later point. But what shall we do about it now? One promising line seems to be this: if we accept one of the alternatives as a *hypothesis* (which we are free to reconsider, revise, or reject afterwards)—namely, the alternative according to which the truth-value of conditionals *does* depend on the truth-values of their components—we shall be able to develop a system of logic which has considerable power in evaluating arguments as being formally valid or not, and which is by and large in accordance with what seems obvious. At worst, this system represents an approximation of the true story concerning formal validity. And besides its practical value as such, it may provide us with tools for getting closer to the true story. (An oversimplification and an approximate theory often make a better theory possible.) At best, it may turn out to be a true story after all.

It is fair to point out right away where such a system is at its weakest. You will note that our rules allow us to infer from the negation of a conditional to its antecedent, and also to the negation of its consequent. Compare Exercises 1(x) and (y) of Chapter 9. So we are allowed to conclude

from:    (1)    it is not the case that if McGovern wins, then there
                will be bad harvests in every country

to:      (2)    McGovern will win

and:     (3)    there won't be bad harvests in every country.

And however desirable these conclusions may be, they don't seem to follow from the premise, which seems pretty clearly true. At best, the conclusions seem to be to varying degrees uncertain. That is, we might be
willing to accept statement (1) as true but unwilling to regard it as guaran-
teeing the truth of (2) and (3). So the system is capable of having us
count certain arguments as formally valid which we are strongly inclined
to reject as invalid.

One remedy for this danger is to pay attention to the significance of conditionals and biconditionals appearing in arguments that we want to
evaluate with this system of rules. For we know how the system treats
them. According to it, (1) is true just in case both (2) and (3) are true. If
one or both of the latter is false or uncertain, then so is (1). Viewed in
this way, the reasoning is valid (and indeed formally so). So the system
cannot mislead us if we treat statements in accordance with it. If there is
a way of interpreting (1) so that it is clearly true, while (2) and (3) are
false or uncertain, then the system does not apply to this interpretation,
and the system cannot mislead us, unless we are careless. There is no real
danger in the system, so long as we are careful.

**4. Summary.** In view of these considerations, let us then adopt the following two principles:

- A conditional is true just in case either its antecedent is false or its
  consequent is true, or both.

- A biconditional is true just in case its left side and its right side have
  the same truth-value.

When these two principles are added to our previous three concerning
negation, conjunction, and disjunction, a truth-value assignment to the
sentential letters assigns a truth-value to *all* of the formulas we have considered so far. So we have a general method for specifying the conditions
under which a statement of a given form would be true or would be false.
And so we have a general method for determining that there are arguments of a given form which are not valid.

## Exercises

3    For each of the following formulas, find a truth-value assignment under which the formula is assigned 'T'; then find a truth-value assignment under which the formula is assigned 'F'.

| | | | |
|---|---|---|---|
| (a) | $P \supset Q$ | (b) | $P \supset (P \supset Q)$ |
| (c) | $\sim P \supset Q$ | (d) | $P \supset (P \equiv Q)$ |
| (e) | $\sim (P \supset Q)$ | (f) | $\sim (P \equiv Q) \supset \sim (P \supset Q)$ |
| (g) | $\sim (\sim P \supset \sim Q)$ | (h) | $(P \vee Q) \supset \sim (P \And R)$ |
| (i) | $P \equiv Q$ | (j) | $\sim ((P \vee Q) \supset \sim (\sim P \And \sim R))$ |
| (k) | $P \equiv \sim Q$ | (l) | $\sim (\sim P \equiv Q)$ |

4    For each of the following argument forms (the last formula being taken as the conclusion, the others as premises) show that there are arguments of that form which are not valid.

(a)
$$P \supset Q$$
$$R \supset \sim S$$
$$S \supset P$$
$$Q \supset R$$

(b)
$$P \supset R$$
$$Q \supset \sim S$$
$$R \supset Q$$
$$P \vee S$$

(c)
$$P \supset Q$$
$$(Q \supset P) \supset P$$
$$P$$

(d)
$$(P \And Q) \supset R$$
$$R \supset S$$
$$Q \And \sim S$$
$$P \equiv \sim R$$

(e)
$$(P \supset Q) \supset R$$
$$S \supset \sim P$$
$$T$$
$$(S \And T) \supset Q$$

(f)
$$\sim (P \And \sim Q) \equiv \sim (\sim S \And \sim T)$$
$$\sim (T \vee Q)$$
$$U \supset (\sim T \supset (\sim S \And P))$$
$$\sim T \equiv U$$

(g)
$$(P \And \sim Q) \vee (P \equiv R)$$
$$\sim Q \supset \sim P$$
$$R$$

(h)
$$(\sim P \supset Q) \supset R$$
$$\sim R$$
$$\sim (Q \supset P)$$

(i)
$$(P \supset Q) \supset Q$$
$$(T \supset P) \supset R$$
$$(R \supset S) \supset \sim (S \supset Q)$$

(j)
$$(P \supset Q) \vee (P \supset \sim Q)$$
$$(P \equiv Q) \vee (P \equiv \sim Q)$$
$$(P \supset Q) \equiv (P \supset \sim Q)$$
$$\sim (\sim P \vee \sim (Q \vee \sim Q))$$

# Chapter 13

## Other Logical Properties

**1. Introduction.** So far we have directed our attention to devising techniques for showing that arguments are formally valid or not formally valid. This is because, from a logical as well as from a practical point of view, these are the most important properties that arguments can have. There is also a further motivation for proceeding in the way we have, which is that other important logical properties and relations can be *defined in terms* of formal validity or the lack thereof. This means, among other things, that the two techniques which we have learned (constructing derivations and providing truth-value assignments) can be applied in the determination of these further logical properties and relations. Our present goal will be to define several of these further logical properties and relations and show how we go about determining whether they are present.

To say that a group of statements is *consistent* (or *compatible*) is to say that there are possible situations in which *all* the statements in the group are true. To say that a group of statements is *inconsistent* (or *incompatible*) is to say that there are no possible situations in which all the statements in the group are true. *Formal inconsistency* and *formal consistency* are related to *inconsistency* and *consistency* in a way very much like the way in which being formally valid and not being formally valid are related to validity and invalidity. Roughly, a group of statements is formally inconsistent if and only if the statements in the group have a form such that *all* groups of statements of that form are inconsistent; and a group of statements is formally consistent if and only if the statements in the group do not have a form such that *all* groups of statements of that form are inconsistent. By retracing our reasoning concerning what it is to be formally valid and not to be formally valid, we see that our methods can be adapted to determine formal inconsistency or formal consistency. Let's see how this works.

**2. Formal Inconsistency.** First, observe that a group of statements is *inconsistent* if and only if there are *no* possible cases in which *all* the statements in the group are true. That is to say, if, in any possible case, all but one of the statements were to be true, the remaining one would have to be false. In other words, if, in any possible case, all but one of the statements were to be true, the *negation* of the remaining one would have to be true. But that is to say that the negation of any one of the statements *follows* from the rest. Also, if the argument to this negation from the rest is *formally valid*, then the statements in the group have a form such that, in any group of statements of that form, the negation of any one of them follows from the rest. But this is to say that the statements in the group have a form such that any group of statements of that form is inconsistent. That is, the group of statements is *formally inconsistent*. In short, to determine that a group of statements is *formally inconsistent*, it suffices to derive the negation of any one of them from the rest.

For example, suppose we want to show that the following group of formulas is inconsistent:

$$P \text{ v } (Q \text{ v } R)$$
$$\sim P$$
$$\sim Q$$
$$\sim R$$

We can do this quite easily by deriving the *negation* of one of these formulas from the rest, as follows:

| | | | |
|---|---|---|---|
| 1 | 1 | $P \text{ v } (Q \text{ v } R)$ | S |
| 2 | 2 | $\sim P$ | S |
| 3 | 3 | $\sim Q$ | S |
| 1,2 | 4 | $Q \text{ v } R$ | 1,2 DS |
| 1,2,3 | 5 | $R$ | 3,4 DS |
| 1,2,3 | 6 | $\sim\sim R$ | 5 DNI |

This shows that any group of statements having this form is inconsistent.

**3. Formal Consistency.** On the other hand, suppose that we can give a truth-value assignment which specifies conditions under which all the statements in a group of statements having a certain form would be true. Then we know that there are groups of statements of that form which are *consistent*. So, not all groups of statements of that form are inconsistent. As we shall soon see, this is *not* yet enough to show that the group of statements is consistent. But it approaches this in that, if we confine our attention to the forms which we have up to now discerned in the statements, we know that there are consistent groups of formulas of those forms. We might put this briefly by saying that the *forms* themselves are consistent. And since our formulas are designed to represent forms, we see that to show that a group of formulas is *consistent* (i.e., that there are

consistent groups of statements having a form represented by those formulas), it suffices to give a truth-value assignment under which all the formulas are assigned 'T'.

For example, to show that the following group of formulas is consistent:

$$P \supset Q$$
$$\sim Q \equiv (R \vee S)$$
$$\sim S \mathbin{\&} \sim P$$
$$\sim R$$
$$Q$$

we need only give the following truth-value assignment:

| | | |
|---|---|---|
| $P$ | — | F |
| $Q$ | — | T |
| $R$ | — | F |
| $S$ | — | F |

Since (as you can easily determine) all five formulas are *true* under this
assignment, the formulas are consistent.

**Exercises**

---

1   Are there any *other* truth-value assignments which show that these five
    formulas are consistent?

---

**4. Logically True, False, and Contingent.** A statement is *logically true* just
in case there are no possible cases in which it is false. We have already
encountered some examples of logical truths, when we discovered that it is
possible to construct derivations in which the last line has *no* supposition
numerals (see Chapter 10). Actually, given just the rules we have so far,
not all logical truths can be derived in this way from no suppositions.
Nonetheless, any theorem of our present system is, as we have argued, a
logical truth. So our preferred method of showing that a formula is a logical truth is to construct a derivation of it from no suppositions.

A statement that is false in all possible cases is said to be *logically false.*
Obviously, the negation of a logically false statement is logically true. So,
we may show a statement to be logically false by deriving its negation
from no suppositions.

A statement that is neither logically true nor logically false is said to be *logically contingent*. We show that a statement is logically contingent by providing *two* truth-value assignments: one in which the statement is true and one in which the statement is false. This shows that the statement isn't always false and isn't always true. Hence, it's logically contingent.

For instance, the following formula is logically contingent:

$$R \text{ v } (S \text{ v } (T \equiv R))$$

**Exercises**

2   Show this. Can you give *several* truth-value assignments of each required sort?

**5. Logical Equivalence.** Two statements are *logically equivalent* just in case they have the same truth-value in every possible situation. In other words, if either one of them is true, then the other one must also be true. But this is to say that each statement *follows from* the other. So, to show that two formulas are equivalent, we need only give a derivation of each one from the other.

If you recall rule $\equiv$I, you will see that two formulas are derivable one from the other just in case the biconditional with one of them as the left side and the other as the right side is a *theorem*. So two formulas are equivalent if their biconditional is a theorem. For example, we can show that the two formulas:

$$P$$
$$\sim\sim P$$

are formally equivalent by constructing the following simple derivation:

| 1 | 1 | $P$ | S (for $\equiv$I) |
|---|---|---|---|
| 1 | 2 | $\sim\sim P$ | 1 DNI |
| 3 | 3 | $\sim\sim P$ | S (for $\equiv$I) |
| 3 | 4 | $P$ | 3 DNE |
| $\Lambda$ | 5 | $P \equiv \sim\sim P$ | 1,2,3,4 $\equiv$I |

**6. Preliminary Summary.** So we have the following results:

(1)   To show that a formula is *implied by* or *follows from* a group of formulas, it suffices to give a derivation having that implied formula as

conclusion and the group of formulas as suppositions.

(2)    To show that a formula is *not implied by* or *does not follow from* a group of formulas, it suffices to give a truth-value assignment under which all the formulas in the group are true and that formula is false.

(3)    To determine that a group of formulas is *formally inconsistent*, it suffices to derive the negation of any one of them from the rest.

(4)    To show that a group of formulas is *formally consistent*, it suffices to give a truth-value assignment under which all the formulas are assigned 'T'.

(5)    To show that a formula is *logically true*, it suffices to give a derivation of it from no suppositions.

(6)    To show that a formula is *logically false*, it suffices to give a derivation of its negation from no suppositions.

(7)    To show that a formula is *logically contingent*, it suffices to give a truth-value assignment under which the formula is assigned 'T', as well as a truth-value assignment under which the formula is assigned 'F'.

(8)    To show that two formulas are *formally equivalent*, it suffices to give a derivation of each from the other.

**7. Truth-Tables Reconsidered**. Truth-tables provide a systematic way to survey all possible truth-value assignments. And they allow us to determine the truth-values of certain formulas in relation to the truth-values of other formulas. Truth-tables may therefore be used to determine the consistency or inconsistency of a group of formulas, the logical truth, falsehood, or contingency of a single formula, the logical equivalence or nonequivalence of two formulas, and indeed whether a formula follows or does not follow from a group of formulas.

The following results should be obvious upon reflection:

(1)    To show that a formula is *implied by* or *follows from* a group of formulas, it suffices to show that there is no row in the truth-table on which the formulas in the group are all true and the implied formula is false.

(2)    To show that a formula is *not implied by* or *does not follow from* a group of formulas, it suffices to show that there is at least one line in the truth-table on which all the formulas in the group are true and that formula is false.

(3)   To determine that a group of formulas is *formally inconsistent*, it suffices to show that there is no row in the truth-table on which all formulas are true.

(4)   To show that a group of formulas is *formally consistent*, it suffices to show that there is at least one row in the truth-table on which all formulas are true.

(5)   To show that a formula is *logically true*, it suffices to show that it is true on every row in a truth-table.

(6)   To show that a formula is *logically false*, it suffices to show that it is false on every row in a truth-table.

(7)   To show that a formula is *logically contingent*, it suffices to show that it is true on at least one row in the truth-table and false on at least one (other) row.

(8)   To show that two formulas are *formally equivalent*, it suffices to show that they have the same truth-value on every row in the truth-table.

For example, suppose we want to show that the following two formulas are logically equivalent:

$$P \text{ v } (Q \text{ v } R)$$
$$(P \text{ v } Q) \text{ v } R$$

We could give a derivation of each from the other, but that would be long and tedious. Instead, we shall construct the following truth-table:

| $P$ | $Q$ | $R$ | $P \text{ v } (Q \text{ v } R)$ | $(P \text{ v } Q) \text{ v } R$ |
|-----|-----|-----|----------------------------------|----------------------------------|
| T | T | T | T | T |
| T | T | F | T | T |
| T | F | T | T | T |
| T | F | F | T | T |
| F | T | T | T | T |
| F | T | F | T | T |
| F | F | T | T | T |
| F | F | F | F | F |

Since both formulas have identical values on each row, the formulas are equivalent, by clause (7) above.

**8. Decision Procedures.** The device of constructing truth-tables thus provides us with a completely mechanical and straightforward way of determining the presence or absence of any of the logical properties and relations we have so far considered. In that sense, the technique of constructing truth-tables is a *decision procedure* for truth-functional logic: if we want to find out whether, for example, a given formula follows from some group of formulas, we need only construct a truth-table in the way outlined above. And you shouldn't need any particular insight or acumen in doing this; if you are constructing a truth-table, you should never need to wonder what the next step should be. At any time, the steps you need to get a complete answer should be completely obvious.

It should be clear, therefore, that we didn't *need* to learn any of the many rules of derivation presented in previous chapters. To find out if a formula follows from a group of formulas, a truth-table would have done just as well. Indeed, constructing truth-tables is a far more mechanical and step-by-step procedure than is constructing derivations. Some of the derivations we have asked you to do have been quite long and complicated. So why have we placed so much emphasis on derivations, and so little on truth-tables?

There are a number of reasons for this. First of all, derivations mirror much more closely than truth-tables the lines of reasoning that we actually go through in our everyday life. Another difference between the two techniques is that derivations are sometimes much more manageable than the corresponding truth-table would be. An argument involving six sentential letters, for instance, would require a truth-table having 64 lines. A derivation, though, might proceed very easily and quickly. So derivations can sometimes save us some work.

But by far the most important difference is that the technique of truth-table construction *cannot* be easily extended into portions of logic beyond truth-functional logic. As we shall see later in this book, derivations allow us to show validity (or inconsistency) in even very advanced portions of logic, where nothing like the mechanical procedures of truth-tables is feasible. So cultivating our skills in constructing derivations will serve us well.

## Exercises

---

3    We have already shown that the following group of formulas is incon-
     sistent (see above, Section 2). Do this again, by deriving the negation of
     the *first* formula from the others.

$$P \text{ v } (Q \text{ v } R)$$
$$\sim P$$
$$\sim Q$$
$$\sim R$$

4    Show that each of the following groups of formulas is *formally incon-
     sistent.*

     (a) $T \supset \sim R, \quad \sim(((S \text{ v } T) \& R) \equiv (S \& R))$

     (b) $\sim(S \text{ v } T), \quad (S \supset T) \supset T$

     (c) $S \equiv \sim S$

     (d) $S, \quad S \supset \sim T, \quad \sim T \supset \sim S$

     (e) $\sim(\sim S \supset (S \supset T)), \quad S \supset T$

     (f) $P \supset Q, \quad R \supset \sim S, \quad S \supset P, \quad Q \supset R, \quad S$

     (g) $(\sim P \supset Q) \supset \sim R, \quad R, \quad \sim Q \supset P$

5    Show that each of the following groups of formulas is *formally con-
     sistent.*

     (a) $P \supset Q, \quad P \supset R, \quad \sim Q \supset \sim R, \quad Q$

     (b) $P \supset Q, \quad (Q \supset P) \supset P, \quad Q$

     (c) $(P \supset Q) \supset R, \quad S \supset \sim T, \quad (\sim S \& T) \supset Q$

     (d) $P \supset R, \quad Q \supset \sim S, \quad R \supset Q, \quad P \supset \sim S$

     (e) $(P \& Q) \supset R, \quad R \supset S, \quad Q \& \sim S, \quad \sim P$

     (f) $(P \& \sim Q) \text{ v } (P \& Q), \quad \sim Q \supset \sim P, \quad R$

     (g) $\sim(P \& \sim Q) \text{ v } \sim(\sim S \& \sim T)$

6    Show that each of the following formulas is *logically false.*

     (a) $P \& \sim P$

     (b) $P \equiv \sim P$

     (c) $(P \& Q) \equiv (\sim P \& Q)$

     (d) $(P \text{ v } \sim P) \supset \sim(P \text{ v } \sim P)$

7    Show that each of the following formulas is *logically contingent.*

    (a)  $P \ \& \ {\sim}Q$

    (b)  $(P \equiv P) \equiv P$

    (c)  $R \ \mathrm{v} \ (S \ \mathrm{v} \ (T \equiv R))$

    (d)  $H \supset {\sim}H$

8    Show that the formulas in each of the following pairs are *formally equivalent*.

    (a)  $P, \quad P \equiv (P \equiv P)$

    (b)  ${\sim}P \ \mathrm{v} \ (Q \ \mathrm{v} \ R), \quad P \supset (Q \ \mathrm{v} \ R)$

    (c)  ${\sim}A \equiv B, \quad {\sim}B \equiv A$

    (d)  $A \ \& \ B, \quad {\sim}(A \supset {\sim}B)$

9    Show that the argument with the first two formulas below as premises and the third as conclusion is *formally valid*. Are the premises consistent?

$$A \equiv (B \supset {\sim}A)$$
$$B$$
$${\sim}B \equiv A$$

10  For each of the arguments in Exercise 1 of Chapter 5, decide whether the argument is valid or invalid. If it is *valid*, give a derivation of the conclusion from the premises. If it is *invalid*, give a truth-value assignment under which the premises are true and the conclusion is false.

11  Do the same for each of the arguments in Exercise 2 of Chapter 5.

12  Explain why an argument whose premises are *inconsistent* must be *valid*.

13  Must an argument which is *valid* have premises which are *inconsistent*?

14  Show that a statement is logically contingent just in case it is consistent *and* its negation is consistent.

15  Show that a statement is *logically false* just in case it is *inconsistent* with every statement (including itself).

16  Show that a statement *follows from* a group of statements just in case its negation is *inconsistent* with that group.

17  Let us introduce a new truth-functional connective, '|', representing the phrase 'neither...nor' (this is sometimes called the *Sheffer stroke*). For instance, the statement 'Neither Alfred nor Bertha is a Democrat' might be represented as '$A \,|\, B$'. The truth-table for this connective is as follows:

| $A$ | $B$ | $A\mid B$ |
|---|---|---|
| T | T | F |
| T | F | F |
| F | T | F |
| F | F | T |

(a) Find a formula containing just the Sheffer stroke, the letter '$A$', and parentheses (if necessary) which is *formally equivalent* to '$\sim A$'.

(b) Find a formula containing just the Sheffer stroke, the letters '$A$' and '$B$', and parentheses (if necessary) which is *formally equivalent* to '$A$ & $B$'.

(c) Do the same for '$A$ v $B$'.

(d) Do the same for '$A \supset B$'.

(e) Do the same for '$A \equiv B$'.

(f) What can you conclude from (a) through (e)?

18 Find a formula that has the following truth-table:

| $A$ | $B$ | $C$ | ? |
|---|---|---|---|
| T | T | T | F |
| T | T | F | T |
| T | F | T | T |
| T | F | F | T |
| F | T | T | F |
| F | T | F | F |
| F | F | T | T |
| F | F | F | F |

# PART III

## Quantificational Logic

Our next goal is to widen the class of logical forms that we can treat. There are three main additional features of statements that we shall now consider: subjects and predicates, the identity predicate, and expressions of quantity ('all', 'some', 'none', and the like). There is a simple and elegant way of representing the logical form of these statements. In addition, we can achieve a complete system of rules by adopting just two rules concerning identity formulas and four concerning quantificational formulas. The resulting system of logic is a very powerful instrument, applicable to a wide variety of problems.

# Chapter 14

## Logical Subjects and Predicates

**1. The Limits of Truth-Functional Logic.** The two chief methods that we have employed in truth-functional logic (constructing derivations and finding truth-value assignments) fail to give us satisfactory answers in all cases that we might consider. A simple kind of example that illustrates this is the argument:

> Greta has peeked at my picture.
> _____
> Someone has peeked at my picture.

Quite obviously, the argument is valid: if the premise is true, the conclusion must also be true. Yet the only logical form that we can isolate at the level of truth-functional logic is this:

$$P$$
$$Q$$

which is not formally valid, as you can easily show with a truth-value assignment. So the method of assigning truth-values is insufficient to give us a full and correct answer here.

The reason for this is that in truth-functional logic we pay attention to the logical form of statements only up to a certain depth, so to speak—i.e., only insofar as a statement can be regarded as compounded out of simpler statements by means of the five statement connectives. Having isolated the logical form of an argument to a certain depth, if we show that *all* arguments of that form are valid, then we have obviously also shown that the argument in question is valid, and indeed formally valid. A similar result holds for formal inconsistency.

But if, having isolated the logical form of an argument to a certain depth, we show that *not all* arguments of that form are valid, we have not thereby shown that the argument is not valid, nor that it is not formally valid. For, we may be able to isolate a deeper form such that indeed *all* arguments of *that* form are valid.[1] (Roughly, this deeper form will be the form so far isolated but with further details discerned.) So, although the argument may have *a* form such that not all arguments of *that* form are valid, it may also have *another* form such that *all* arguments of this new form *are* valid. Thus, if we have isolated a logical form only up to a certain depth, the test for absence of formal validity is not conclusive. And similarly for formal consistency.

At the level of truth-functional logic, the premise and conclusion in the argument above are both statements which are not compounded of simpler *statements*. That is to say, neither one counts as a negation, a conjunction, a disjunction, etc. But a deeper look shows that the statements *are* compounded of other parts, such as 'Greta', 'someone', 'has peeked at my picture'. In addition, all arguments whose premise and conclusion have a similar structure are valid. That is, the argument would remain valid even if we replaced 'Greta' by 'Bill', or 'has peeked at my picture' by 'will buy me a fine present'. This indicates that the argument is not only valid, but also *formally* valid, if we take into regard this deeper logical form.

Our present goal, then, is to learn how to isolate such deeper logical forms. A little later, we shall give special emphasis to the role of such phrases as 'everything', 'something', 'nothing', 'everyone', 'someone', 'none', 'everywhere', 'whenever', 'every', 'some', 'all', 'no', and similar phrases. This takes us into what is called *quantificational logic*. Until we tackle such phrases head on, however, you may consider yourself to be studying *identity logic*, for reasons which will soon become clear.

**2. Grammatical v. Logical Subjects.** The most striking division of many statements which are not compounded of simpler statements is the intuitively obvious one into the grammatical subject and the grammatical predicate. For example, the premise of the preceding argument divides naturally into 'Greta' and 'has peeked at my picture'. But there are other portions of such statements which resemble grammatical subjects in at least two logically interesting ways:

● These portions can be brought into the grammatical subject position through transformations which do not appreciably alter the meaning of the original statement. In other words, we can find another statement with substantially the same meaning and having these portions in the grammatical subject position.

---

[1] Notice that this is a different kind of "depth" from that discussed in Chapter 4, Sec. 4.

- These portions behave in the same way as grammatical subjects in inferences involving 'everything', 'something', etc.

For example, the premise of the argument above can be "transformed" into:

My picture has been peeked at by Greta.

Also, we may infer from that premise:

Greta has peeked at something.

Because of these logically interesting features, such portions of statements are regarded in logic as being on a par with grammatical subjects, and both are called *logical subjects* of the statement. So both 'Greta' and 'my picture' count as logical subjects. The "rest" of the statement (what you get when you remove the logical subjects) is called the *logical predicate*. Subject to further qualifications below, we can say that a logical subject is any part of a statement that purports to designate a single, definite individual or thing. And, the logical predicate of a non-molecular statement is what remains when you remove the logical subject(s).

**3. Representing Logical Subjects and Predicates.** Because grammatical subjects thus lose their pre-eminence, they are represented in precisely the same way as other logical subjects. A logical subject is represented by a *lower*-case letter chosen from the range '$a$' to '$t$'. Thus, for instance, we might represent the logical subject 'Greta' with the letter '$g$' and the logical subject 'my picture' with the letter '$m$'.

Representing a logical predicate is slightly more complicated, since a logical predicate contains certain "gaps" indicating the removal of one or more logical subjects. For instance, when we remove the logical subjects from the statement:

Greta has peeked at my picture.

we are left with the phrase 'has peeked at'. It will be useful if we indicate *where* logical subjects were removed from the original statement to get this phrase. We can do this easily by replacing the logical subjects by circled numerals, as follows:

① has peeked at ②

This will be our standard way of specifying logical predicates, which we shall then represent with *upper*-case letters.[2] Finally, we represent non-

---

[2] Taking full advantage of the "expanded English alphabet". Thus, predicate letters may be written with subscripts, if necessary.

molecular *statements* by writing the letter representing the logical predicate followed directly by the letter(s) representing the logical subject(s). Thus, it is natural to symbolize the statement:

Greta has peeked at my picture.

as:

$$Pgm$$

Similarly, we may represent the statement:

Clothilda has given my picture to Penelope.

as:

$$Gcmp$$

In giving such representations, we must pay special attention to the *order* of the logical subjects. In a simple statement about giving (such as the second statement just above), there are always (though perhaps at times only implicitly) three logical subjects: one representing the *giver*, one representing the thing *given*, and one representing the *receiver*.[3] Generally we shall put the giver first, the object given second, and the receiver third. This amounts to isolating the following logical predicate:

①  gave  ②  to  ③

In this case, we may symbolize:

Penelope has given my picture to Greta.

as:

$$Gpmg$$

And:

The picture was given to Greta by John

---

[3] There is no requirement that these three things all be distinct from one another. In a society that permitted human enslavement, one could, for instance, give oneself to someone else. It still makes sense, however, to distinguish what is given from what does the giving, and a good symbolization should reflect that they *are* the same. So we might represent the statement that Alfred gave himself to Clothilda as '*Gaac*'.

as

$$Gjmg$$

In all these cases, the circled numerals in the specification of the logical predicate indicate that the logical subjects must be written in the order: giver, given, receiver.

But there is no reason that we should restrict ourselves always to having things in this order. For certain purposes, it may be more useful to put the letter representing the thing given in the first place. In that case, we might adopt the order: given, receiver, giver. This amounts to isolating the logical predicate:

③ gave ① to ②

And we would symbolize the two statements above as

$$Gmpg$$

and

$$Gmgj$$

For most purposes, however, we shall choose to number the gaps in a logical predicate in order from left to right.

**4. Expanded Phrase-Books.** Whenever we represent logical form, we must append to our representation an indication of how our symbols are to be understood. In truth-functional logic we did this by means of phrase-books matching statement-letters with statements. We shall now extend the idea of a phrase-book so that we may also match *logical predicate letters* with logical predicates (marked in the way illustrated above to indicate the order in which we are to write their logical subjects); and we match *logical subject letters* (also called *individual constants*) with logical subjects, which are usually names or phrases purporting to stand for a single specified thing (or person, etc.). We can then represent various statements, employing in this process the special symbols of truth-functional logic. Thus we might have the following expanded phrase-book:

| | | |
|---|---|---|
| $W$ | : | Things have turned out well. |
| $N$ | : | ① is nice |
| $L$ | : | ① likes ② |
| $G$ | : | ① gave ② to ③ |
| $g$ | : | Greta |

$j$  :   John
$p$  :   Penelope
$i$  :   I
$m$  :   my picture

Then we may symbolize the following statements as indicated:

(a)   Greta didn't give my picture to Penelope.

$$\sim Ggmp$$

(b)   My picture is nice and Greta likes it.

$$Nm \ \& \ Lgm$$

(c)   If John gave my picture to Greta, then Penelope was given it by Greta.

$$Gjmg \supset Ggmp$$

(d)   Neither I nor John gave my picture to Greta.

$$\sim(Gimg \ \text{v} \ Gjmg)$$

(e)   If my picture is not nice but Greta likes it, then she is not nice.

$$(\sim Nm \ \& \ Lgm) \supset \sim Ng$$

(f)   If Greta gave my picture to Penelope, then things have turned out well if and only if the picture was given by Penelope to me.

$$Ggmp \supset (W \equiv Gpmi)$$

**5. Logical Subjects Reconsidered.** We should note that in certain circumstances, phrases that *look* like logical subjects should not be counted as logical subjects. This is similar to the situation in truth-functional logic when we encountered certain statements that *looked* (for instance) like negations, but which we decided not to classify as negations. We have tentatively characterized a logical subject as any word or phrase that purports to designate a single definite individual, place, item, or thing. But we shall *not* count such words or phrases as genuine logical subjects when (1) they occur as parts of other such phrases, (2) they occur in "modal" contexts, or (3) they occur in "intentional" contexts. Let us explain what each of these means.

Sometimes, a phrase that appears to designate a single individual item contains *another* such word or phrase. For example, the phrase 'the father of Alfred' contains the word 'Alfred'. Similarly, the phrase 'the abbé' occurs as part of the phrase 'the first person ever to confess to the abbé'. In such cases, we shall agree not to count as a logical subject the word or phrase which is contained within the longer phrase. Hence, in the phrase 'the first person ever to confess to the abbé', we do not count 'the abbé' as a logical subject. This is the simplest kind of "candidate" logical subject that does not count as a "genuine" logical subject. Of course, the longer phrase, 'the first person ever to confess to the abbé', is itself a logical subject.

The second case of candidate logical subjects which do not qualify as genuine logical subjects concerns the occurrence of such phrases in *modal contexts*. Modal contexts are those introduced by such locutions as 'it is possible that', 'it is necessary that', 'it is very likely that' and the like. For example, in the statement:

It is possible that the abbé misheard his first confessee.

the phrases 'the abbé' and 'the abbé's first confessee' both occur within the context of the modal phrase 'it is possible that'. Neither one of these, therefore, is to count as a logical subject. The best we can do at present is to count such a statement as non-molecular.

A similar fate befalls apparent logical subjects when they occur in a *psychological* or *intentional* context. It is difficult to say precisely what counts as an intentional context, but these coincide roughly with the object of someone's thinking, supposing, surmising, believing, hoping (etc.) something. Another way of putting this is to say that any such phrase which follows a "verb of the head" is only an apparent and not a real logical subject. For example, the phrase 'Madame de Chablis thinks that' introduces an intentional context. Hence, we will not count the occurrence of the phrase 'the abbé' in the statement:

Madame de Chablis thinks that the abbé is a murderer.

as a genuine logical subject. The phrase 'Madame de Chablis' *does* however qualify as a genuine logical subject, since it does not follow the intentional verb 'thinks that'.

The second and third cases isolated, in which apparent logical subjects occur within modal contexts or intentional contexts, introduce complexities which are beyond the scope of this book. In fact, deciding how to deal with such cases is one of the more difficult problems in the philosophy of logic. But the first case, in which apparent logical subjects occur as part of other logical subjects, *can* be treated straightforwardly in several different ways. We shall consider two of them in Chapters 23 and 25.

**6. Derivations and Truth-Value Assignments.** We noticed above that the resources of truth-functional logic do not give us correct answers concerning *all* arguments. But as long as the statements we deal with do not contain phrases like those listed at the end of Section 1 and do not contain phrases of the kind just considered,[4] the resources of truth-functional logic *do* in fact suffice to determine formal validity, formal invalidity, formal consistency, and formal inconsistency. In particular, as we have already observed, a derivation in truth-functional logic shows conclusively validity or inconsistency, as the case may be. All we need to do is to treat the newly-introduced formulas in such a way that a formula consisting of a logical predicate letter followed by a suitable number of individual constants behaves just like a sentential letter. In other words, such formulas are treated like non-molecular formulas, taking care to note that if there is *any* difference at all between two such formulas, they must be treated as if they were *distinct* sentential letters. (Thus, '*Gabb*' and '*Gaba*' must be treated as different formulas.) So we might have the following derivation:

| | | | |
|---|---|---|---|
| 1 | 1 | *Gaba* ∨ *Gabb* | S |
| 2 | 2 | *Gaba* ⊃ *Haa* | S |
| 3 | 3 | *Gabb* ⊃ *Haa* | S |
| 4 | 4 | *Gaba* | S (for vE) |
| 2,4 | 5 | *Haa* | 2,4 MPP |
| 6 | 6 | *Gabb* | S (for vE) |
| 3,6 | 7 | *Haa* | 3,6 MPP |
| 1,2,3 | 8 | *Haa* | 1,4,5,6,7 vE |

This derivation shows conclusively that the formula on the last line *follows from* the formulas on the first three lines.

It is also the case that truth-value assignments suffice to determine invalidity and consistency of these kinds of statements. All we need to do is assign truth-values to formulas consisting of a logical predicate letter followed by the appropriate number of individual constants just as if these new sorts of formulas were sentential letters. Thus, we can show the invalidity of the argument:

*Faa* ∨ *Gabc*
*Faa*
*Gabc*

---

[4] Or the identity predicate to be considered in the next chapter.

using the following truth-value assignment:

$$Faa \quad - \quad T$$
$$Gabc \quad - \quad F$$

But for further developments this simple method will not suffice, and we shall need to introduce a new method, that of *semantical assignments.*

**Exercises**

1    In each of the following statements, determine which words or phrases are logical subjects. If there are any *apparent* logical subjects which are not *genuine* logical subjects, explain why not.

(a)   It is necessary that Charlie go to the bank, if we are to be paid today.

(b)   Alfred is hunting for the man who stole his wristwatch.

(c)   Bertha lives next to the tallest person in Berkeley.

(d)   The first person to walk on the moon grew up in Wapakoneta, Ohio.

(e)   Dunforth was deceived by a man of slight build.

(f)   The latest poem attributed to Shakespeare was probably not written by him.

2    Symbolize each of the following arguments using the *new* kind of phrase-book, and show with a derivation that the argument so symbolized is valid. (You will want to use a separate phrase-book for each part.)

(a)   If Alfred arrived on time, then he saw both Bertha and Clothilda. If he saw Clothilda, he gave her the code book and she gave him the sealed envelope. If he saw Bertha, he gave her the sealed envelope if Clothilda gave it to him. But Alfred didn't give Bertha the sealed envelope. So Alfred did not arrive on time.

(b)   Either New York is farther from Boston than San Francisco is from Los Angeles, or New York is farther from Atlanta than it is from Chicago. In the former case, Alfred will arrive sooner than Mary. In the latter, Susan will arrive sooner than Peter. But if Susan arrives sooner than Peter, then Alfred won't arrive sooner than Mary. So New York is farther from Boston than San Francisco is from Los Angeles if and only if New York is not farther from Atlanta than it is from Chicago.

(c)   If Alfred loves Bertha, then he loves her better than himself. If Alfred loves Bertha better than himself, then she loves him but not better than herself. So either Alfred does not love Bertha or she does not love him better than herself.

(d) If Peter is a friend of Susan's and Susan is a friend of Jill's, then Peter is a friend of Jill's. Also, if Peter is a friend of Susan's, then he goes to her parties. But if he goes to Susan's parties, Susan goes to Jill's. And if Susan goes to Jill's parties, then Susan is her friend and does not tell tales about her. Well, if Susan doesn't, then Peter does—unless Jill tells tales about herself. So unless Jill tells tales about herself, if Peter is a friend of Susan's, he is a friend of Jill's who tells tales about her!

(e) Either Alfred is rich and supports Bertha or she is rich and supports him. If either is rich, Charlie was able to pay his debts to Dunforth. But if Dunforth was paid by Charlie and Bertha supports Alfred, then she will elope with Dunforth. So Bertha won't elope with Dunforth only if Alfred is rich.

3   In each of the arguments of the previous exercise, replace the conclusion by the corresponding one below; then show by means of a truth-value assignment that the resulting argument is *not* valid.

(a) Clothilda didn't give Alfred the sealed envelope.

(b) New York is not farther from Atlanta than it is from Chicago.

(c) If Bertha loves Alfred, then he loves her.

(d) Peter is either not a friend of Susan's or not of Jill's.

(e) It is not the case that both Alfred and Bertha are rich.

# Chapter 15

## Identity Statements

**1. Identity.** The simplest class of arguments for which the resources of truth-functional logic do not suffice to show validity or inconsistency is the class of arguments containing *identity statements*. An identity statement is a statement which asserts that a given thing (person, etc.) is the very same thing (person, etc.) as such and such a thing. For example:

> The first person to confess to the abbé **is** the marquis.
> Alfred **was** the only person Clothilda asked to dance.
> Bertha **is** Dunforth's only daughter.
> The square root of 9 **is identical with** the cube root of 27.

An identity statement can be regarded as consisting of two logical subjects (not necessarily distinct) and a logical predicate expressing identity. If we agree to use the usual symbol '=' to represent the logical predicate '① is identical to ②', then we might symbolize the first statement as:

$$f = m$$

To see that the resources of truth-functional logic are insufficient to handle such statements, consider the following argument:

> The first person to confess to the abbé is the marquis.
> The person who first confessed to the abbé is a murderer.
> _____
> The marquis is a murderer.

If we represent this argument using the resources of truth-functional logic, and then evaluate the argument using the techniques of truth-functional logic, the verdict will be that it is *not* valid. For, the symbolization within truth-functional logic will have the pattern:

$$I$$
$$F$$
$$M$$

This is because none of these statements contains any distinguishable *statements* as components so all must therefore be classified as *non-molecular*. But if we want to symbolize the argument using the devices of the last chapter together with the extension introduced above, we get a phrase-book like:

$$M \; : \quad \text{①} \text{ is a murderer}$$
$$f \; : \quad \text{the first person to confess to the abbé}$$
$$m \; : \quad \text{the marquis who just entered}$$

in which case the argument may be symbolized as:

$$f = m$$
$$Mf$$
$$Mm$$

The identity sign '=' is meant to represent what we earlier called a "special phrase" (see Chapter 3). It functions exactly as a predicate letter, except that we write it *between* the two logical subjects in question. And, since this symbol *always* represents the logical predicate '① is identical to ②', we shall conveniently omit it from our phrase-books. We shall also allow ourselves the notational convention of writing the *negation* of an identity statement by affixing the negation sign to the identity sign itself. So, for instance, we shall write '$a \neq b$' where we would otherwise have written '$\sim a = b$'. (Note carefully that we have *not* introduced parentheses in the latter case, since the formula '$a = b$' is non-molecular and therefore *unary*.)

2. **Identity Rules.** With the addition of two very obvious rules concerning identity, we can show that the argument discussed above is in fact *valid*. The first rule is SI, the rule of self-identity:

---

SI        Any formula consisting of the identity sign (=) flanked by occurrences of the *same* individual constant may be entered on a line, with *no* supposition numerals.

---

For, everything is identical to itself, and the truth of this does not depend on any suppositions. An example of the application of SI is:

(e)

$$Fac \ \& \ {\sim}Fbd$$
$$a = b$$
$$\sim c = d$$

(f)

$$(P \lor Q) \supset a = b$$
$$\sim P \supset a = c$$
$$\sim Q \supset b = c$$
$$a = b$$

(g)

$$a = b$$
$$Fa \lor (a = b \ \& \ Gab)$$
$$\sim Q \supset {\sim}(b = b \ \& \ Gbb)$$
$$Fb \supset Q$$
$$Q$$

(h)

$$Fab \supset (b = a \supset Fbb)$$

(i)

$$a = b \supset b = a$$

(j)

$$(a = b \ \& \ b = c) \supset a = c$$

(k)

$$a = b \supset (b \neq c \supset c \neq a)$$

(l)

$$(Fa \ \& \ {\sim}Fb) \supset a \neq b$$

3 For each of the following arguments, represent its logical form and give a derivation to show that it is formally valid.

(a) The first person to confess to the abbé was a murderer. The marquis was the first person ever to confess to the abbé. Therefore, the marquis is a murderer.

(b) Given that the first person to confess to the abbé was a murderer, either the marquis is a murderer or else the marquis was not the first person ever to confess to the abbé.

(c) If both the abbé and the prelate from Paris hear the confession of the marquis, then the abbé is not the prelate from Paris. If the prelate from Paris does not hear the confession of the abbé, then the prelate from Paris hears the confession of the marquis. Either the abbé hears the confession of the marquis or the prelate from Paris hears his own confession. Therefore, if the abbé is the prelate from Paris, then the prelate from Paris hears his own confession.

$$\Lambda \ \Big| \quad 6 \quad m = m \qquad\qquad\qquad\qquad \text{SI}$$

The second rule of identity is rule L, for "Leibniz' Law". Suppose that Alfred is the tallest person in Berkeley. Suppose also that the tallest person in Berkeley owes his landlord two months rent. What can we conclude from these two suppositions? Surely it must be obvious that *Alfred* owes his landlord two months rent. In other words, whatever is true of the tallest person in Berkeley is also true of Alfred, precisely because Alfred is identical with the tallest person in Berkeley. Generally, we have the following rule L:

---

L  Given two lines (not necessarily distinct or in that order), the first of which is an identity statement and the second of which contains at least one of the individual constants occurring in the first, infer any result of replacing in the second line any number of occurrences of one of the individual constants occurring in the first line by occurrences of the other individual constant occurring in the first line. As supposition numerals of the inferred line, take all those of the two given lines.

---

For if $a$ is the same thing as $b$, then whatever properties $a$ has, $b$ also has. An example of the application of rule L is:

$$1,2 \ \Big| \quad 7 \quad m = f$$

$$2,3,5 \ \Big| \quad 12 \quad Ff \supset (a = f \equiv {\sim}Gmff)$$

$$1,2,3,5 \ \Big| \quad 17 \quad Fm \supset (a = m \equiv {\sim}Gmfm) \qquad 7,12 \ \text{L}$$

where we see that three occurrences of '$f$' have been replaced by occurrences of '$m$' in the inference from line (12) to line (17).

**3. Example.** Suppose that we wish to construct a derivation from the three premises:

$$Fab \supset Hbc$$
$$a = c$$

$$Fcb \equiv q = q$$

to the following conclusion:

$$Hba$$

As always, we shall begin by writing in our premises as suppositions and the conclusion as the desired goal:

| 1 | 1 | $Fab \supset Hbc$ | S |
|---|---|---|---|
| 2 | 2 | $a = c$ | S |
| 3 | 3 | $Fcb \equiv q = q$ | S |
|   |   | $Hba$ | |

There isn't much we can do to work backwards, since the desired goal is non-molecular. So let us apply our working forward strategies:

| 1 | 1 | $Fab \supset Hbc$ | S |
|---|---|---|---|
| 2 | 2 | $a = c$ | S |
| 3 | 3 | $Fcb \equiv q = q$ | S |
| 3 | 4 | $Fcb \supset q = q$ | 3 ≡E |
| 3 | 5 | $q = q \supset Fcb$ | 3 ≡E |
|   |   | $Hba$ | |

We can get the antecedent of line (5) by rule SI, and then apply MPP, as follows:

| 1 | 1 | $Fab \supset Hbc$ | S |
|---|---|---|---|
| 2 | 2 | $a = c$ | S |
| 3 | 3 | $Fcb \equiv q = q$ | S |
| 3 | 4 | $Fcb \supset q = q$ | 3 ≡E |
| 3 | 5 | $q = q \supset Fcb$ | 3 ≡E |
| Λ | 6 | $q = q$ | SI |
| 3 | 7 | $Fcb$ | 5,6 MPP |
|   |   | $Hba$ | |

It would be helpful if we could get the antecedent of line (1). But this is easy, if we apply rule L to lines (2) and (7):

| 1 | 1 | $Fab \supset Hbc$ | S |
|---|---|---|---|
| 2 | 2 | $a = c$ | S |
| 3 | 3 | $Fcb \equiv q = q$ | S |
| 3 | 4 | $Fcb \supset q = q$ | 3 ≡E |
| 3 | 5 | $q = q \supset Fcb$ | 3 ≡E |
| Λ | 6 | $q = q$ | SI |
| 3 | 7 | $Fcb$ | 5,6 MPP |
| 2,3 | 8 | $Fab$ | 2,7 L |
|   |   | $Hba$ | |

Now we can apply MPP and finish up with a further application of rule L:

| 1 | 1 | $Fab \supset Hbc$ | S |
|---|---|---|---|
| 2 | 2 | $a = c$ | S |
| 3 | 3 | $Fcb \equiv q = q$ | S |
| 3 | 4 | $Fcb \supset q = q$ | 3 ≡E |
| 3 | 5 | $q = q \supset Fcb$ | 3 ≡E |
| Λ | 6 | $q = q$ | SI |
| 3 | 7 | $Fcb$ | 5,6 MPP |
| 2,3 | 8 | $Fab$ | 2,7 L |
| 1,2,3 | 9 | $Hbc$ | 1,8 MPP |
| 1,2,3 | 10 | $Hba$ | 2,9 L |

### Exercises

1   Which line(s), if any, are not actually needed in the derivation ju above? How do you recognize an unnecessary line in a derivation?

2   In each of the following groups of formulas, derive the last one from t others (if any). You may use derived truth-functional rules.

(a)
$$Fa \supset a = b$$
$$Fa \supset Gb$$
$$Fa \supset Ga$$

(b)
$$Fab \supset a = b$$
$$Gab \supset Fab$$
$$Gab \supset Gbb$$

(c)
$$a = b$$
$$Fac \lor Fbc$$
$$Fac \& Fbc$$

(d)
$$a = b$$
$$Fab \supset (Gab \ \& \ b = c$$
$$P \supset Fbb$$
$$P \supset Gbc$$

# Chapter 16

# Truncated Semantical Assignments

**1. Truth and Falsity.** As long as we deal only with statements in which phrases like 'every', 'some', etc., do not appear, we can determine that an argument is formally invalid, or that a group of statements is formally consistent, merely by providing an appropriate truth-value assignment. This holds true even when we begin to notice the division of statements into logical subject(s) and a logical predicate. It is only when we take into account statements involving phrases like 'every', 'some', etc., or the identity predicate 'is identical to', that we need a new technique, that of *semantical assignments*. But semantical assignments can also be used to show the absence of formal validity and the presence of formal consistency in cases that involve statements not containing these phrases. And indeed it is easiest to become familiar with the techniques involved in giving semantical assignments in these simpler cases. So we will begin there.

The connection between truth-value assignments and semantical assignments may be explained in this way: in truth-value assignments, we represent possible situations by specifying that the statements symbolized by certain sentential letters are to be true or false. In semantical assignments, we represent the features of a possible situation in greater detail; we are not concerned with just truth and falsity, but also with *other* features which are themselves relevant to the truth or falsity of certain statements.

What features of situations are relevant to a statement's being either true or false? Let us take a simple case. The statement:

Berkeley is in California

is *true*, and it is true because of three facts:

(1)    a logical subject of the statement, the word 'Berkeley', is correctly used to refer to a certain object, namely a certain city;

(2)   the remaining logical predicate, the phrase '① is in California', is correctly applied to any member of a certain class of objects, namely the things that are located in California; and

(3)   the object picked out as in (1) is a member of the class of objects picked out as in (2).

Further, the two statements:

Berkeley is in Nevada
Reno is in California

are *false* because the objects picked out by their logical subjects are not members of the classes picked out by their corresponding logical predicates. Thus, we see that we can specify a possible situation in which certain statements would be true and others false by specifying three things:

(1)   what objects their logical subjects pick out

(2)   what classes of objects their logical predicates pick out

(3)   whether the objects picked out by their logical subjects are members of the classes picked out by the logical predicates.

This threefold specification is the main idea of a *semantical assignment*. Consider for example the three formulas:

$$Fa$$
$$Gb$$
$$Hc$$

Are there three statements of which these formulas might be representations, such that it is possible for the first two to be true and the third false? Even without specifying what these statements might be, we can say this much: if we consider some situation in which the constant '$a$' picks out an object which is in the class picked out by '$F$', '$b$' picks out an object which is a member of the class picked out by '$G$', and '$c$' is *not* a member of the class picked out by '$H$', then the first two statements will be true and the last one will be false. So to specify a situation under which certain formulas will correspond to true statements and other formulas to false statements, we need only specify which *object* corresponds to each individual constant occurring in the formulas in question, and which *class* of objects corresponds to each logical predicate.

Since this will hold true no matter what objects we consider, it will be convenient to restrict our attention to *natural numbers*. So, to specify the conditions under which some given formulas are true or false, we need to say which number corresponds to each individual constant and which class of numbers corresponds to each logical predicate. In doing this, we are giving what we shall call a *truncated semantical assignment*.[1] For example:

$$
\begin{array}{ccl}
F & - & \{1,2,3\} \\
G & - & \{1,2,3\} \\
H & - & \{1\} \\
\\
a & - & 1 \\
b & - & 2 \\
c & - & 3
\end{array}
$$

Here we can see that: the object picked out by '*a*' (namely, 1) is a member of the set picked out by '*F*'; the object picked out by '*b*' (namely, 2) is a member of the set picked out by '*G*'; but the object picked out by '*c*' (namely, 3) is *not* a member of the set picked out by '*H*'. Consequently, in this semantical assignment the formulas '*Fa*' and '*Gb*' are true, but the formula '*Hc*' is false.

**2. Examples.** This idea fits in well with our previous study of the connectives of truth-functional logic. For example, in the following list, *with three exceptions*, all the odd-numbered formulas are true with respect to the truncated semantical assignment given immediately above, and all the even-numbered ones are false under that assignment.

| | | | |
|---|---|---|---|
| (1) | $\sim Hc$ | (8) | $(Fa \supset Gb) \supset Hc$ |
| (2) | $Fa \,\&\, Hc$ | (9) | $Hc \equiv \sim Fa$ |
| (3) | $\sim Fa \lor \sim Hc$ | (10) | $(\sim Fa \lor Hc) \equiv \sim(Gb \lor \sim Gc)$ |
| (4) | $\sim(\sim Fa \lor \sim Fb)$ | (11) | $Fb \equiv \sim Hb$ |
| (5) | $(Fa \,\&\, Gb) \lor \sim Hc$ | (12) | $\sim((Fc \equiv Gc) \supset \sim Hb)$ |
| (6) | $(Fa \lor Gb) \,\&\, Hc$ | (13) | $Fc \supset (Ga \supset (Ha \supset (\sim Ha \lor \sim Hc)))$ |
| (7) | $(Hc \supset Fa) \supset Gb$ | (14) | $\sim\sim Hc \supset (\sim Hc \supset Hc)$ |

---

[1] This is a "truncated" semantical assignment since we shall later extend the present specification by adding certain new features. See Chapter 19.

## Exercises

---

1    Find the three exceptions.

---

3. **Multiple Logical Subjects.** So far we have considered splitting a statement into only *one* logical subject and the remaining logical predicate. What happens when we find more than one logical subject in a statement? If we think of the statement 'Berkeley is in California' as consisting of two logical subjects (namely, 'Berkeley' and 'California') together with the logical predicate

$$\textcircled{1} \text{ is in } \textcircled{2}$$

we see that the statement is true just in case the objects picked out by the two logical subjects, *taken in the order in which we number the corresponding slots in the logical predicate*, belong to what is picked out by the logical predicate. Notice that the *order* in which we consider the two logical subjects is important: it is true that Berkeley is in California, but false that California is in Berkeley. So we need some way of indicating, when we specify a semantical assignment, how the various objects picked out by the individual constants are to be ordered when we specify the classes corresponding to the logical predicates. For this we use the device of *ordered couples*. We shall represent the ordered couple whose first term is the number 1 and whose second term is the number 2 as '<1,2>'. We shall require, then, that logical predicates containing two logical subjects have classes of ordered couples assigned to them in a truncated semantical assignment, those containing three have ordered triples assigned to them, and so on.[2] When we speak of a class of ordered couples, ordered triples, and so on—more generally, a class of ordered *n*-tuples—we are *not* excluding a class which has *none* of them in it: the *empty set*. And we shall say that a statement is true under such a semantical assignment just in case the ordered *n*-tuple consisting of the objects picked out by the logical subjects taken in the order specified is a member of the class of ordered *n*-tuples picked out by the logical predicate. For example, we can show that the statement 'Berkeley is in California' is formally consistent. First we symbolize it in accordance with the phrase-book:

---

[2] We shall represent the ordered *triple* consisting of the numbers 1, 2, and 3 in that order as '<1,2,3>', and so on for ordered quadruples, quintuples, etc.

$$I: \qquad ① \text{ is in } ②$$
$$b: \qquad \text{Berkeley}$$
$$c: \qquad \text{California}$$

Thus we get the formula '*Ibc*', and this formula is true under the truncated semantical assignment:

$$I \qquad - \qquad \{<1,2>, <2,1>\}$$

$$b \qquad - \qquad 1$$
$$c \qquad - \qquad 2$$

So, by showing that there is at least one truncated semantical assignment under which the given formula is true, we have shown that the formula is *formally consistent*. Notice that with respect to this same semantical assignment, the formula '*Icb*', which symbolizes the statement 'California is in Berkeley', is also true. We can, if we wish, also provide a truncated semantical assignment with respect to which the first formula is true and the second false, thus showing that 'California is in Berkeley' does not follow from 'Berkeley is in California'. Thus:

$$I \qquad - \qquad \{<1,2>\}$$

$$b \qquad - \qquad 1$$
$$c \qquad - \qquad 2$$

It is easy to generalize these ideas. Consider the truncated semantical assignment:

$$F \qquad - \qquad \{1,3\}$$
$$G \qquad - \qquad \{<2,1>, <3,3>\}$$
$$H \qquad - \qquad \{<1,2,3>, <2,3,1>, <3,1,2>\}$$

$$a \qquad - \qquad 3$$
$$b \qquad - \qquad 2$$
$$c \qquad - \qquad 1$$

Here we see that under this assignment, all the following odd-numbered formulas are true and all the even-numbered formulas are false, *with three exceptions:*

| | | | |
|---|---|---|---|
| (1) | *Fc* | (8) | *Hacb* ⊃ (*Habc* v *Fb*) |
| (2) | *Gcb* | (9) | *Gcb* ≡ *Haca* |
| (3) | ~*Hbca* | (10) | *Hcba* ⊃ ~*Hcba* |
| (4) | *Fb* v *Habc* | (11) | ~(*Fb* ⊃ (*Gab* v (*Gbb* ≡ *Hcab*))) |
| (5) | ~*Gcc* | (12) | *Gab* ≡ *Gba* |
| (6) | ~*Gaa* | (13) | (*Fb* v *Gab*) v (*Habc* ⊃ ~*Hbac*) |
| (7) | ~*Haaa* | (14) | ~*Gaa* v (~*Hccc* ≡ *Gaa*) |

**Exercises**

---

  2   Find the three exceptions.

---

**4. Identity Statements.** Given what we have already said, it should be obvious how to deal with a formula involving the identity sign, '='. A formula such as '$f = m$' will be *true* in a semantical assignment just in case the very same object is assigned to both '$f$' and '$m$' in that assignment. And such a formula is *false* just in case the two constants are assigned different objects. Consider, for example, the following semantical assignment:

$$
\begin{aligned}
F &\quad - \quad \{1,2,3\} \\
G &\quad - \quad \{1,3\} \\
\\
a &\quad - \quad 1 \\
b &\quad - \quad 2 \\
c &\quad - \quad 1
\end{aligned}
$$

Under this assignment, the following formulas are all *true*:

$$
\begin{aligned}
a &= c \\
b &\neq a \\
Fa &\equiv a = c \\
a = b &\supset (Ga \equiv Gb)
\end{aligned}
$$

And under this assignment, the following formulas are all *false*:

$$a = b$$
$$Fa \equiv a \neq c$$
$$a = c \equiv b = c$$
$$a = c \supset (Fa \equiv Gb)$$

It follows from what we have said that a formula such as '$m = m$' is true in *all* semantical assignments, since the individual constants on each side of the identity sign must always be assigned the same object. This is the primary reason that we adopted the rule SI in Chapter 15. Without rule SI, we would have been unable to prove these obviously true statements as theorems of logic.

**Exercises**

---

3   For each of the following formulas, determine whether it is true or false under the truncated semantical assignment given:

$$F \quad - \quad \{1,2\}$$
$$G \quad - \quad \{<1,2,3>, <1,2,2>, <1,2,1>,$$
$$<1,1,3>, <1,1,2>, <1,1,1>\}$$
$$H \quad - \quad \{<3,1>, <2,2>, <1,2>, <1,3>\}$$

$$a \quad - \quad 1$$
$$b \quad - \quad 3$$
$$c \quad - \quad 2$$

(a)  *Fa & Gaba*

(b)  *~(Hbb & Fc) ⊃ ~ (Gaaa v Fb)*

(c)  *~Fa v (Fc & Hba)*

(d)  *(Hbc & Hcb) v (~Hbc & ~Hcb)*

(e)  *Gabc ⊃ Gcba*

(f)  *(Fa v Fb) v (~Fa ⊃ ~Fb)*

(g)  *Fa ⊃ (Gabb ⊃ Hab)*

(h)  *Gbcc & ~Gccb*

(i)  *Fb ≡ (Fc ≡ ~Gabc)*

(j)  *Gaaa ⊃ (Gaaa ⊃ Gaaa)*

(k)  *~(Fa v Fc) v ~(Hab v Hac)*

(l)  *(Fa ⊃ Fa) ⊃ ~(Hbb ⊃ Hbb)*

4   For each of the following groups of formulas, construct a truncated
    semantical assignment under which *all* the formulas in that group are
    true; then construct a truncated semantical assignment under which all
    the last formula in the group is false and the rest (if any) are true. Use
    numbers as objects in your assignments, and keep the number of
    numbers you use as small as possible.

(a)          *Fa* & (*Habc* v *Gbb*)          (b)          *Faa* ⊃ (*Ha* ⊃ *Gba*)

(c)    ~(*Fab* &*Gc*) ⊃ ~(*Fba* & ~*Gc*)    (d)    *Faaa* & (*Faba* ⊃ ~*Fbab*)
         *Fab* ⊃ (*Fab* ⊃ *Habc*)                   (*Faba* v *Fbbb*) ≡ ~*Fbaa*
              ~*Hcba* v ~*Gc*                        *Fbaa* ⊃ (*Faaa* ⊃ ~*Fabb*)

(e)             *Habc* ⊃ *Faa*             (f)          *Ha* ≡ (*Fab* ≡ ~*Gba*)
                *Habb* ⊃ ~*Faa*

5   Decide which of the following formulas are *theorems* and which are *not*.
    For each theorem, give a derivation of it from the empty set (Λ). For
    each non-theorem, give a semantical assignment under which it is false.

(a)  (*a* = *b* & *b* ≠ *d*) ⊃ *a* = *d*

(b)  *Fa* ≡ (*a* = *b* & *Fb*)

(c)  (*a* = *b* & *Haa*) ⊃ *Hab*

(d)  *a* = *b* v *b* ≠ *a*

(e)  (*Fbc* & ~*Fcb*) ⊃ *b* ≠ *c*

# Chapter 17

## Quantifiers

**1. Quantity.** The method of representing logical subjects and logical predicates developed in Chapter 14 can be extended naturally to the representation of statements containing certain phrases expressing *quantity*, such as 'all', 'every', 'some', 'at least one', 'no more than three' and related phrases. These kinds of phrases occur in arguments such as the following two, which fall within the province of *quantificational*, or *predicate*, logic:

> Some Rosecrucians eat quiche.
> All Rosecrucians are men.
> _____
> Some men eat quiche.

> All kittens are cuddly and warm.
> Whatever is warm may also be dangerous.
> _____
> Some kittens may be dangerous.

Not all statements containing expressions of quantity are this simple; an example of a more complicated argument that also falls within the province of quantificational logic is:

> Everyone is friendly to everyone.
> If someone is friendly to a person, then he gives that person gifts.
> _____
> Someone gives himself gifts and is friendly to himself.

This argument is in fact valid, though that may not be obvious to you. In quantificational logic, as in truth-functional logic, we show that such an argument is valid by reducing it to "simpler" lines of argument. So ultimately we shall need to isolate certain rules of derivation applicable to quantified statements. But our first job in the study of the logic of quantity is to learn how to represent the *logical form* of such statements.

**2. Expressions of Quantity.** Because of the added complexity of quantificational logic, we shall approach this task in two stages. Here in this chapter, we shall learn how to represent the logical form of non-molecular statements involving *one* expression of quantity. All of the statements in the first two lines of argument above are of this sort. Then, in Chapter 18, we shall extend what we learn to statements involving *two or more* such expressions. The premises of the third argument above are of this sort.

Let us begin by noting that the major quantifying expressions may be grouped into two types, which we shall hereafter call *expressions of universality* and *expressions of existence*. The primary expression of universality is 'all', and the primary expression of existence is 'some', though (as we shall see) there are many other examples of both types. A statement whose truth-functional form is non-molecular and which contains one expression of universality will be called a *universal generalization*. Similarly, a statement whose truth-functional form is non-molecular and which contains one expression of existence will be called an *existential generalization*. We can then say that the essential step taken in moving from truth-functional logic to quantificational logic is the subdivision of the non-molecular category into universal generalizations, existential generalizations, and what we might call *still others*.

**3. Expressions of Universality.** Let us consider first some examples of expressions of universality. In the list below, these expressions are indicated in **boldface**.

> **All** cows chew grass.
>
> Bertha talked with **everyone** at the soirée.
>
> Alfred has not done **all** of his homework exercises.
>
> **Everyone** is bored by a dull or silly movie.
>
> Not **everybody** loses in a lottery.
>
> **Everything** was destroyed by the hurricane.
>
> **Anyone** who studies can pass logic.
>
> **Whatever** you do, it probably won't work.
>
> Young professors are **invariably** snooty.
>
> **Without exception**, dandelions bloom in the spring.

If **a** pig is hot, it wallows in the mud.

**Each one of us** ought to be proud of Alfred's skills.

**Dogs** are carnivorous.

**Everything is such that** it either costs too much or is not worth having.

One distinctive feature of these statements is that they can all be easily paraphrased into statements of the *last* kind listed above, that is, of the form:

Everything is such that ...it...

For instance, we can straightforwardly rephrase the statement about the hurricane as:

Everything is such that it was destroyed by the hurricane.

And, without too much violence, the first statement can be paraphrased as:

Everything is such that, if it is a cow, then it chews grass.

Further, the second statement may be rephrased as:

Everything is such that, if it was a person at the soirée, then Bertha talked with it.

The relevance of this paraphrasing is that we shall represent the phrase 'everything is such that' with what is called a *universal quantifier*. A universal quantifier is the symbol '$\forall$' together with a lower-case letter from '$u$' to '$z$', henceforth to be called a *variable*. For example, '$\forall x$'.

To represent a statement like those in this list, paraphrase the statement as indicated above, replace the phrase 'everything is such that' by a universal quantifier, and prefix this quantifier to whatever formula represents the *rest* of the paraphrasis. Then, in this "remainder", replace occurrences of the pronoun 'it', 'he', 'she', 'they' (and the like) with occurrences of the same variable that occurs in the quantifier. The resulting formula represents the logical form of the original statement.

To see how this works in practice, consider the following phrase-book:

$C$ :   ① is a cow
$D$ :   ① was destroyed by the hurricane
$G$ :   ① chews grass

Then we can represent the logical form of these statements as follows:

(a)   Everything is such that it was destroyed by the hurricane.

$$\forall x Dx$$

(b)   Everything is such that, if it is a cow, then it chews grass.

$$\forall x (Cx \supset Gx)$$

(c)   All cows were destroyed by the hurricane.

$$\forall x (Cx \supset Dx)$$

(d)   Everything destroyed by the hurricane was a cow.

$$\forall x (Dx \supset Cx)$$

(e)   Everything is a cow and was destroyed by the hurricane.

$$\forall x (Cx \ \& \ Dx)$$

(f)   Every cow is a cow.

$$\forall x (Cx \supset Cx)$$

(g)   Every cow that chews grass was destroyed by the hurricane.

$$\forall x ((Cx \ \& \ Gx) \supset Dx)$$

Even more complicated forms are possible, but before considering some of them, let's take a look at expressions of existence.

**4. Expressions of Existence.** The following statements all contain expressions of existence:

**Some** cows chew grass.

**There are** cows who chew grass.

Bertha talked with **some of** the people at the soirée.

**At least one person** saw the murder.

Doris was chased by **a** dog.

**There is** an even prime number.

Bacon is **sometimes** eaten at dinner.

If **someone** wins the lottery, Bertha will be sad.

**There exist** even prime numbers.

If **anyone** eats sushi, then wasabi must be ordered.

**A** man came to the door.

**Something is such that** it chews grass.

With statements containing one such expression of existence, our goal will be to paraphrase, as above, until we are left with a statement of the form:

Something is such that ...it...

We represent this phrase with an *existential quantifier*, formed by associating the special symbol '∃' with a *variable*. For example, '∃$u$'. The last statement will then be represented by the formula:

$$\exists y Gy$$

The first statement above may be paraphrased as:

Something is such that it is a cow and it chews grass.

in which case it will be represented as:

$$\exists x(Cx \ \& \ Gx)$$

Once again, study the following examples to see how the existential quantifier is used to represent expressions of existence:

(a)   Some cows were destroyed by the hurricane.

$$\exists x(Cx \ \& \ Dx)$$

(b)   If a cow was destroyed by the hurricane, then something was destroyed by the hurricane.

$$\exists x(Cx \ \& \ Dx) \supset \exists y Dy$$

(c)    Some cows destroyed by the hurricane did not chew grass.

$$\exists z((Cz \ \& \ Dz) \ \& \ \sim Gz)$$

**5. Further Examples.** So far, then, our procedure for determining the logical form of non-molecular statements involving one expression of quantity may be summarized as follows:

(1)    Paraphrase the given statement so that it begins either with the phrase 'everything is such that' or with the phrase 'something is such that'.

(2)    Determine the logical form of the remaining part of the paraphrasis, replacing pronouns such as 'it', 'he', 'she', etc., by a *variable.*

(3)    Prefix the appropriate quantifier containing the variable selected in step (2).

Of course, to get to a *non-molecular* statement involving one expression of quantity, you may first need to sift through some truth-functional form. For instance, we might represent the two statements:

Everyone is happy if he is rich.
Everyone is happy if everyone is rich.

with the formulas, respectively:

$$\forall x (Rx \supset Hx)$$
$$\forall x Rx \supset \forall y Hy$$

It is important to appreciate the difference between these two formulas. While the latter *is* a conditional, the former one is *not*, although it *contains* a conditional. In this respect, the quantifiers are rather like the negation sign; just as:

$$\sim (Fab \supset Gab)$$

is *not* a conditional, so also:

$$\forall y (Fay \supset Gyb)$$

is not a conditional. The quantifiers behave like the negation sign with respect to parentheses as well: just as we did not need parentheses around unary formulas like '$P$' in order to apply the negation sign to it, so also we do not need parentheses around non-molecular formulas like '$Hu$' to apply a quantifier to it. To apply the existential quantifier, we write simply '$\exists u Hu$'. But just as we *did* need parentheses around:

$$P \ \& \ Q$$

to apply negation to it to get:

$$\sim(P \ \& \ Q)$$

so we also need parentheses around:

$$Fay \supset Gyb$$

to apply a quantifier to it:

$$\forall y\,(Fay \supset Gyb)$$

To appreciate the difference between applying a quantifier to a formula and applying it to just a part of it, compare:

$$\forall x\,(Hx \supset Hg)$$
$$\forall x Hx \supset Hg$$

Consider the following situation: some people are happy, some are not, and Greta is among those who are not happy. In this situation, the first formula is false. This formula may be read: pick anyone you choose, if that person is happy, then so is Greta. But in the situation described, this is false; if we choose a happy person, the first formula requires that if that person is happy, then so is Greta (and by our understanding of the conditional, this is false in the situation described). The second formula may be read: if everyone is happy, then so is Greta, and this is obviously true. So the formulas are not equivalent.

Let's look at a few more examples. Consider the following phrase-book:[1]

| | | |
|---|---|---|
| $G$ | : | ① is a guard |
| $N$ | : | ① is nice |
| $P$ | : | ① is patient |
| $G$ | : | ① gave ② to ③ |
| | | |
| $g$ | : | Greta |
| $m$ | : | my picture |
| $p$ | : | Penelope |

---

[1] Notice that the letter '$G$' here represents *two* different logical predicates. No confusion should result, since for any given occurrence of '$G$', the number of individual constants following the predicate letter clearly indicates which logical predicate it symbolizes.

Using the procedure described above, you may easily turn the following statements into the corresponding formulas:

(a)    Some guard is nice.

$$\exists x(Gx \ \& \ Nx)$$

(b)    Someone is a guard, and someone is nice.

$$\exists xGx \ \& \ \exists yNy$$

(c)    Every guard is nice.

$$\forall x(Gx \supset Nx)$$

(d)    Some patient guard is nice.

$$\exists x((Gx \ \& \ Px) \ \& \ Nx)$$

(e)    Every patient guard is nice.

$$\forall x((Gx \ \& \ Px) \supset Nx)$$

(f)    Greta gave something to Penelope.

$$\exists yGgyp$$

(g)    Some guard who has given my picture to Penelope is nice.

$$\exists x((Gx \ \& \ Gxmp) \ \& \ Nx)$$

(h)    Every guard who has given my picture to Penelope is nice.

$$\forall x((Gx \ \& \ Gxmp) \supset Nx)$$

**6. Caution.** You may have noticed that several quantifying expressions (for instance 'a' and 'anyone') occur on *both* of the above lists. This realization has the healthy effect of keeping us from proceeding too mechanically in representing logical form. We simply *cannot* say that the word 'anyone' indicates universality and must be represented with a universal quantifier; *nor* can we say that the word 'a' indicates existence and must be represented with an existential quantifier. When confronted by a phrase such as 'a man' (or 'a pig'), we must attend to the meaning of the entire statement and must decide whether this phrase could be replaced by the phrase 'at least one man'. If so, then we may classify that occurrence as an expression of existence. If, on the other hand, we cannot replace the word 'a' by 'at least one' without significantly altering the meaning of the original statement, then we should classify it as an expression of universality.

In addition to this general advice, there is the following observation: a statement which *looks* like a conditional, but which contains an indefinite pronomial cross-reference, is probably a universal generalization of a conditional.[2] For instance, the statement:

If a man lives in Denver, then he likes skiing.

might look like a conditional, but there is an indefinite pronomial cross-reference from the candidate consequent to the candidate antecedent. So this statement is not a conditional, but a universal generalization of a conditional. We might represent it, given an appropriate phrase-book, as follows:

$$\forall z (Dz \supset Lz)$$

7. **Other Quantifying Phrases**. The two basic sorts of quantifier phrases that we have already isolated, 'everything is such that' and 'something is such that', can in fact be used to represent a variety of similar phrases. For instance, the statement:

No alligator lives in the Arctic.

can be paraphrased into the statement:

Everything is such that, if it is an alligator, then it does not live in the Arctic.

Accordingly, we may represent its logical form as:

$$\forall x (Ax \supset {\sim}Lxa)$$

Similarly, to say:

Only fish have both scales and bones.

is to say:

Everything is such that, if it has both scales and bones, then it is a fish.

---

[2] Or a universal generalization of a universal generalization...of a conditional.

In that case, we may represent the logical form as:

$$\forall w((Sw \ \& \ Bw) \supset Fw)$$

Of particular note is the word 'except', which serves mainly to *exclude* certain situations. Together with the techniques of Chapter 15, we can represent the statement:

Everyone except Bertha was destroyed by the hurricane

with the formula:

$$\forall x(x \neq b \supset Dx)$$

This representation leaves it open as to whether Bertha was destroyed by the hurricane; it says merely that anyone *different from* Bertha was destroyed. This would be an appropriate representation if we knew nothing about Bertha's state of health, but were sure that everyone *else* had been destroyed by the hurricane. If we want to make sure that our representation includes the fact that Bertha was not destroyed, we might give the following:

$$\forall x(x \neq b \supset Dx) \ \& \ {\sim}Db$$

This formula is logically equivalent to:

$$\forall x(x \neq b \equiv Dx)$$

but we shall not be in a position to prove this until Chapter 21.

Similarly, given the phrase-book:

$$
\begin{array}{lll}
L & : & \text{①  lives on land} \\
M & : & \text{①  is a mammal} \\
W & : & \text{①  is a whale}
\end{array}
$$

the statement:

All mammals except whales live on land.

might be represented as:

$$\forall y((My \ \& \ {\sim}Wy) \supset Ly)$$

In general, phrases like those schematized below are to be represented by the corresponding schematic formula:

(a)   Some A is such that ...it...

$$\exists x (Ax \; \& \; \cdots x \cdots )$$

(b)   Some A which is B is such that ...it...

$$\exists x ((Ax \; \& \; Bx) \; \& \; \cdots x \cdots )$$

(c)   Every A is such that ...it...

$$\forall x (Ax \supset \cdots x \cdots )$$

(d)   Every A which is B is such that ...it...

$$\forall x ((Ax \; \& \; Bx) \supset \cdots x \cdots )$$

(e)   Every A except B is such that ...it...

$$\forall x ((Ax \; \& \; {\sim}Bx) \supset \cdots x \cdots )$$

(f)   Every A except $b$ is such that ...it...

$$\forall x ((Ax \; \& \; x \neq b) \supset \cdots x \cdots )$$

(g)   No A is such that ...it...

$$\forall x (Ax \supset {\sim} \cdots x \cdots )$$

(h)   Only A is such that ...it...

$$\forall x ( \cdots x \cdots \supset Ax)$$

**8. Restricting Quantifiers.** So far we have stipulated that the universal and existential quantifiers are to be understood as representing the phrases 'everything is such that' and 'something is such that', respectively. Occasionally, however, this stipulation leads to needless complexity in our representations, if the things under discussion are all of a uniform sort. To see this, consider the following argument:

All persons with myopia are dangerous.
A dangerous person should be put in jail.

---

All myopic persons should be put in jail.

Given the following phrase-book:

$$
\begin{array}{rl}
D : & \text{① is dangerous} \\
J : & \text{① should be put in jail} \\
M : & \text{① is myopic} \\
P : & \text{① is a person}
\end{array}
$$

when we paraphrase the first statement into our preferred form, we get something like:

Everything is such that, if it is a person and is myopic, then it is dangerous.

Accordingly, we might arrive at the following representations of logical form for these statements:

$$\forall x((Px \ \& \ Mx) \supset Dx)$$
$$\forall x((Px \ \& \ Dx) \supset Jx)$$
$$\forall x((Px \ \& \ Mx) \supset Jx)$$

The unnecessary complexity arises from our having to include the letter '$P$' (representing the predicate '① is a person') in all three cases. If our attention is restricted here to persons, then it may be tedious to have to include this predicate all the time. To avoid this, we may stipulate that all predicates and quantifiers are to be understood as applying only to persons. This is called "restricting the application of the quantifiers". To announce that in some particular case we have chosen to do this, we include the following line at the top of our phrase-book:[3]

$$\forall \exists :: \text{① is a person}$$

In this case, the three formulas above may be simplified to:

$$\forall x(Mx \supset Dx)$$
$$\forall x(Dx \supset Jx)$$

---

[3] The double colon '::' indicates that this is a restriction of the quantifiers, not a specification of a logical predicate.

$$\forall x (Mx \supset Jx)$$

In a situation such as this, the quantifiers are now to be understood as representing the phrases 'everyone is such that' and 'someone is such that'. So we may represent a statement like:

Bertha talked with everyone at the soirée.

as follows:

$$\forall x (Sx \supset Tbx)$$

You may not, however, adopt this simplification if there are objects discussed to which the restricting predicate you have selected does *not* apply. For instance, if we wanted to represent the statement:

Some nice person gave the cat to Bertha.

we should not give:

$$\exists x (Nx \ \& \ Gxcb)$$

since the item represented by the individual constant '$c$' is not a person. Instead, we should give the formula:

$$\exists x ((Px \ \&Nx) \ \& \ Gxcb)$$

**9. Summary.** We may sum this chapter up by remarking that we now have a fairly uniform procedure for passing step by step from a statement of ordinary English which contains a single expression of quantity to its symbolization. Some quantifying expressions, like 'most' or 'a few', cannot easily be handled by our present method of representing logical form, but very many quantifying expressions can be dealt with in the ways illustrated. Our procedure involves constant attention to the intended meaning of the original statement, and there is this rule of thumb: at each step try to put an as yet unsymbolized portion of a statement into one of the forms:

Everything is such that ...it...

Something is such that ...it...

and represent these by means of the forms:

$$\forall v \ \cdots \ v \ \cdots$$

$$\exists v \ \cdots \ v \ \cdots$$

Unfortunately, the only reasonably routine procedure for going in the *reverse* direction and obtaining ordinary statements from symbolizations is to try various ordinary statements which are plausible candidates and see whether, by means of the above procedure, they would be plausibly symbolized in that way. Fortunately, with practice and familiarity the symbolizations become intelligible in themselves even when one is hard pressed to come up with an ordinary statement that they might be symbolizations of. This is especially true with multiple quantification, as we shall see in the next chapter.

There is, however, at least the following informal "check" you can run on your formulas: it almost *never* happens that a straightforward English statement is represented with an existential quantifier governing a conditional. In other words, a representation having the form:

$$\exists v ( \cdots \supset \cdots )$$

should be avoided. By glancing back over the examples given in this chapter, you will see that universal quantifiers naturally accompany *conditionals* and that existential quantifiers naturally accompany *conjunctions*. That is to say, the formulas schematized below are *very common* representations of everyday English statements classified as universal or existential generalizations:

$$\forall v ( \cdots \supset \cdots )$$
$$\exists v ( \cdots \& \cdots )$$

If you arrive at a formula like the existential generalization of a conditional above, you should review your paraphrase carefully and critically. It is probably wrong.

## Exercises

---

1  As illustrated in the text above, paraphrase each of the following statements until you have a statement which begins with the phrase 'everything is such that' or the phrase 'something is such that'.

   (a)  Someone is rich and famous.

   (b)  Everyone is rich and famous.

   (c)  Doris was chased by a dog.

   (d)  Young professors are invariably snooty.

   (e)  Bacon is sometimes eaten at dinner.

    (f)  Dogs are carnivorous.

    (g)  At least one person saw the murder.

2    Construct a single phrase-book and represent the logical form of each of the following statements in accordance with that phrase-book. Some of the statements may be ambiguous; whenever you detect an ambiguity, symbolize the alternative readings in order of decreasing plausibility.

    (a)  Bertha is a logic student and works hard.

    (b)  Some logic students work hard.

    (c)  Some hard workers study both computer science and logic.

    (d)  If Bertha is a logic student, then she works hard.

    (e)  All logic students work hard.

    (f)  Only logic students work hard.

    (g)  Every computer science student works hard.

    (h)  Every computer science student except Alfred works hard.

    (i)  Some computer science students do not work hard.

3    Do the same for each of the following statements.

    (a)  Some logic student scored higher than Alfred.

    (b)  Alfred scored higher than some logic student.

    (c)  Some logic student scored higher than himself.

    (d)  No one scored higher than himself.

    (e)  Bertha scored higher than every logic student.

    (f)  No one except Alfred scored higher than Bertha.

4    First, construct a phrase-book and represent the logical form of each of the statements below, using quantifiers which are *unrestricted* in application. Then, modify your phrase-book by restricting the quantifiers in some reasonable way; represent the logical form in accordance with the new phrase-book.

    (a)  Some planet revolves around the Earth, and that is the moon.

    (b)  The only planet revolving around the Earth is the moon.

    (c)  The Earth revolves around no planet which revolves around Jupiter.

    (d)  If a planet revolves around Jupiter, it doesn't revolve around the Earth.

    (e)  Some planet revolves around both Jupiter and the Earth.

5    Construct an appropriate phrase-book and represent the logical form of each of the statements below. (You may assume that all quantifiers are restricted to persons.)

(a)  Someone likes Alfred, but it isn't Clothilda.

(b)  If Greta likes Clothilda, then someone likes Clothilda.

(c)  Alfred likes Clothilda and everyone Clothilda likes.

(d)  If Bertha likes Alfred, then she likes everybody.

(e)  If someone other than Alfred likes Bertha, then she doesn't like him.

(f)  If everyone likes Alfred, then Greta likes someone.

(g)  No one likes Bertha only if she doesn't like herself.

6    Let us consider a third quantifier, '$\mathbb{N}$' (the "non-existential" quantifier), which represents the phrase 'nothing is such that...'. For example, the formula '$\mathbb{N}x(Fx \mathbin{\&} Gx)$' might represent the statement 'nothing is both flaky and gooey'. Can you define the universal and existential quantifiers introduced above in terms of this non-existential quantifier alone?

# Chapter 18

## Multiple Quantification

**1. Multiple Quantifying Expressions.** So we have developed a fairly uniform way of representing non-molecular statements in which there is *one* expression of quantity. Now we shall extend this to more complicated cases involving multiple quantifying expressions, like the following statements:

> Everyone likes someone.
> Anyone who likes someone is generous to someone.
> Every girl who has given something to every boy is nice.
> Someone likes everyone who has read something by Joyce.
> Bertha gave a trophy to everyone on the team.

As in the previous chapter, we shall represent such expressions using the universal and existential quantifiers. But the added complexity of such statements makes room for numerous ambiguities and alternative readings, so it is best to approach multiply-quantified statements with special care. For instance, does the last statement above say that Bertha gave *one* trophy to the whole team, or *many* trophies, one to each member? Both of these are quite possible. Contextual factors (or general knowledge about the world) may make one of these possibilities more plausible than the other, but sometimes we simply cannot tell which of several interpretations is the best. Nonetheless, our system of representing logical form is well-equipped to make these alternative readings clear, by assigning *different* formulas to each one. Let's see how this works.

**2. Inward Paraphrasing.** The general technique for moving from English statements containing several expressions of quantity to formulas which represent their logical forms is that of "paraphrasing inward", which by now should be familiar to you. Consider the statement as a whole, and decide what kind of statement it is. Then turn your attention to the *parts* of the original statement and decide what kinds of statements or phrases they are. Continue this inward paraphrasing until all the parts of the original statement have been categorized; now that you have a complete description of the logical form, it is a simple matter to construct a formula representing it.

In practice this technique is relatively straightforward. Consider the statement:

Everyone likes someone.

It should be clear that this statement has no *truth-functional* structure; on the basis of the sixfold classification given in Chapter 4, we should classify it as non-molecular (or "other"). On the basis of our expanded statement classification, we might classify this statement as a *universal generalization*, since in uttering this statement, we are saying: choose anyone you like, there is someone whom that person likes. So we may paraphrase the original statement as:

Everyone is such that he likes someone.

At this point, since there are multiple quantifying expressions, we should remove the pronoun 'he' and replace it with a variable, as follows:

Every $x$ is such that $x$ likes someone.

Now we have to deal with the phrase '$x$ likes someone'. But we already know how to do this:

Every $x$ is such that someone is such that $x$ likes him.

Finally, replacing the newly-emerged pronoun 'him' with a *different* variable, we get:

Every $x$ is such that some $y$ is such that $x$ likes $y$.

in which case we may give the following formula as a representation of the logical form of the original statement:

$$\forall x \exists y Lxy$$

By contrast, in the statement:

Someone likes everyone.

we are saying: there is someone such that no matter whom you choose, that first person likes the second. If we use arrows pointing from the person who does the liking to the person who is liked, we have something like the following contrast:

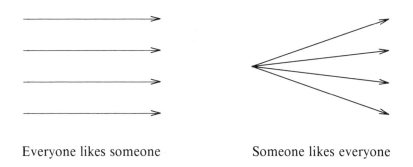

Everyone likes someone                    Someone likes everyone

And we may represent this existential generalization as:

$$\exists x\,\forall y Lxy$$

As before, it is completely arbitrary which variable you use to construct a quantifier and to signal occurrences of universality or existence in the formula following the quantifier, but you should choose *different* variables if you have more than one quantifier in a given formula. If, for instance, we tried to represent 'everyone likes someone' as:

$$\forall x\,\exists x Lxx$$

we could not tell whether it was the liker or the person liked who has universality attributed to him. So always choose different variables if you need more than one quantifier in representing some statement.[1]

Consider next the two statements:

Everyone is liked by someone.

and

Someone likes everyone.

Surely there are senses in which these do *not* mean the same thing. On perhaps the most natural reading, the first says that no matter whom we pick, there is someone who likes that person. The second claims rather that there is someone such that no matter whom we pick, the person likes the person we pick. In this way, the first statement is most naturally read

---

[1] In view of this advice, we would be remiss if we did not allow ourselves an *infinite* stock of variables. As with sentential and predicate letters, we shall allow variables to be written with or without numerical subscripts. So '$x_1$' and '$x$' are considered *different* variables.

as a universal statement, the second as an existential statement. Since in a universal statement, the universal quantifier must precede all other quantifiers, the statement 'everyone is liked by someone' is represented as:

$$\forall x \exists y Lyx$$

And in an existential statement, the existential quantifier must precede all other quantifiers. So 'someone likes everyone' is represented as:

$$\exists y \forall x Lyx$$

Here we see that the *order* in which the quantifiers occur is very important in the representation of logical form. Once again, study the following examples carefully:

(a)     Everyone likes someone.

$$\forall u \exists v Luv$$

(b)     Someone is liked by everyone.

$$\exists w \forall x Lxw$$

(c)     Everyone is liked by someone.

$$\forall y \exists z Lzy$$

(d)     Someone likes everyone.

$$\exists u \forall v Luv$$

(e)     Someone is nice and likes my picture.

$$\exists u (Nu \ \& \ Lum)$$

(f)     Someone is nice and someone likes my picture.

$$\exists u Nu \ \& \ \exists v Lvm$$

(g)     Everyone is either nice or likes my picture.

$$\forall u (Nu \ v \ Lum)$$

(h)     Either everyone is nice or everyone likes my picture.

$$\forall u Nu \ v \ \forall v Lvm$$

(i)   Everyone likes himself.

$$\forall u L u u$$

(j)   Everyone likes everyone.

$$\forall u\,\forall v L u v$$

(k)   Someone likes himself.

$$\exists u L u u$$

(l)   Someone likes someone.

$$\exists u\,\exists v L u v$$

Note the difference between the fifth and sixth statements, (e) and (f). The sixth statement is a conjunction and is represented accordingly. The fifth statement is however *not* a conjunction; it is an existential generalization of a conjunction. As we shall see in the next chapter, these two formulas are not equivalent. (Similar remarks apply to the seventh and eighth statements.)

**3. Further Examples**. The important thing to remember in all of this is that phrases of the form:

> Everything is such that ...it...
>
> Something is such that ...it...

are almost always represented as:

$$\forall u \ \cdots u \cdots$$
$$\exists u \ \cdots u \cdots$$

So, for complicated cases like those we have been considering, it is best to try to rephrase the given statement into one or the other of these two forms. Let us go through another example, which should be self-explanatory:

(1)                         Everyone gave something to everyone.

(2)                     Everyone is such that he gave something to everyone.

(3)                         $\forall u$  $u$ gave something to everyone.

(4)                     $\forall u$ something is such that $u$ gave it to everyone.

(5)                         $\forall u \exists v$  $u$ gave $v$ to everyone.

(6)                     $\forall u \exists v$ everyone is such that $u$ gave $v$ to him.

(7)                         $\forall u \exists v \forall w$  $u$ gave $v$ to $w$.

(8)                             $\forall u \exists v \forall w Guvw$

It should be noted that in passing from (3) to (4), we had to make a choice
as to how to interpret the phrase:

$$u \text{ gave something to everyone}$$

We chose:

$$\text{something is such that } u \text{ gave it to everyone}$$

whereas we could instead have chosen:

$$\text{everyone is such that } u \text{ gave something to him}$$

in which case we would have proceeded as follows:

(5')                         $\forall u \forall w$  $u$ gave something to $w$

(6')                     $\forall u \forall w$ something is such that $u$ gave it to $w$

(7')                         $\forall u \forall w \exists v$  $u$ gave $v$ to $w$

(8')                             $\forall u \forall w \exists v Guvw$

The ambiguity at step (4) only reflects the ambiguity of the original
English statement, as we can see on reflection. Is it that everyone took
some particular thing and gave it to everyone (presumably, successively
and with returns)—our first reading—or is it that everyone gave each person something or other (and not necessarily the same thing in each
case)—our second choice. Such ambiguity is common in ordinary
language and is resolved in our system of symbolization. As we have
already mentioned, context and other considerations often make one alternative more plausible than another. In the example above, the *second*
alternative is clearly the more plausible one.

**4. Pronomial Cross-Reference.** We need to pay special attention to the symbolization schema when there is a pronomial cross-reference from the grammatical predicate into the grammatical subject. For example, we have the following concrete cases:

(a)    Some girl who knows a boy loves him.

$$\exists x (Gx \; \& \; \exists y((Kxy \; \& \; By) \; \& \; Lxy))$$

(b)    Every girl who knows a boy loves him.

$$\forall x (Gx \supset \forall y (Kxy \supset (By \supset Lxy)))$$

(c)    Every girl who knows a boy who loves her loves him.

$$\forall x (Gx \supset \forall y (Kxy \supset (By \supset (Lyx \supset Lxy))))$$

(d)    Some girl who knows a boy who loves her loves him.

$$\exists x (Gx \; \& \; \exists y (((Kxy \; \& \; By) \; \& \; Lyx) \; \& \; Lxy))$$

Make sure that you can apply the technique of "paraphrasing inward" to these statements in such a way that you arrive at the representations listed. Notice also that some of these statements may be ambiguous.

**Exercises**

---

1    Construct a suitable phrase-book and represent the two different interpretations of the statement alluded to in Section 1:

       Bertha gave a trophy to everyone on the team.

Can you think of any *other* plausible interpretations?

2    Represent the logical form of the following statements, using the phrase-book provided:

$P$ :    ① is a philosopher
$C$ :    ① contradicts ②

$h$ :    Hegel
$b$ :    Berkeley

(a)    All philosophers contradict Hegel.

(b)  No one is a philosopher unless he contradicts some philosopher.

(c)  No philosopher contradicts himself.

(d)  Hegel contradicts every other philosopher.

(e)  There is a philosopher whom every philosopher contradicts.

(f)  Hegel contradicts every philosopher whom Berkeley does not.

3    Using the phrase-book provided below, represent the logical form of
     each of the following statements. If you detect any ambiguities,
     represent the form of *each* statement that might have been intended,
     starting with the most plausible.

$$
\begin{array}{rl}
B : & ① \text{ is a boy} \\
G : & ① \text{ is a girl} \\
G : & ① \text{ gave } ② \text{ to } ③ \\
H : & ① \text{ is happy} \\
L : & ① \text{ loves } ② \\
N : & ① \text{ is nice}
\end{array}
$$

(a)  Some girl who has given something to every boy is nice.

(b)  Every girl who has given something to every boy is nice.

(c)  Some girl who has given something to some boy is nice.

(d)  Every girl who has given something to some boy is nice.

(e)  Every girl who has given something to every boy loves some boy
     who has given something to every girl.

(f)  Some girl who loves a boy who loves her is happy.

(g)  Every girl who loves a boy who loves her is happy.

4    Supply an appropriate phrase-book of the restricted sort and symbolize
     the following statements. If you detect any ambiguities, represent *each*
     of the statements that might have been intended, in order of decreasing
     plausibility.

(a)  Anyone who likes someone is a friendly person.

(b)  Anyone who likes everyone is generous to someone.

(c)  Anyone who does not like anyone is not generous to anyone.

(d)  If anyone both likes a person and is liked by that person, then he is
     happy.

(e)  If anyone both likes a person and is liked by a person, then he likes
     himself.

(f)  If anyone likes anyone, then he is generous to him.

(g)  If anyone likes anyone, then someone is friendly.

(h)  If everyone likes everyone, then everyone is happy.

(i)  If someone does not like anyone, then not everyone is liked by everyone.

(j)  If someone likes someone, then he is friendly.

(k)  If someone likes someone and is liked by him, then they are generous to each other.

(l)  No one who likes someone is ungenerous to him.

5    Throughout our discussion of existential statements, we have not distinguished between grammatical singulars and plurals. That is to say, we have used the formula:

$$\exists v F v$$

to represent both 'there is a fish' and 'there are fish'. It turns out, however, that in combination with the devices of Chapter 15, we can represent the existence of more than one thing which is $F$, e.g., as:

$$\exists x \exists y ((Fx \ \& \ Fy) \ \& \ x \neq y)$$

Find representations of each of the following statements, using the phrase-book provided:

$F$ :    ① is a fish
$I$ :    ① is in ②

$s$ :    San Francisco Bay

(a)  There is at least one fish in San Francisco Bay.

(b)  There are at least two fish in San Francisco Bay.

(c)  There is at most one fish in San Francisco Bay.

(d)  There are at most two fish in San Francisco Bay.

(e)  There is exactly one fish in San Francisco Bay.

(f)  There are exactly two fish in San Francisco Bay.

(g)  There are at least three fish in San Francisco Bay.

# Chapter 19

## Semantical Assignments

**1. Domains.** The next question to tackle is how to represent in a semantical assignment the truth or falsity of statements having forms which need to be represented with the aid of quantifiers, such as:

$$\exists x F x$$
$$\forall x F x$$

It should be obvious that the first statement can be made true by having at least one object in the set assigned to the predicate letter '$F$'. But what about the second statement? Certainly this statement can be made true if we arrange it that *all* objects are in the set assigned to '$F$'. But this way of putting things is a bit vague. For one thing, it isn't at all clear what we are to count as an object, or what objects in fact there are. In particular, it is advantageous:

- to have a clear and easy way of indicating whether or not *all* objects are in a particular set,

- to keep down the number of objects we have to take into account,

- to be able to consider possible situations in which there are fewer objects than there in fact are,[1]

- to rely as little as possible on having to know what objects there in fact are.

These advantages can be secured by including in our semantical assignments a feature designed to indicate which objects are supposed to exist in the possible situation being considered. We do this by choosing a set of objects as the "domain" of that semantical assignment. The objects in the domain are just those objects which we suppose to exist in that possible situation. Accordingly, all the objects assigned to the individual constants

---

[1] What about possible situations in which there are *more* objects than there in fact are? See Chapter 24.

must be included in the domain, as well as all objects found in the sets
assigned to the predicate letters (or found in ordered couples occurring in
sets assigned to predicate letters, etc.). We specify the domain of a
semantical assignment by writing a bold letter 'D', and assigning to some
set of objects. As before, we shall always use natural numbers as the elements of our domain. For example:

$$\mathbf{D} \quad - \quad \{1,2,3,4\}$$

$$
\begin{array}{lll}
F & - & \{1,2,3,4\} \\
G & - & \{1,3,4\} \\
H & - & \{<1,4>, <2,3>, <3,2>\} \\
I & - & \Lambda \\
J & - & \{<1,2>, <2,2>, <3,2>, <4,2>\}
\end{array}
$$

$$
\begin{array}{lll}
a & - & 3 \\
b & - & 2 \\
c & - & 1 \\
d & - & 4
\end{array}
$$

An existential generalization is true in a semantical assignment just in
case the generalizatum[2] is true for *at least one* object in the domain. And
a universal generalization is true in a semantical assignment just in case
the generalizatum is true for *all* objects in the domain. Accordingly, the
following formulas are all true under this semantical assignment:

$$
\begin{array}{ll}
\forall x Fx & \exists x Gx \\
\forall x Jxb & \sim\exists x Hxc \\
\forall x (Fx \lor Gx) & \forall y (Gy \lor Hxa) \\
\forall x \exists y Jxy & \exists x \forall y Jyx \\
\exists x \exists y ((Gx \,\&\, Gy) \,\&\, x \neq y) & Gb \supset \forall x Gx \\
\forall x \forall y (Hxy \supset x \neq y) & \exists x \exists y (Hxy \equiv Jxy)
\end{array}
$$

And the following formulas are all false under this semantical assignment:

$$
\begin{array}{ll}
\forall x Gx & \exists y Iyy \\
\forall x (Fx \equiv Gx) & \forall x \exists y Hxy \\
\forall x \forall y Hxy & \forall x \forall y Jxy \\
\forall x \forall y (Hxy \equiv x \neq y) & \forall x \forall y (Hxy \equiv Jxy)
\end{array}
$$

---

[2] That is, the formula of which it is a generalization.

**2. Examples**. For very simple cases, the best way to tell whether a formula is true or false under a given semantical assignment is just this: try to put into words what the formula "says", then see whether that expresses a truth or a falsehood about the assignment. For instance, the formula:

$$\forall x Gx$$

intuitively "says" that everything in the domain is $G$, and by inspection we see that this is not true, since the number 2 is in the domain but not in the set assigned to '$G$'. And the formula:

$$\forall x \forall y (Hxy \supset x \neq y)$$

intuitively "says" that if one thing $H$'s a second, then they are not identical. This *is* true, since none of the ordered pairs in the set assigned to '$H$' has both elements the same.

For more complicated formulas, however, it may be rather difficult to see what the formula in question says, and we need some more systematic approach. In such cases, a procedure for determining whether a formula is true or false under a given semantical assignment goes along the following lines. Consider the formula:

$$\forall x (Jxx \supset \exists y (Ixy \ \& \ {\sim}Fy))$$

with respect to the semantical assignment given above. This formula comes out true if and only if *every* object in the domain is such that, when '$x$' is regarded as picking *it* out, the generalizatum:

$$Jxx \supset \exists y (Ixy \ \& \ {\sim}Fy)$$

comes out true. So there are four cases to consider:

$$
\begin{array}{ccc}
x & \rightarrow & 1 \\
x & \rightarrow & 2 \\
x & \rightarrow & 3 \\
x & \rightarrow & 4
\end{array}
$$

In the first, third, and fourth cases, the antecedent '$Jxx$' comes out false, so the whole conditional comes out true. (Recall that a conditional is true under some semantical assignment if and only if either the antecedent is false or the consequent is true, or both.) In the second case (when '$x$' is assigned the number 2), the antecedent comes out true, so we need to see whether the consequent also comes out true. Now the formula:

$$\exists y\,(Ixy\ \&\ {\sim}Fy)$$

will come out true if and only if *some* object in the domain is such that, when it is assigned to '$y$' and 2 is assigned to '$x$', the formula:

$$Ixy\ \&\ {\sim}Fy$$

comes out true. Again, there are four subcases to consider, namely:

$$
\begin{array}{ccc}
y & \rightarrow & 1 \\
y & \rightarrow & 2 \\
y & \rightarrow & 3 \\
y & \rightarrow & 4 \\
\end{array}
$$

Since everything in the domain is also in the set assigned to '$F$', none of these assignments to '$y$' will make the formula '${\sim}Fy$' true; it follows that none of these assignments will make the conjunction true. Hence the existential is never true, and the original formula is *false* under the semantical assignment given. In general, this step-by-step procedure will enable us to decide even for very complicated formulas whether or not they are true under some given semantical assignment.

**3. Invalidity.** Now that we know how to determine the truth-value of a formula under a given semantical assignment and how to find a semantical assignment under which a given formula has a desired truth-value, we may apply this knowledge to show that certain arguments representable in quantificational logic are *invalid*. As in truth-functional logic, to show that an argument is not formally valid, we first determine the logical form of the argument and then give a semantical assignment under which the premises are all true and the conclusion is false. Consider, for example, the following simple argument:

> All cats see well at night.
> Bertha is not a cat.
> _____
> Bertha does not see well at night.

Using methods learned previously, we can give the following three formulas as a representation of the logical form of this argument:

$$\forall x\,(Cx \supset Sx)$$
$$\sim\!Cb$$
$$\sim\!Sb$$

In the following semantical assignment, both premises are true while the conclusion is false:

$$\mathbf{D} \quad - \quad \{1,2\}$$

$$C \quad - \quad \{2\}$$
$$S \quad - \quad \{1,2\}$$

$$b \quad - \quad 1$$

This assignment shows that the argument is not formally valid. Since it does not have a more detailed form that is valid, we can say that the original argument is *invalid*.

**4. Consistency.** Finally, let us note that we are now able to show that certain groups of formulas containing quantifiers are *consistent*. We do this by providing a semantical assignment under which all of the formulas are true. For example, the following group of formulas is consistent:

$$\exists x G x$$
$$\exists x {\sim} G x$$

since we can give the following semantical assignment under which both are true:

$$\mathbf{D} \quad - \quad \{1,2\}$$

$$G \quad - \quad \{1\}$$

We are also in a position to show that certain pairs of formulas involving quantifiers are *not logically equivalent*. We do this by providing a semantical assignment under which one of the formulas is true and the other formula is false. Consider for example the two formulas discussed in Chapter 18:

$$\exists u (N u \ \& \ L u m )$$
$$\exists u N u \ \& \ \exists v L v m$$

Under the semantical assignment given below, the first formula is false, yet the second is true. Hence they are not logically equivalent, just as we earlier claimed.

$$\mathbf{D} \quad - \quad \{1,2\}$$

$$L \quad - \quad \{<2,1>\}$$
$$N \quad - \quad \{1\}$$

$$m \quad - \quad 1$$

## Exercises

1    Consider the following semantical assignment:

$$\mathbf{D} \quad - \quad \{1,2,3\}$$

$$F \quad - \quad \{1,2,3\}$$
$$G \quad - \quad \{1,3\}$$
$$H \quad - \quad \Lambda$$
$$I \quad - \quad \{<1,1>, <2,2>, <3,3>\}$$
$$J \quad - \quad \{<1,2>, <2,2>, <3,2>\}$$

$$a \quad - \quad 2$$
$$b \quad - \quad 2$$
$$c \quad - \quad 1$$

Under this assignment, with a few exceptions, the odd-numbered formulas below are true and the even-numbered ones are false.  Find the exceptions.

| | | | |
|---|---|---|---|
| (1) | $\exists x Fx$ | (13) | $\forall x \exists y Jxy$ |
| (2) | $\exists x Hxx$ | (14) | $\exists x \forall y Jyx$ |
| (3) | $\exists x Ixx$ | (15) | $\exists x \forall y Jxy$ |
| (4) | $\sim\exists x Jxx$ | (16) | $\forall x (Fx \supset Gx)$ |
| (5) | $\exists x Jcx$ | (17) | $\forall x (Gx \supset Fx)$ |
| (6) | $\exists x Jxc$ | (18) | $\forall x ((Jax \lor Jbx) \supset Fx)$ |
| (7) | $\exists x \exists y Jxy$ | (19) | $\forall x ((Jxa \lor Jxb) \supset Fx)$ |
| (8) | $\sim\exists x Gx$ | (20) | $\forall x \forall y (Jxy \supset Ixy)$ |
| (9) | $\forall x Gx$ | (21) | $\forall x (Jxx \supset Ixx)$ |
| (10) | $\forall x Fx$ | (22) | $\forall x (\sim Hxx \supset Jxx)$ |
| (11) | $\forall x Ixx$ | (23) | $\forall x (Hxx \supset Jxx)$ |
| (12) | $\forall x \forall y Jxy$ | (24) | $\forall x (Gx \supset \exists y Ixy)$ |

2    Give a semantical assignment under which the following formula is *true*:

$$\forall x (Jxx \supset \exists y (Ixy \ \& \ {\sim}Fy))$$

3    For each of the following groups of formulas, give a semantical assign-
     ment under which all the formulas in the group are true. Then give a
     (different) semantical assignment under which the *last* formula in each
     group is *false* and the rest (if any) are *true*.

(a)            $\forall x (Fx \supset Gx)$            (b)            $\forall x (\exists y Fxy \supset \forall z Gxz)$

(c)            $\forall x (Fx \supset Gx)$            (d)            $\forall x (\exists y Fxy \supset Gxx)$
               $\exists y Gy$                                        ${\sim}\exists y Gyy$

(e)            $\forall x \forall y (Fxy \supset Gxy)$   (f)        $\forall x \forall y (Fxy \supset (Gxx \supset Gyy))$

(g)            $\forall x \forall y (Fxy \supset Gyx)$   (h)        $\forall x \forall y (Fxy \supset \exists z Gxz)$

(i)            $\forall x (Fx \supset Gx)$            (j)                      $\exists y Fy$
               $\forall y (Fy \supset {\sim}Gy)$                             $\exists y (Fy \supset Gy)$
                                                                              $\exists u Gu$

4    Show that the following two formulas are *not* logically equivalent:

$$\forall u (Nu \ v \ Lum)$$
$$\forall u Nu \ v \ \forall v Lvm$$

# Chapter 20

# Derivations with Quantifiers

**1. Derivations**. In quantificational logic, as in truth-functional logic, we show that an argument is formally valid by constructing a chain of simpler arguments, each of which is obviously formally valid, starting with the given premises and ending with the desired conclusion. That is, our goal is to construct a *derivation* of the conclusion from the premises. Similarly, we show that a group of formulas is formally inconsistent by deriving the negation of any one of them from the rest. So our next major task is to specify certain rules of derivation which we may use in these ways.

First, however, let us observe that our rules for truth-functional logic are applicable without modification to our extended stock of formulas. For example, consider the following simple argument:

> Every cat is friendly to every cat.
> If every cat is friendly to every cat,
> then some cat basks in the sun and some cat is content.
> _____
> Some cat basks in the sun.

Even if we isolate *as much* logical form as we know how to, we can already show this argument to be formally valid, by constructing the following derivation:

| | | | |
|---|---|---|---|
| 1 | 1 | $\forall x \forall y Fxy$ | S |
| 2 | 2 | $\forall x \forall y Fxy \supset (\exists u Bu \ \& \ \exists v Cv)$ | S |
| 1,2 | 3 | $\exists u Bu \ \& \ \exists v Cv$ | 1,2 MPP |
| 1,2 | 4 | $\exists u Bu$ | 3 &E |

This is because our rules for truth-functional logic are applicable to *all* statements having certain logical forms. The formula on line (2) is a conditional, regardless of the fact that its antecedent and consequent have more complex logical forms than we were able to represent in truth-functional logic. Since, therefore, its antecedent occurs on line (1), we may infer its consequent by MPP. Similarly, line (3) is a conjunction, so we may infer either conjunct by &E. And so on.

But we need additional rules to capture the validity of arguments, such as those at the beginning of Chapter 17, which depend on the presence of phrases like 'everything', 'something', etc. We shall adopt just *four* basic quantificational rules and no derived rules. In this chapter, we consider the two easiest quantificational rules.

**2. Rule $\forall$E.** The first quantificational rule takes its inspiration from the fact that if *everything* has some attribute or property, then certainly Greta, or Michael, or the Campanile, or whatever, must have that property. In other words, if everything has some property, then any particular thing you care to consider must have that property. Schematically, if we are given some universal generalization:

$$\forall x \;\; \cdots \; x \; \cdots$$

we may drop the quantifier and replace the '$x$' throughout by the letter representing 'Greta'. So we get:

$$\cdots \; g \; \cdots$$

To make this procedure precise, we adopt the following rule:

---

$\forall$E         Given a *universal generalization* whose initial quantifier contains some variable, infer the result of dropping the initial quantifier (together with any pair of parentheses which are now outermost, if any) and replacing *all* occurrences of that variable by occurrences of some one and the same individual constant.[1] As supposition numerals of the inferred line, take all those of the given line.

---

Examples:

$$
\begin{array}{cc|ll}
1 & & 1 & \forall xFx \\
1 & & 2 & Fb \\
\end{array}
\qquad\qquad
\begin{array}{l}
\text{S} \\
1\ \forall\text{E}
\end{array}
$$

---

[1] Recall that the (individual) *variables* are the lower-case letters '$u$' through '$z$', and that the *individual constants* are the lower-case letters '$a$' through '$t$', with or without numerical subscripts.

$$1,2 \mid \quad 5 \quad \forall x Gaxab$$

$$1,2 \mid \quad 13 \quad Gaaab \qquad\qquad\qquad\qquad 5\ \forall E$$

$$1,5 \mid \quad 10 \quad \forall x(\exists y Aby \ \lor\ \forall z Bbax)$$

$$1,5 \mid \quad 12 \quad \exists y Aby \ \lor\ \forall z Bbaa \qquad\qquad 10\ \forall E$$

$$2 \mid \quad 3 \quad \forall u \forall z Fuz$$

$$2 \mid \quad 8 \quad \forall z Fqz \qquad\qquad\qquad\qquad 3\ \forall E$$

Note that this rule does *not* allow you to remove just any universal quantifier and replace the associated variable with an individual constant. It states that the formula must itself be a universal generalization. In particular, you cannot apply this new rule to just *part* of a formula. So, for example, the following is **not** a correct application of rule $\forall E$:

$$
\begin{array}{c|ccl}
1 & 1 & \forall u Gu \supset \forall z Fz & \text{S} \\
1 & 2 & \forall u Gu \supset Fa & 1\ \forall E\ \textbf{not correct!}
\end{array}
$$

Nor is the following correct:

$$
\begin{array}{c|ccl}
1 & 1 & \forall u Gu \supset \forall z Fz & \text{S} \\
1 & 2 & Ga \supset \forall z Fz & 1\ \forall E\ \textbf{not correct!}
\end{array}
$$

## Exercises

1   Show that the formula '$\forall u Gu \supset Fa$' does in fact *follow from* the formula '$\forall u Gu \supset \forall z Fz$' (even though it cannot be derived in one step as attempted above).

2    Can you give a derivation of the formula '*Ga* ⊃ ∀*zFz*' from the formula
'∀*uGu* ⊃ ∀*zFz*'?

---

**3. Rule ∃I.** The second rule corresponds to the following line of reasoning: if *Greta* (or Michael, or the Campanile, or whatever) has some property, then certainly *something* has that same property. In other words, if we are given a line in which the constant '*g*' representing 'Greta' occurs,

$$\cdots g \cdots$$

then we can conclude:

$$\exists x \cdots x \cdots$$

For example, suppose we say:

Greta gave my picture to Penelope.

From this statement we may deduce a variety of other statements, among which are:

Someone gave my picture to Penelope.
Greta gave my picture to someone.

In symbols, we may say that from:

$$Ggmp$$

we may conclude, respectively:

$$\exists xGxmp$$
$$\exists xGgmx$$

So we may adopt the following rule:

---

∃I          Given any formula containing occurrences of a given individual constant, infer the result of replacing *some* (and perhaps *all*) occurrences of that individual constant by occurrences of one and the same *fresh* variable, enclosing the whole in parentheses if necessary, and prefixing the existential quantifier containing that variable. As supposition numerals of the inferred line, take all those of the given line.

---

Examples:

$$
\begin{array}{lll}
1 & \quad 1 \quad Fq & \qquad\qquad S \\
1 & \quad 2 \quad \exists xFx & \qquad\qquad 1\ \exists I
\end{array}
$$

$$
1,4 \quad\Big| \quad 5 \quad Gaaab
$$

$$
1,4 \quad\Big| \quad 13 \quad \exists zGzazb \qquad\qquad 5\ \exists I
$$

$$
1,6,7 \quad\Big| \quad 11 \quad \forall x(\exists yAby \ \text{v} \ \forall zBbaz)
$$

$$
1,6,7 \quad\Big| \quad 15 \quad \exists v\forall x(\exists yAby \ \text{v} \ \forall zBvaz) \qquad\qquad 11\ \exists I
$$

**4. Examples.** With these two new rules, together with our old rules for truth-functional logic, we can now construct derivations showing that certain arguments are valid, that certain statements are inconsistent, or that certain formulas are theorems. Let us give an example of each of these uses of our rules $\forall E$ and $\exists I$.

Let us begin by showing the validity of the following simple argument:

> Mefisto is a cuddly and warm kitten.
> Whatever is warm may also be dangerous.
> _____
> Some kittens may be dangerous.

We may represent its logical form as:

$$
Km \ \& \ (Cm \ \& \ Wm)
$$
$$
\forall x(Wx \supset Dx)
$$
$$
\exists x(Kx \ \& \ Dx)
$$

And the following simple derivation shows the argument to be formally valid:

| | | | |
|---|---|---|---|
| 1 | 1 | $Km$ & $(Cm$ & $Wm)$ | S |
| 2 | 2 | $\forall x(Wx \supset Dx)$ | S |
| 1 | 3 | $Km$ | 1 &E |
| 1 | 4 | $Cm$ & $Wm$ | 1 &E |
| 1 | 5 | $Wm$ | 4 &E |
| 2 | 6 | $Wm \supset Dm$ | 2 $\forall$E |
| 1,2 | 7 | $Dm$ | 5,6 MPP |
| 1,2 | 8 | $Km$ & $Dm$ | 3,7 &I |
| 1,2 | 9 | $\exists x(Kx$ & $Dx)$ | 8 $\exists$I |

Consider next the following pair of statements:

Every philosopher contradicts every philosopher.
Hegel, who is a philosopher, contradicts no one.

These statements are inconsistent, as we may show with the following derivation:

| | | | |
|---|---|---|---|
| 1 | 1 | $\forall x(Px \supset \forall y(Py \supset Cxy))$ | S |
| 2 | 2 | $Ph$ & $\forall x\sim Chx$ | S (for RAA) |
| 1 | 3 | $Ph \supset \forall y(Py \supset Chy)$ | 1 $\forall$E |
| 2 | 4 | $Ph$ | 2 &E |
| 1,2 | 5 | $\forall y(Py \supset Chy)$ | 3,4 MPP |
| 1,2 | 6 | $Ph \supset Chh$ | 5 $\forall$E |
| 1,2 | 7 | $Chh$ | 4,6 MPP |
| 2 | 8 | $\forall x\sim Chx$ | 2 &E |
| 2 | 9 | $\sim Chh$ | 8 $\forall$E |
| 1 | 10 | $\sim(Ph$ & $\forall x\sim Chx)$ | 2,7,8 RAA |

By deriving the *negation* of the second statement from the first statement, we have shown that the two statements are formally inconsistent.

Finally, we may illustrate proving quantificational *theorems* with the following simple derivation:

| | | | |
|---|---|---|---|
| 1 | 1 | $\forall xFx$ | S (for CP) |
| 1 | 2 | $Fa$ | 1 $\forall$E |
| 1 | 3 | $\exists yFy$ | 2 $\exists$I |
| $\Lambda$ | 4 | $\forall xFx \supset \exists yFy$ | 1,3 CP |

This shows that the formula on the last line follows from no suppositions and is therefore a theorem of quantificational logic.

**5. Strategy Hints.** As usual, there are straightforward strategy hints that can help guide our derivation construction. If you want to prove an existential generalization, one way to go about it is first to try to prove some formula from which the existential generalization can be obtained by application of rule $\exists$I. (We shall call such a formula an *instance* of the generalization.) For example, if you want to derive the formula:

$$\exists y(Fy \; \& \; Gy)$$

from some suppositions, you might try first to derive '$Fa \; \& \; Ga$' from them. There is, however, a certain risk in this strategy, for an instance of an existential generalization might not be derivable from the given suppositions, even though the existential generalization itself is.[2]

A more generally useful hint is this: if one of the available lines as you are working *forward* in a derivation is a universal generalization, write in an instance of the generalization in accordance with rule $\forall$E. Exactly *which* instance you write in will usually depend on what is already in your derivation and where you hope to get to; often, however, it is useful to take instances involving constants which *already* occur in the derivation. So we have:

☞   If you are given (or have already derived) a universal generalization, derive an instance of the generalization involving a constant which seems useful.

☞   If the desired formula is an existential generalization, try to derive an instance of the generalization; then apply $\exists$I.

You may want to review the sample derivations given above to see how these hints came into play. Let us further illustrate their use by showing that the following formula is a *theorem* of quantificational logic:

$$\sim\forall x(Fx \; \& \; \sim\exists yFy)$$

How shall we begin? We are given no suppositions, so we shall have to generate some ourselves. Let us try the standard RAA approach:

| 1 | 1 | $\forall x(Fx \; \& \; \sim\exists yFy)$ | S (for RAA) |
|---|---|---|---|
| $\Lambda$ | | $\sim\forall x(Fx \; \& \; \sim\exists yFy)$ | |

---

[2] Recall the similar situation that arose in connection with rule $\forall$I, in Chapter 8.

Now we can apply the first strategy hint. Since no constants yet appear in our partial derivation, we must introduce one, as follows:

| 1 | 1 | $\forall x(Fx \ \& \sim\exists y Fy)$ | S (for RAA) |
|---|---|---|---|
| 1 | 2 | $Fa \ \& \sim\exists y Fy$ | 1 $\forall$E |
| | | | |
| $\Lambda$ | | $\sim\forall x(Fx \ \& \sim\exists y Fy)$ | |

We should probably break the conjunction on line (2) apart:

| 1 | 1 | $\forall x(Fx \ \& \sim\exists y Fy)$ | S (for RAA) |
|---|---|---|---|
| 1 | 2 | $Fa \ \& \sim\exists y Fy$ | 1 $\forall$E |
| 1 | 3 | $Fa$ | 2 &E |
| 1 | 4 | $\sim\exists y Fy$ | 2 &E |
| | | | |
| $\Lambda$ | | $\sim\forall x(Fx \ \& \sim\exists y Fy)$ | |

Our goal, of course, is to derive a pair of contradictory formulas. Since (at this point) there is nothing we can do with line (4), we might try to derive its negatum. This is quite simple, and we may finish up as follows:

| 1 | 1 | $\forall x(Fx \ \& \sim\exists y Fy)$ | S (for RAA) |
|---|---|---|---|
| 1 | 2 | $Fa \ \& \sim\exists y Fy$ | 1 $\forall$E |
| 1 | 3 | $Fa$ | 2 &E |
| 1 | 4 | $\sim\exists y Fy$ | 2 &E |
| 1 | 5 | $\exists y Fy$ | 3 $\exists$I |
| $\Lambda$ | 6 | $\sim\forall x(Fx \ \& \sim\exists y Fy)$ | 1,4,5 RAA |

## Exercises

3   Show that the following argument forms are valid by finding a derivation of the last formula in each group from the remaining.

(a)          $\forall u Fu$          (b)          $\forall u \forall v Fuv$
             $\exists u Fu \supset \forall v Gv$                    $\exists z Fzz$
             $\exists v Gv$

(c)          $\forall x Fxx$          (d)          $\forall u \forall v Fuv$
             $\exists u \exists v Fuv$                    $\forall u \forall v(Fuv \supset Guv)$
                                           $\exists u \exists v Guv$

(e)   $\forall u \forall v Fuv$    (f)   $\exists u Fu \supset \forall v Gv$
   $\forall u \forall v (Fuv \supset Guv)$     $\forall u Fu \supset \exists u Gu$
   $\exists u (Guu \ \& \ Fuu)$

(g)   $\forall u \forall v Fuv$    (h)   $\forall u \forall v (Fuv \supset Guv)$
   $\forall u \forall v (Fuv \supset Guv)$     $Fab$
   $\exists u \exists v (Fuu \ \& \ Guv)$     $\exists u \exists v Guv$

(i)   $\exists y Fay \supset \forall u Gub$    (j)   $\forall u \forall v Fuv$
   $Fab$     $\forall w (\forall v Fwv \supset Gw)$
   $\exists x Gxx$     $\exists u Gu$

(k)   $\forall x Fx$    (l)   $\sim \exists x Fx$
   $\sim \forall x \sim Fx$     $\sim \forall x Fx$

# Chapter 21

# Universal Generalization

**1. Intuitive Motivation.** We are ready for the third of the four basic rules governing derivations in quantificational logic. It is a little more complicated than the first two, but generally quite easy to apply. Suppose we have the two statements:

> (1) Everyone is either happy or nice.
> (2) Everyone is unhappy.

Now consider Greta. From these two statements we may infer both:

> (3) Greta is either happy or nice.
> (4) Greta is unhappy.

from which we may conclude (by a step analogous to the rule DS):

> (5) Greta is nice.

Here is the central point: we chose Greta just as an *example* to illustrate consequences that (1) and (2) would have for any particular case. It should be clear that we could have reached a conclusion analogous to (5) about anyone else. For instance, we could have drawn similar conclusions about Clothilda:

> (3′) Clothilda is either happy or nice.
> (4′) Clothilda is unhappy.
> (5′) Clothilda is nice.

Since we can replicate this line of reasoning about *anyone at all*, we can infer:

> (6) Everyone is nice.

Note that (6) does *not* follow solely from (5), or from (5′); it *does* however
follow from (5), or from (5′), together with the fact that we could have
drawn a similar conclusion about anyone. We must of course be careful
*not* to draw this conclusion if the line of reasoning cannot be exactly
reproduced about any other person. In other words, we must be careful
that nowhere in the line of reasoning leading to (5) have we in any way
depended on suppositions *specifically about Greta*, and that our ultimate
conclusion, in this case (6), contains no mention of Greta. Both of these
restrictions insure that the line of reasoning *can* be reproduced exactly
about Clothilda, and about Penelope, etc.

**2. Precise Formulation.** We may, then, frame the following rule:

---

∀I          Given a formula containing occurrences of some individual
constant, infer the result of replacing *all* occurrences of that
constant by a variable that is *fresh* to that formula, enclosing
the whole in parentheses if necessary, and prefixing to the
result the universal quantifier containing that variable, *provided that* the individual constant in question occurs in none of
the suppositions of the given line. As supposition numerals of
the inferred line, take all those of the given line.

---

Here are three examples. The first derivation formalizes the line of reasoning (1) through (6) above:

| | | | |
|---|---|---|---|
| 1 | 1 | $\forall u (Hu \lor Nu)$ | S |
| 2 | 2 | $\forall w \sim Hw$ | S |
| 1 | 3 | $Hg \lor Ng$ | 1 ∀E |
| 2 | 4 | $\sim Hg$ | 2 ∀E |
| 1,2 | 5 | $Ng$ | 3,4 DS |
| 1,2 | 6 | $\forall u Nu$ | 5 ∀I |

| | | | |
|---|---|---|---|
| 1 | 1 | $\forall x Fx$ | S |
| 1 | 2 | $Fa$ | 1 ∀E |
| 1 | 3 | $\forall u Fu$ | 2 ∀I |

$$\vdots \qquad \vdots$$

$$3 \mid \quad 3 \quad Aab \qquad\qquad\qquad\qquad\qquad S$$

$$\vdots \qquad \vdots$$

$$7 \mid \quad 7 \quad \forall z\,(\exists yAzy \supset \forall xBxb\,) \qquad\qquad S$$

$$\vdots \qquad \vdots$$

$$3,7 \mid \quad 12 \quad Bcb$$

$$\vdots \qquad \vdots$$

$$3,7 \mid \quad 15 \quad \forall uBub \qquad\qquad\qquad\qquad 12 \; \forall I$$

$$\vdots \qquad \vdots$$

Note that in using this rule it is necessary to survey the entire derivation in order to determine that the individual constant in question does not occur in any of the suppositions of the given line. Note also that other constants may well occur in those suppositions. In this last example, for instance, the individual constant in question is '$c$'. It is therefore acceptable that the constant '$b$' occurs in both of the suppositions of line (12), and that '$a$' occurs in one of them.

**3. Strategy Hints.** Associated with rule $\forall I$ is the following strategy hint: if the desired conclusion is a universal generalization, try to derive an instance of the generalization in which the constant that will be replaced by a variable in the application of $\forall I$ does *not* occur in any of the given suppositions. For example, suppose that we want to derive the formula:

$$\forall x\,(Fx \supset Ix\,)$$

from the two formulas:

$$\forall x\,((Fx \; v \; Gx\,) \supset Hx\,)$$
$$\forall x\,(Hx \supset Ix\,)$$

The desired conclusion is a universal generalization, so we might try to derive an instance of it. Since no constants at all occur in the two suppositions, we may choose any instance we like:

$$1 \mid \quad 1 \quad \forall x\,((Fx \; v \; Gx\,) \supset Hx\,) \qquad S$$
$$2 \mid \quad 2 \quad \forall x\,(Hx \supset Ix\,) \qquad\qquad S$$

$$\qquad\qquad Fa \supset Ia$$
$$\qquad\qquad \forall x\,(Fx \supset Ix\,)$$

This instance is itself a conditional, so we continue as follows:

| 1 | 1 | $\forall x((Fx \lor Gx) \supset Hx)$ | S |
| 2 | 2 | $\forall x(Hx \supset Ix)$ | S |
| 3 | 3 | $Fa$ | S (for CP) |
| | | $Ia$ | |
| | | $Fa \supset Ia$ | |
| | | $\forall x(Fx \supset Ix)$ | |

Now we must begin to work forward in our derivation. We have two universal generalizations as suppositions, so we may apply rule $\forall$E. We also have '$Fa$' as a supposition, and we want to get '$Ia$', so we should probably replace the variable by the constant '$a$':

| 1 | 1 | $\forall x((Fx \lor Gx) \supset Hx)$ | S |
| 2 | 2 | $\forall x(Hx \supset Ix)$ | S |
| 3 | 3 | $Fa$ | S (for CP) |
| 1 | 4 | $(Fa \lor Ga) \supset Ha$ | 1 $\forall$E |
| 2 | 5 | $Ha \supset Ia$ | 2 $\forall$E |
| | | $Ia$ | |
| | | $Fa \supset Ia$ | |
| | | $\forall x(Fx \supset Ix)$ | |

Now it is a simple matter to fill in the intermediate steps. We may get the antecedent of line (4) quite easily, and then apply MPP:

| 1 | 1 | $\forall x((Fx \lor Gx) \supset Hx)$ | S |
| 2 | 2 | $\forall x(Hx \supset Ix)$ | S |
| 3 | 3 | $Fa$ | S (for CP) |
| 1 | 4 | $(Fa \lor Ga) \supset Ha$ | 1 $\forall$E |
| 2 | 5 | $Ha \supset Ia$ | 2 $\forall$E |
| 3 | 6 | $Fa \lor Ga$ | 3 vI |
| 1,3 | 7 | $Ha$ | 4,6 MPP |
| 1,2,3 | 8 | $Ia$ | 5,7 MPP |
| 1,2 | 9 | $Fa \supset Ia$ | 3,8 CP |
| 1,2 | 10 | $\forall x(Fx \supset Ix)$ | 9 $\forall$I |

The constant '$a$' does not occur in line (10) or in any supposition of line (9); hence, rule $\forall$I is correctly applied.

So remember:

☞ If the desired conclusion is a universal generalization, try to derive an instance of it containing in the appropriate location a constant which does not occur in any given supposition.

**Exercises**

---

1   In each item, derive the last formula from the other(s).

(a)     $\forall x (Fx \supset Gx)$          (b)          $\forall x (Gx \supset \sim Fx)$
        $\forall x (Gx \supset \sim Hx)$                      $\forall x (Hx \supset Gx)$
        $\forall x (Fx \supset \sim Hx)$                      $\forall x (Fx \supset \sim Hx)$

(c)     $\forall x (Fx \equiv Gx)$          (d)          $\forall x (Fx \equiv Gx)$
        $\forall x (Fx \supset Gx)$                           $\forall x Fx \equiv \forall x Gx$

(e)     $\forall x (Fx \supset Gx)$          (f)          $\forall x (P \supset Fx)$
        $\forall x Fx \supset \forall x Gx$                  $P \supset \forall x Fx$

(g)     $\forall x ((Fx \vee Gx) \supset Hx)$   (h)          $P \supset \forall x Fx$
        $\forall x \sim Hx$                                  $\forall x (P \supset Fx)$
        $\forall x \sim Fx$

---

2   In each item, derive the last formula from the other(s).

(a)     $\forall x \forall y Hxy$           (b)          $\forall x (Fx \,\&\, Gx)$
        $\forall y \forall x Hxy$                            $\forall x Fx \,\&\, \forall x Gx$

(c)     $\forall x Fx \vee \forall x Gx$    (d)    $\forall x \forall y \forall z ((Hxy \,\&\, Hyz) \supset Hxz)$
        $\forall x (Fx \vee Gx)$                              $\forall x \sim Hxx$
                                                             $\forall x \forall y (Hxy \supset \sim Hyx)$

(e)     $\forall u \forall v Fuv$           (f)          $\sim \forall x \sim \forall y Fxy$
        $\forall u Fuu$                                      $\forall y \sim \forall x \sim Fxy$

(g)     $\forall u Lug$                     (h)          $\forall u Fuu$
        $\forall u \forall w (Lwu \supset Luw)$             $\forall u (\exists v Fuv \supset \forall v Fuv)$
        $\forall u Lgu$                                      $\forall u \forall v Fuv$

---

# Chapter 22

# Existential Instantiation

**1. Intuitive Motivation.** The last of the four basic rules that we shall adopt for quantificational logic is motivated by the following sort of reasoning. Suppose that we are given:

(1) Someone is both nice and happy.

First let us suppose that this lucky individual is Greta. Of course, this might not in fact be true, but we can surely *suppose* it. Then we have:

(2) Greta is both nice and happy.

from which we may conclude (by a line of reasoning analogous to rule &E):

(3) Greta is happy.

and from this we may then conclude:

(4) Someone is happy.

To be sure, our conclusion at this stage rests on the *supposition* that we made on line (2) to the effect that it is *Greta* who is the lucky person who is both nice and happy. But according to (1), *there is someone* who is both nice and happy—even if it isn't Greta. Now if our reasoning about Greta is such that a corresponding line of reasoning could be constructed that leads to the same conclusion, *no matter whom* we supposed the lucky individual to be, then since the truth of (1) requires that at least one of these suppositions be true, the truth of (1) requires that the conclusion to which they all lead be true. In other words, we may infer (4) not from the supposition (2), but from (1).

What has just been said may be rephrased as follows: consider *all* the lines of reasoning which are just like the one about Greta, except for the changes that must be made because they start with a supposition about some other person, say Penelope or Michael. If they *all* lead to the same conclusion, then if *any one* of the suppositions in question were to be true, the conclusion would also have to be true. But if (1) were to be true, then indeed *at least one* of the suppositions in question *would* have to be true. So, if (1) were true, the conclusion would have to be true.

So we see that if (a) starting with the supposition which says of a particular specified individual that it is such-and-such, we obtain a certain conclusion, and (b) we can be sure that we could obtain that conclusion by a corresponding line of reasoning, starting with the supposition that said of any other specified individual that it is such-and-such, then that conclusion follows from the statement that *someone* is such-and-such.

**2. Precise Formulation.** Now, how can we be sure about point (b)? We can be sure about it if the line of reasoning mentioned in point (a) satisfies three conditions:

• The particular individual in question (Greta, in our example) is not specifically mentioned in the given statement that *someone* is such-and-such.

• The conclusion does not retain any traces of our having started with a supposition about that particular individual.

• The conclusion does not rest on *any* further suppositions about that individual.

These of course are restrictions on our everyday lines of reasoning. In the following rule, these three conditions are rephrased into the three restrictions:

○ The individual constant in the *second* given line which replaces occurrences of a variable in the *first* given line is to be *fresh*—in the sense that it does not occur in the *first* given line.

○ That individual constant does *not* occur in the *third* given line.

○ That individual constant does *not* occur in any supposition of the *third* given line other than the *second* line.

We may, then, frame the following rule:

∃E                   Given three lines such that

(1)    the formula on the first is an *existential generalization*;
(2)    the formula on the second line is a supposition and is
       also the result of taking the formula on the first line and
       omitting the initial existential quantifier (and a pair of
       parentheses that are outermost—if any) and replacing *all*
       occurrences of the variable which is contained in the om-
       itted existential quantifier by occurrences of some one
       *fresh* (to that formula) individual constant;
(3)    the third is a formula which has the second line among
       its suppositions but which does *not* contain the individu-
       al constant in question.

Infer a line which has on it the same formula as that on the
third given line, provided that the individual constant in question does not occur in any of the suppositions of the third line
other than the second given line.

As supposition numerals of the inferred line, take all those of
the first given line together with the result of omitting the *line*
numeral of the second given line from the supposition
numerals of the third given line.

Here are three examples. The first derivation formalizes the line of reasoning (1) through (4) above:

| 1 | 1 | $\exists u(Hu$ & $Nu)$ | S |
|---|---|---|---|
| 2 | 2 | $Hg$ & $Ng$ | S (for ∃E) |
| 2 | 3 | $Hg$ | 2 &E |
| 2 | 4 | $\exists uHu$ | 3 ∃I |
| 1 | 5 | $\exists uHu$ | 1,2,4 ∃E |

| 1 | 1 | $\exists uFubu$ | S |
|---|---|---|---|
| 2 | 2 | $Faba$ | S (for ∃E) |
| 2 | 3 | $\exists yFyba$ | 2 ∃I |
| 2 | 4 | $\exists x\exists yFybx$ | 3 ∃I |
| 1 | 5 | $\exists x\exists yFybx$ | 1,2,4 ∃E |

The individual constant in question here is '*a*'. Hence the rule is not
violated by the fact that '*b*' occurs in the original supposition on line (1)
and in the supposition for ∃E on line (2).

$$
\begin{array}{rrll}
2 & 2 & \forall x\,\forall y Axy & \text{S} \\
3 & 3 & Aab \supset \exists u\,\forall v Buv & \text{S} \\[2ex]
5 & 5 & \forall u\,\forall v(Buv \supset Cuv) & \text{S} \\[2ex]
2,3 & 8 & \exists u\,\forall v Buv & \\[2ex]
10 & 10 & \forall v Bcv & \text{S (for } \exists \text{E)} \\[2ex]
5,10 & 16 & \exists u\,\forall v Cuv & \\
2,3,5 & 17 & \exists u\,\forall v Cuv & 8,10,16\ \exists \text{E}
\end{array}
$$

The individual constant in question here is '$c$'. So '$a$' and '$b$' may well occur in line (3), as well as any of the lines omitted. Note once again that in using this rule it is necessary to survey the entire derivation up to this point to determine that the individual constant in question does not occur in any of the suppositions of the *third* given line other than the *second* given line. If the constant in question *does* occur in any of the suppositions of that line (other than the second line), then we may *not* apply the rule.

**3. Example.** Suppose that we want to find a derivation from the premise:

$$\forall x (Fx \supset Gx)$$

to the conclusion:

$$\sim\!\exists x (Fx\ \&\ \sim\!Gx)$$

As always, we begin by working backward. Since the conclusion is a negation, we might think to go straight into an RAA strategy; we should therefore suppose the negatum of the desired conclusion, as follows:

$$
\begin{array}{rrll}
1 & 1 & \forall x (Fx \supset Gx) & \text{S} \\
2 & 2 & \exists x (Fx\ \&\ \sim\!Gx) & \text{S (for RAA)} \\[2ex]
& & \sim\!\exists x (Fx\ \&\ \sim\!Gx) &
\end{array}
$$

Now we need to work forward. We have a universal generalization, an existential generalization, and nothing else. Which should we work on first? Generally, if you have a situation like this, you should introduce an instance of the existential generalization as a new supposition *before* you introduce an instance of the universal generalization (as allowed by ∀E). The reason for this is quite simple: ∃E has restrictions on its application, and to be safe we should always introduce an instance involving a constant which does not yet occur in the derivation. Rule ∀E, on the other hand, has no restrictions; we are free to introduce an instance involving any constant we like. So let us take as a new supposition an instance of line (2) involving a fresh constant:

| | | | |
|---|---|---|---|
| 1 | 1 | $\forall x(Fx \supset Gx)$ | S |
| 2 | 2 | $\exists x(Fx \,\&\, \sim Gx)$ | S (for RAA) |
| 3 | 3 | $Fa \,\&\, \sim Ga$ | S (for ∃E) |
| | | $\sim\exists x(Fx \,\&\, \sim Gx)$ | |

Now it should be obvious which instance of line (1) we need to derive by rule ∀E:

| | | | |
|---|---|---|---|
| 1 | 1 | $\forall x(Fx \supset Gx)$ | S |
| 2 | 2 | $\exists x(Fx \,\&\, \sim Gx)$ | S (for RAA) |
| 3 | 3 | $Fa \,\&\, \sim Ga$ | S (for ∃E) |
| 1 | 4 | $Fa \supset Ga$ | 1 ∀E |
| | | $\sim\exists x(Fx \,\&\, \sim Gx)$ | |

It is then easy to derive two express contradictories, as required by our earlier adoption of an RAA strategy:

| | | | |
|---|---|---|---|
| 1 | 1 | $\forall x(Fx \supset Gx)$ | S |
| 2 | 2 | $\exists x(Fx \,\&\, \sim Gx)$ | S (for RAA) |
| 3 | 3 | $Fa \,\&\, \sim Ga$ | S (for ∃E) |
| 1 | 4 | $Fa \supset Ga$ | 1 ∀E |
| 3 | 5 | $Fa$ | 3 &E |
| 3 | 6 | $\sim Ga$ | 3 &E |
| 1,3 | 7 | $Ga$ | 4,5 MPP |
| | | $\sim\exists x(Fx \,\&\, \sim Gx)$ | |

We cannot, however, apply RAA yet, since the supposition for RAA, line (2), is not a supposition of either of the express contradictories. But we know how to solve that problem: insert the Nevada marriage and divorce. So we get:

| | | | |
|---|---|---|---|
| 1 | 1 | $\forall x(Fx \supset Gx)$ | S |
| 2 | 2 | $\exists x(Fx \ \& \ {\sim}Gx)$ | S (for RAA) |
| 3 | 3 | $Fa \ \& \ {\sim}Ga$ | S (for $\exists$E) |
| 1 | 4 | $Fa \supset Ga$ | 1 $\forall$E |
| 3 | 5 | $Fa$ | 3 &E |
| 3 | 6 | ${\sim}Ga$ | 3 &E |
| 1,3 | 7 | $Ga$ | 4,5 MPP |
| 1,2,3 | 8 | $Ga \ \& \ \exists x(Fx \ \& \ {\sim}Gx)$ | 2,7 &I |
| 1,2,3 | 9 | $Ga$ | 8 &E |

$${\sim}\exists x(Fx \ \& \ {\sim}Gx)$$

Now we *can* apply RAA:

| | | | |
|---|---|---|---|
| 1 | 1 | $\forall x(Fx \supset Gx)$ | S |
| 2 | 2 | $\exists x(Fx \ \& \ {\sim}Gx)$ | S (for RAA) |
| 3 | 3 | $Fa \ \& \ {\sim}Ga$ | S (for $\exists$E) |
| 1 | 4 | $Fa \supset Ga$ | 1 $\forall$E |
| 3 | 5 | $Fa$ | 3 &E |
| 3 | 6 | ${\sim}Ga$ | 3 &E |
| 1,3 | 7 | $Ga$ | 4,5 MPP |
| 1,2,3 | 8 | $Ga \ \& \ \exists x(Fx \ \& \ {\sim}Gx)$ | 2,7 &I |
| 1,2,3 | 9 | $Ga$ | 8 &E |
| 1,3 | 10 | ${\sim}\exists x(Fx \ \& \ {\sim}Gx)$ | 2,5,9 RAA |

$${\sim}\exists x(Fx \ \& \ {\sim}Gx)$$

Notice that we have succeeded in deriving the desired formula, but we have not succeeded in deriving it from line (1) alone. What should we do? Remember that $\exists$E allows us to swap supposition numerals in appropriate circumstances. So let's apply $\exists$E:

| 1 | 1 | $\forall x (Fx \supset Gx)$ | S |
|---|---|---|---|
| 2 | 2 | $\exists x (Fx \ \& \ {\sim}Gx)$ | S (for RAA) |
| 3 | 3 | $Fa \ \& \ {\sim}Ga$ | S (for $\exists$E) |
| 1 | 4 | $Fa \supset Ga$ | 1 $\forall$E |
| 3 | 5 | $Fa$ | 3 &E |
| 3 | 6 | ${\sim}Ga$ | 3 &E |
| 1,3 | 7 | $Ga$ | 4,5 MPP |
| 1,2,3 | 8 | $Ga \ \& \ \exists x (Fx \ \& \ {\sim}Gx)$ | 2,7 &I |
| 1,2,3 | 9 | $Ga$ | 8 &E |
| 1,3 | 10 | ${\sim}\exists x (Fx \ \& \ {\sim}Gx)$ | 2,5,9 RAA |
| 1,2 | 11 | ${\sim}\exists x (Fx \ \& \ {\sim}Gx)$ | 2,3,10 $\exists$E |

$${\sim}\exists x (Fx \ \& \ {\sim}Gx)$$

The restrictions on rule $\exists$E are satisfied: the constant '$a$' does not occur in line (2), line (10), or in any supposition of line (10). But we are still not done, for line (11) follows from lines (1) and (2), not from line (1) alone. Still, the derivation can be completed with one further application of RAA:

| 1 | 1 | $\forall x (Fx \supset Gx)$ | S |
|---|---|---|---|
| 2 | 2 | $\exists x (Fx \ \& \ {\sim}Gx)$ | S (for RAA) |
| 3 | 3 | $Fa \ \& \ {\sim}Ga$ | S (for $\exists$E) |
| 1 | 4 | $Fa \supset Ga$ | 1 $\forall$E |
| 3 | 5 | $Fa$ | 3 &E |
| 3 | 6 | ${\sim}Ga$ | 3 &E |
| 1,3 | 7 | $Ga$ | 4,5 MPP |
| 1,2,3 | 8 | $Ga \ \& \ \exists x (Fx \ \& \ {\sim}Gx)$ | 2,7 &I |
| 1,2,3 | 9 | $Ga$ | 8 &E |
| 1,3 | 10 | ${\sim}\exists x (Fx \ \& \ {\sim}Gx)$ | 2,5,9 RAA |
| 1,2 | 11 | ${\sim}\exists x (Fx \ \& \ {\sim}Gx)$ | 2,3,10 $\exists$E |
| 1 | 12 | ${\sim}\exists x (Fx \ \& \ {\sim}Gx)$ | 2,2,11 RAA |

This derivation illustrates, incidentally, that the last line of a derivation using rule $\exists$E need *not* be an existential generalization. What $\exists$E does require is that there be an existential generalization somewhere in the derivation and an instance of that generalization written in as a supposition. The formula that you derive using rule $\exists$E can be of any type at all.

From the preceding discussion, the following strategy hint should be easy to understand:

☞   If you are given (or have already derived) an existential generalization, introduce an instance of that generalization involving a constant which does not yet occur in the derivation; when you have
derived your desired conclusion from that instance (and perhaps
other formulas), apply ∃E.

## Exercises

1   In each item, derive the last formula from the other(s).

    (a)             ∀x(Fx ⊃ Gx)      (b)         ∀x(Fx ⊃ (Gx & Hx))
                           ∃x~Gx                           ∃xFx
                           ∃x~Fx                          ∃xGx

    (c)        ∀x((Fx v Gx) ⊃ Hx)     (d)         ∀x(Gx ⊃ Fx)
                           ∃x~Hx                 ∃x(Gx & ~Hx)
                           ∃x~Fx                 ∃x(Fx & ~Hx)

    (e)             ∀x∃y∀zFxyz       (f)         ∃x∃y∀zFxyz
                         ∀x∀z∃yFxyz              ∀z∃x∃yFxyz

    (g)          ∀xFx & ∃xGx       (h)        ∀xFx v ∃xGx
                       ∃x(Fx & Gx)               ∃x(Fx v Gx)

2   In each item, derive the second formula from the first.

    (a)             ~∀xFx        (b)          ∃x~Fx
                       ∃x~Fx                  ~∀xFx

    (c)             ~∃xFx       (d)          ∀x~Fx
                       ∀x~Fx                  ~∃xFx

3   In each item, derive the last formula from the others.

    (a)         ∀x(x ≠ a ⊃ Fx)     (b)        ∀x(Hx ≡ Gx)
                          Fa                    ∃x(Hx & Fx)
                         ∀xFx                  ∃x(Gx & Fx)

    (c)                 Fa       (d)             ∃xFx
                        ∃x x ≠ a                  ~∃xGx
       ∀x∀y((Fx & Fy) ⊃ x = y)       ∀x(Fx ⊃ (Gx v Hx))
                       ∃x~Fx                    ∃xHx

# PART IV

## Philosophical Logic

There are some arguments which are formally valid (that is, which possess a form such that all arguments of that form are valid) but whose form in virtue of which they are valid involves details of structure that we have not yet systematically attended to. It is possible to enhance our standard truth-functional and quantificational logics in relatively straightforward ways so that we *can* both represent the deeper form and demonstrate the validity of such arguments. These additions to the systems of logic developed in Parts II and III are somewhat technically complicated and lead to philosophical questions that cannot usefully be neglected. Our goal in this part is to consider several extensions to the logic developed so far and to discuss a few of the deeper, more philosophical issues raised by these additions.

# Chapter 23

## Functors

**1. Complex Logical Subjects**. One kind of argument which is formally valid but whose form involves details of structure which we have not yet considered is that in which the unattended-to details of structure involve complex logical subjects. Consider, for example, the following argument:

> The person who first confessed to the abbé was a murderer.
> _____
> The person who first confessed to someone was a murderer.

This argument is formally valid.[1] And so is the following argument having the same premise and a different conclusion:

> The person who first confessed to the abbé was a murderer.
> _____
> Someone who confessed to the abbé was a murderer.

But we are so far unable to represent the forms of these arguments in such a way as to be able to show that they are formally valid. This is because in both cases the formal validity depends on the presence of complex logical subjects such as 'the first person who confessed to the abbé'. So far we simply have no way of dealing with complex logical subjects.

There are two main ways of dealing with such complexity:

(1)   We may take account only of occurrences of logical subjects within logical subjects—e.g., of the occurrence of 'the abbé' within 'the first person who confessed to the abbé'—and of quantification related to such positions. This approach represents complex logical subjects by so-called *functors* or *operation symbols*.

---

[1] The conclusion here is to be understood as: someone's first confessee was a murderer. There is, of course, another reading, namely: the first person ever to confess was a murderer. But understood this second way, the conclusion obviously does not follow from the premise.

(2) Or, we may take account *also* of the occurrence of logical predicates—e.g., the occurrence of 'confessed' within 'the first person who confessed to the abbé'. This way represents complex logical subjects by so-called *definite descriptions*. This approach is discussed in Chapter 25.

**2. Functors.** We may proceed as follows. On analogy with our way of regarding a statement as resulting from the insertion of logical subjects into numbered slots of a logical predicate, we may regard a complex logical subject as resulting from the insertion of logical subjects into the numbered slots of something called a *functor*. For example, we may regard 'the first person who confessed to the abbé' as resulting from the insertion of 'the abbé' into the slot numbered '1' of the functor:

the first person who confessed to ①

and we may regard 'what the marquis said to the abbé' as resulting from the insertion of 'the marquis' and 'the abbé', respectively, into the 1-numbered and the 2-numbered slots of the functor:

what ① said to ②

A functor is *of degree n* just in case it has $n$ distinct numbered slots. We shall use lower-case English letters '$a$' through '$t$' with the numeral $n$ as *superscript* (and, if necessary, numerical subscripts) to represent functors of degree $n$. Thus we can construct an expanded sort of phrase-book by including functors. For example:

$$A \quad : \quad ① \text{ is awful}$$
$$M \quad : \quad ① \text{ is a murderer}$$
$$S \quad : \quad ① \text{ shocked } ②$$

$$f^1 \quad : \quad \text{the first person who confessed to } ①$$
$$s^2 \quad : \quad \text{what } ① \text{ said to } ②$$

$$a \quad : \quad \text{the abbé}$$
$$m \quad : \quad \text{the marquis}$$

With the added expressive power that this phrase-book gives us, we may now represent statements involving complex logical subjects. For instance:

(a)  The first person who confessed to the abbé was a murderer.

$$Mf^1a$$

(b)   What the marquis said to the abbé was awful.

$$As^2ma$$

(c)   What the first person to confess to the abbé said to the abbé was awful.

$$As^2f^1aa$$

(d)   The abbé was shocked by what the first person to confess to him said to him.

$$Ss^2f^1aaa$$

When we get to statements such as these last two, it can sometimes be rather difficult to see what is being said. To discern the structure of a formula such as (d), we must survey the string of individual constants and functors *from right to left*, paying attention to the superscripts of the functors and finding the logical subjects (which may themselves be complex) which occupy the appropriate slots. Let us call individual constants and the results of replacing the appropriate number of (perhaps complex) logical subjects into the slots of a functor *terms*. Our goal is to isolate the various terms in cases such as (d). We have:

$$S \quad s^2 \quad f^1 \quad a \quad a \quad a$$

The square underlinings indicate the various terms occurring in the formula, and the levels of square underlinings indicate which terms are the "immediate" logical subjects (or "arguments") of which expressions.

As before, positions occupied by logical subjects may also be occupied by variables, and these variables may be bound by quantifiers. Note that quantifiers may be applied only to *whole* statements, never to terms alone. Thus we can represent the first argument at the beginning of this chapter with the two formulas:

$$Mf^1a$$
$$\exists xMf^1x$$

## Exercises

---

1 Represent the logical form of each of the following statements. As usual, if you detect ambiguities in a statement, represent each of the plausible readings of the statement.

    (a) If Alfred is friendly, then his mother is friendly.

    (b) Someone's mother is friendly.

    (c) Everyone's mother is friendly.

    (d) If a person is friendly, then his mother is friendly.

    (e) A person's father is friendly if and only if his mother is not friendly.

    (f) If a person's father is friendly, then his maternal grandmother is friendly.

    (g) If someone is a grandfather, then he is friendly.

    (h) All grandmothers are friendly.

    (i) Only grandmothers are friendly.

2 Represent the logical form of each of the following statements.

    (a) If a number is odd, then its square is odd.

    (b) The sum of any two odd numbers is even.

    (c) The sum of the squares of two odd numbers is even.

    (d) The sum of the three pairwise products of any three odd numbers is not even.

    (e) The product of a number and the number which is the product of a second and third numbers is the same number as the product of the number which is the product of the first and second numbers and the third number.

---

**3. Revised Rules.** To deal with this newly-revealed structure, we must enrich our rules of inference. A standard way of doing this is very simple. We stipulate that the rules SI, L, $\exists$I, and $\forall$E are to be understood as applying not merely to individual constants, but to *any* terms whatsoever, as long as those terms do not contain variables. For example:

$$\Lambda \quad | \quad 1 \quad s^2f^1aa = s^2f^1aa \qquad\qquad \text{SI}$$

$$1,2,4 \mid \quad 5 \quad Mf^1a \text{ \& } Gbf^1a$$

$$7 \mid \quad 11 \quad f^1a = g^2ag^2bc$$

$$1,2,4,7 \mid \quad 15 \quad Mf^1a \text{ \& } Gbg^2ag^2bc \qquad\qquad 5,11 \text{ L}$$

$$1,5 \mid \quad 10 \quad \forall x(Fx \text{ \& } Gf^1x)$$

$$1,5 \mid \quad 14 \quad Ff^1a \text{ \& } Gf^1f^1a \qquad\qquad 10 \ \forall E$$

$$1,5 \mid \quad 14 \quad Ff^1a \text{ \& } Gf^1f^1a \qquad\qquad 10 \ \forall E$$

$$1,5 \mid \quad 17 \quad \exists x(Ff^1x \text{ \& } Gf^1f^1a) \qquad\qquad 14 \ \exists I$$
$$1,5 \mid \quad 18 \quad \exists y\exists x(Ff^1x \text{ \& } Gy) \qquad\qquad 17 \ \exists I$$

Note that the rules $\forall I$ and $\exists E$ remain *unchanged*. They apply, as before, only to *individual constants*. We shall consider in detail why this is so in Section 6 below.

**4. Invalidity.** Of course, not all arguments involving functors are formally valid, so we need to have some way of establishing formal *invalidity*. As before, our preferred method of doing this is to provide a semantical assignment in which the premises (if any) are all true and the conclusion is false. But we need to expand our previous characterization of a semantical assignment, since it does not tell us how to deal with terms involving functors.

Recall that in a semantical assignment, individual constants are always to be assigned some element of the domain. We may now generalize this by requiring that each *term* occurring in a given argument is to be assigned some element of the domain. But we have not yet specified which element of the domain this shall be in the case of terms which are not individual constants. Consider the following semantical assignment:

$$\mathbf{D} \quad - \quad \{1,2,3,4\}$$

$$F \quad - \quad \{1,2,3,4\}$$
$$G \quad - \quad \{<1,2>,<2,2>,<4,3>\}$$

$$a \quad - \quad 1$$
$$b \quad - \quad 3$$

It is easy to see that in this semantical assignment the formula '$Gab$' is *false*, since the ordered couple $<1,3>$ is *not* in the set assigned to the predicate letter '$G$'. But we cannot yet tell, for instance, whether the formula '$Gf^1ab$' is true or false. This is because we do not yet know what object in the domain is to be assigned to the term '$f^1a$'. So we need some way of figuring out what objects are to be assigned to terms containing functors.

Let us restrict our attention for the moment to functors of degree 1. Recall that functors (of any degree) are used in the representation of complex logical subjects. When a functor of degree 1 is prefixed to a term, the resulting string is also a term. Thus a functor of degree 1 is a device for denoting some object on the basis of a relationship that that object holds to some object. In a semantical assignment, then, we must indicate, for each object in the domain, which object bears this relationship to that object. We shall do this as follows. To each functor of degree 1, we shall assign a set of ordered *pairs* satisfying two conditions:

(i)     each element of the domain must occur as the first element of at least one ordered pair in this set;

(ii)    each element of the domain must occur as the first element of at most one ordered pair in this set.

Any set of ordered pairs satisfying both of these conditions may be called a *function* of degree 1. So we may say that in a semantical assignment, we are to assign a function of degree 1 to each functor of degree 1. Accordingly, we might add to the semantical assignment above the following entry:

$$f^1 \quad - \quad \{<1,3>,<2,2>,<3,2>,<4,1>\}$$

The *first* elements in these ordered pairs jointly comprise the domain of the semantical assignment, as required by condition (i) above. And the *second* element in each ordered pair is the object assigned to a term beginning '$f^1$', if the first element in that pair is assigned to the term to which this functor is prefixed. So for instance the object assigned to the term

'$f^1a$' is 3. This is because the term to which the functor is prefixed is '$a$'; in the semantical assignment given above, '$a$' is assigned the number 1. The ordered pair in the set assigned to '$f^1a$' which has 1 as its *first* element also has 3 as its *second* element. So, in the semantical assignment above, with the added specification of the assignment to '$f^1$', the object assigned to the term '$f^1a$' is 3. And the formula '$Gf^1ab$' is false, since the ordered pair <3,3> is not in the set assigned to '$G$'.

Generally there are many functions that might be assigned to the functor '$f^1$'. Some other possibilities are:[2]

$$f^1 \quad - \quad \{<1,3>,<2,4>,<3,2>,<4,2>\}$$
$$f^1 \quad - \quad \{<1,4>,<2,3>,<3,3>,<4,4>\}$$
$$f^1 \quad - \quad \{<1,2>,<2,2>,<3,2>,<4,2>\}$$

It is easy to see that the formula '$Gf^1ab$' is true in the semantical assignment having the second of these three functions as the extension of '$f^1$' and false in the other two.

**5. Higher Degree Functors.** Extending these ideas to functors of degree $n$, for $n \geq 2$, is straightforward. We shall require that each functor of degree $n$ be assigned an $n$-placed *function*. An $n$-placed function is a set of ordered $(n+1)$-tuples satisfying the following two conditions:

(i)   each $n$-tuple of elements of the domain must coincide with the first $n$ elements of at least one ordered $(n+1)$-tuple in this set;

(ii)  each $n$-tuple of elements of the domain must coincide with the first $n$ elements of at most one ordered $(n+1)$-tuple in this set.

As with the simpler case above, these two conditions merely serve to ensure that one and only one element of the domain be assigned to each term occurring in an argument.

For example, suppose that we have a line of reasoning whose logical form can be represented using a functor of degree 2, say $g^2$:

$$\forall x (Fg^2xa \equiv Hx)$$
$$\exists z \exists y Hg^2zy$$
$$\exists x \forall y Hg^2xy$$

---

[2] A function like the third one, which has the same second element in each ordered pair, is often called a *constant* function.

The following assignment shows that the argument having the first two formulas as premises and the last as conclusion is formally invalid:

$$\mathbf{D} \quad - \quad \{1,2\}$$

$$F \quad - \quad \{1\}$$
$$H \quad - \quad \{2\}$$
$$g^2 \quad - \quad \{<1,1,2>,<1,2,1>,<2,1,1>,<2,2,2>\}$$

$$a \quad - \quad 1$$

**6. Caution.** As a final illustration, let us consider why we are *not* allowed to apply the rules ∀I and ∃E to terms which are not individual constants. The reason is one that should be familiar from previous chapters: if we *do* allow these two rules to apply to any terms whatsoever, then the rules will be *unsound*. We may show this by giving a derivation in which the restriction is violated, and then showing that in fact the conclusion in that derivation does not follow from the premises. So, suppose that we did allow rule ∀I to apply to any term. We could then, for instance, construct the following **incorrect** derivation:

| | | | |
|---|---|---|---|
| 1 | 1 | $Ga$ | S |
| 2 | 2 | $\forall x(Gx \supset Gf^1x)$ | S |
| 2 | 3 | $Ga \supset Gf^1a$ | 2 ∀E |
| 1,2 | 4 | $Gf^1a$ | 2,3 MPP |
| 2 | 5 | $Gf^1a \supset Gf^1f^1a$ | 2 ∀E |
| 1,2 | 6 | $Gf^1f^1a$ | 4,5 MPP |
| 1,2 | 7 | $\forall xGf^1x$ | 6 ∀I |

Here we have violated the restriction that rule ∀I *not* be applied to terms which are not individual constants (for we applied it to '$f^1a$'). We may now show that violating this restriction leads to an unsound rule of inference, by showing that the argument with the formulas on lines (1) and (2) as premises and the formula on line (7) as conclusion is formally invalid. The following semantical assignment does this:

$$\mathbf{D} \quad - \quad \{1,2\}$$

$$G \quad - \quad \{1\}$$
$$f^1 \quad - \quad \{<1,1>,<2,2>\}$$

$$a \quad - \quad 1$$

Perhaps a bit more intuitively, we may think of the first formula as representing the statement 'Alfred is generous', and the second formula as representing 'The father of anyone who is generous is also generous'. It clearly does not follow that every father is generous; yet this is what the last formula would represent.

You might think that what has really gone wrong here is not that we have applied rule ∀I to terms which are not individual constants, but that the *spirit* (if not the *letter*) of the original restriction on rule ∀I has been violated. Although strictly speaking the term '$f^1a$' does not occur in the given premises, nonetheless a term *contained within it* (viz., '$a$') does. But the following derivation shows that it is not at all essential that we chose a derivation having this feature:

$$
\begin{array}{cc|cll}
1 & & 1 & \forall x G f^1 x & S \\
1 & & 2 & G f^1 a & 1\ \forall E \\
1 & & 3 & \forall x G x & 2\ \forall I \\
\end{array}
$$

Here once again we have applied rule ∀I to a term which is not an individual constant. And, as before, line (3) does not follow from line (1). So, violating this restriction can lead to unwanted derivations even when the individual constant contained within the term generalized on does *not* occur in the premise(s).

**7. The Need for Functors.** Each time we *add* something like functors to the standard quantificational logic developed in Part III, we should ask ourselves whether the additions are worth the trouble. For in order to allow ourselves to represent a bit more logical form than we could before, we have complicated both our symbolizations and our rules of derivation. So we might wonder whether these changes are really necessary.

In the case of functors, the answer is 'no'. That is to say, we do not *have* to add functors to our system of logic in order to be able to show that certain arguments involving complex logical subjects are or are not valid. This is not particularly easy to prove, but it is true in virtue of the following two facts: (1) functors may be dispensed with in favor of *definite descriptions*; and (2) definite descriptions may be dispensed with in favor of normal quantificational theory together with identity theory. We will see exactly what this means in Chapter 25, but in the meantime you should at least know that functors are a dispensable luxury.

Why have we spent so much time developing the theory of functors? There are two reasons for this. First, the device of function symbols, or functors, allows us to represent the logical form of certain statements in a very natural way. And the changes to our rules of derivation are, all in all, relatively minor and straightforward. Second, this device will prove to be very useful in our discussion of the metatheory of logic (Part V). So it is good that you should get acquainted with the idea beforehand.

## Exercises

---

3    Represent the logical form of each of the following statements.

   (a)  The negation of the negation of something is a negation of something.

   (b)  Some negations follow from their negata.

   (c)  Negations of what is true are not true.

   (d)  A conjunction is true if and only if both of its conjuncts are true.

   (e)  If you have a formula and another (not necessarily distinct), then the conjunction, disjunction, and biconditional of the first and second are formulas.

   (f)  Negations of all formulas are formulas.

   (g)  The conditional of one formula as antecedent and another as consequent is itself a formula.

   (h)  The negation of a true negation is not true.

   (i)  If something follows both from the left disjunct and from the right disjunct of a disjunction, then it follows from the disjunction.

   (j)  The formula consisting of a predicate-letter followed by two individual constants is true if and only if the ordered couple of the thing assigned to the first individual constant and the thing assigned to the second individual constant is a member of the set which is assigned to the predicate letter.

4    Decide, for each of the following 24 formulas, whether it is true or false under the given semantical assignment.

$$
\begin{array}{lll}
\mathbf{D} & - & \{1,2,3\} \\
F & - & \{1,3\} \\
G & - & \{1,3\} \\
f^1 & - & \{<1,1>, <2,3>, <3,2>\} \\
g^1 & - & \{<1,2>, <2,1>, <3,2>\} \\
h^2 & - & \{<1,1,2>, <1,2,1>, <1,3,2>, \\
& & \ \ <2,1,3>, <2,2,2>, <2,3,1>, \\
& & \ \ <3,1,1>, <3,2,2>, <3,3,2>\} \\
a & - & 2 \\
b & - & 3 \\
\end{array}
$$

| | | | |
|---|---|---|---|
| (a) | $\exists x Fg^1 x$ | (b) | $\forall x \exists y h^2 xy \neq x$ |
| (c) | $\exists x Fh^2 xx$ | (d) | $\exists x \forall y (Fx \equiv Gf^1 y)$ |
| (e) | $\exists x h^2 xx = g^1 x$ | (f) | $\exists x \forall y x = y$ |
| (g) | $\sim\exists x h^2 xx = x$ | (h) | $\forall x (Ff^1 x \supset Gx)$ |
| (i) | $\exists x Fh^2 xx$ | (j) | $Fh^2 g^1 f^1 ag^1 b$ |
| (k) | $Gh^2 ab$ | (l) | $\forall x \forall y (Gh^2 xy \equiv Fh^2 xy)$ |
| (m) | $\exists x \exists y Fh^2 xy$ | (n) | $\forall x Gf^1 h^2 xx$ |
| (o) | $\sim\exists x Gf^1 x$ | (p) | $\forall x \forall y h^2 xy = h^2 yx$ |
| (q) | $\forall x \sim Gf^1 x$ | (r) | $\forall x (Fg^1 x \equiv Gf^1 x)$ |
| (s) | $\forall x (x \neq a \supset Ff^1 x)$ | (t) | $\forall x \sim Gh^2 xx$ |
| (u) | $Ff^1 a \equiv Gg^1 b$ | (v) | $\forall x (Gf^1 x \supset Fx)$ |
| (w) | $\forall x Gh^2 xf^1 x$ | (x) | $\forall x Fxx$ |

5   Suppose that the domain of some semantical assignment has three members. How many distinct functions are there which could be assigned to a functor of degree 2? Of degree 3?

6   Show that each of the following argument forms is valid.

| | | | |
|---|---|---|---|
| (a) | $\forall x Fg^1 x$ | (b) | $\forall x (Bf^1 x \supset Bx)$ |
| | $\forall x Fg^1 g^1 x$ | | $\forall x Bf^1 f^1 f^1 x$ |
| | | | $\forall x Bx$ |
| (c) | $\forall x Fx$ | (d) | $\forall x (\exists y\, x = f^1 y \vee \exists z\, x = m^1 z)$ |
| | $\forall x Fg^1 x$ | | $\forall x (Mf^1 x \ \& \ Fm^1 x)$ |
| | | | $\forall x (Mx \vee Fx)$ |
| (e) | $\forall x \forall y Fg^2 xy$ | (f) | $\forall x \forall y (x = f^1 y \equiv y = f^1 x)$ |
| | $\forall x Fg^2 xx$ | | $\forall x Ff^1 x$ |
| | | | $\forall x Fx$ |

(g)          $\exists x Fx$                    (h)          $\forall x (Ax \supset Bx)$
      $\forall x (Fx \supset Gh^2 xx)$                      $\forall x (Bx \supset Bf^1 x)$
             $\exists x Gx$                              $\forall x (Ax \supset Bf^1 f^1 f^1 x)$

(i)       $\forall x \forall y Fxy$              (j)          $\forall x (Ax \supset Bx)$
   $\forall x \forall y \forall z Fg^1 f^2 xy f^2 xg^1 z$          $\forall x (\sim Ax \supset \exists y (By \ \& \ x = f^1 y))$
                                                        $\forall x (Bx \supset Bf^1 x)$
                                                             $\forall x Bx$

(k)       $\forall x \exists y Fg^2 xy$           (l)        $\exists x \forall y \forall z \ x = g^2 yz$
       $\forall x \forall y \ g^2 xy = g^2 yx$              $\forall x \forall y Fg^2 xyg^2 xyg^2 xy$
          $\forall x \exists y Fg^2 yx$                        $\exists x Fg^2 xxxx$

(m)          $\exists x Fg^1 x$                 (n)          $\forall x \forall y Ff^2 xy$
   $\forall x (Fx \supset \forall y (x = g^1 y \supset Gy))$      $\forall x \forall y \ f^2 m^1 xm^1 y = m^1 f^2 xy$
             $\exists x Gx$                                $\forall x \forall y Fm^1 f^2 xy$

(o)       $\forall x \ f^1 x = x$               (p)        $\forall x \forall y \ f^1 x = f^1 y$
        $\forall x \exists y \ x = f^1 y$              $\exists x \forall y (\exists z y = f^1 z \equiv x = y)$

(q)       $\forall x \exists y \ x = f^1 y$         (r)        $\sim \forall x \forall y f^1 x \neq f^1 y$
             $\forall x Ff^1 x$
             $\forall x Fx$

(s)         $\forall x \ x = f^1 x$              (t)        $\forall x \forall y \ f^1 x = f^1 y$
          $\forall x \ x = f^1 f^1 x$                     $\exists x \ x = f^1 f^1 x$

(u)     $\forall x \forall y (x = y \supset f^1 x = f^1 y)$

7    Show that each of the following argument forms is invalid.

(a)          $\forall x Fg^1 x$                 (b)          $\forall x \exists y Fg^2 xy$
             $\forall x Fx$                              $\forall y \exists x Fg^2 xy$

(c)          $\forall x Fg^2 xx$                (d)        $\forall x \forall y \exists z \ z \neq g^2 xy$
          $\forall x \forall y Fg^2 xy$

(e)      $\sim \forall x \forall y \exists z \ z = g^2 xy$    (f)        $\sim \forall x \forall y \exists z \ z \neq g^2 xy$

(g)          $\exists x Fx$                    (h)          $\exists x Fg^1 x$
       $\forall x (Fh^1 x \supset Gx)$            $\forall x (Fg^1 x \supset \forall y (x = g^1 y \supset Gy))$
             $\exists x Gx$                                $\forall x Gx$

(i)       $\exists x \forall y \ x = f^1 y$          (j)        $\sim \exists x \forall y \ x = f^1 y$

(k)     $\forall x \forall y (f^1 x = f^1 y \supset x = y)$    (l)        $\forall x \ x \neq f^1 x$

(m)          $\forall x Bf^1 f^1 f^1 x$            (n)    $\forall x (\exists y x = f^1 y \ v \ \exists z x = m^1 z)$
       $\forall x (Bf^1 f^1 x \supset Bf^1 x)$                $\forall x (Mf^1 x \ v \ Fm^1 x)$

$$\forall x Bx \qquad\qquad\qquad \forall x(Mx \lor Fx)$$

(o)  $\forall x \forall y\ f^2xy = f^2yx$  (p)  $\forall x \forall y\ f^2xy = f^2yx$
     $\exists x\ x = f^2xx$                  $\sim\!\exists x\ x = f^2xx$

(q)  $\forall x \exists y \exists z\ x = f^2yz$  (r)  $\forall x\ f^1x = x$
                                                  $\forall x \forall y\ f^1x = f^1y$

(s)  $\forall x \forall y\ f^2xy = f^2yx$  (t)  $\forall x \forall y\ f^1x \neq f^1y$

8   Suppose that we prohibited the application of rule $\forall$I *only* with regard
    to terms containing either an individual constant *or a functor* occurring
    in the premises.  Would the resulting rule be unsound?

---

# Chapter 24

## Vacuous Logical Subjects

**1. The Problem.** The simple way of dealing with complex logical subjects introduced in the previous chapter involves problems which we must now examine. Consider the following (intuitively true) statement:

(1)    Pegasus is a flying horse.

It is natural to represent this statement with the formula:

(2)    $Hp$ & $Fp$

Now, from this, using rule $\exists$I, we may infer:

(3)    $\exists x (Hx$ & $Fx)$

which seems to be the (intuitively false) statement that there is (was or will be) a flying horse. Thus we are presented with a puzzle. It *seems* that

(a)    the premise is *true*
(b)    the conclusion is *false*
(c)    the argument is *valid*.

But we know that this is impossible. Actually, we are also tacitly exploiting a fourth item that also *seems* to be the case, namely

(d)    statement (1) has a *form* which is correctly represented by formula (2).

The problem has to do with phrases which appear to be logical subjects (let us call such phrases *apparent logical subjects*) but which in fact fail to denote anything (let us call such phrases *vacuous*). The trouble is that there is (or was, or will be) no object, Pegasus, corresponding to the word 'Pegasus'.[1] There are four main ways of dealing with this problem, each of

---

[1] The word 'Pegasus' does not stand for a word or an idea, because words and ideas *do*

which consists in *denying* one of the four items that *seem* to be the case. We may consider these to be options from among which we may choose the one we like best. Each of them is, however, problematic to some degree.

**2. Option I.** Premise (1) is *false*. Why? Well, at the very least, the statement contains a vacuous logical subject. One might try accepting the view that statements which contain vacuous apparent logical subjects are *always false*. This, however, conflicts with the Law of the Excluded Middle, which is provable as a theorem of logic using our rules:

$$(Hp \ \& \ Fp) \ v \ \sim(Hp \ \& \ Fp)$$

We cannot (it seems) count this as true while counting both disjuncts as false (or even merely as not true). One might try accepting the modified thesis that all *atomic* statements (i.e., statements consisting solely of apparent logical subjects and one logical predicate) containing vacuous apparent logical subjects are false, and that all others have truth-values depending on these in the usual way. So we would count '*Fp*' as false and '*~Fp*' as true. But suppose that there is a predicate '*U*' which is "universal" in the sense that it is true of everything, that is, such that we have:

$$\forall x U x$$

If we count '*Up*' as false, then '*~Up*' will be true, and we will be able to infer:

$$\exists x \sim U x$$

which must be false. Indeed, we do have such predicates; self-identity is one of them, for we can prove:

$$\forall x \ \ x = x$$

As a last resort, we might try adopting the thesis that all *atomic* statements with vacuous apparent logical subjects are *false* if their predicates are "non-universal", and *true* otherwise. But this procedure is unsatisfactory, for several reasons. First, it is clearly *ad hoc* and has no better justification than that it helps us out of the problem of vacuous apparent logical subjects. Second, it is highly unintuitive in its assignation of truth-values, since we have to count 'Pegasus is a flying horse' as false, but 'Pegasus is not a flying horse' as true. Third, there seem to be problems

---

exist but are *not* flying horses, whereas Pegasus *is* (supposed to be) a flying horse and does *not* exist.

about which predicates are to classified as "genuinely atomic", as well as difficulties in determining whether a predicate is "universal" or not. Finally, as if this were not enough, there is the following problem. If we consider self-identity statements, whether we consider '$p = p$' as true or false, we are able to derive a falsehood, either '$\exists x\ x = p$' or '$\exists x\ x \neq p$'. So we must at least make the further provision that apparent identity statements involving vacuous apparent logical subjects are not to be regarded as genuine identity statements and are not to be symbolized at all by formulas (so that if '$p$' is used to represent a vacuous logical subject, then '$p = p$', '$p = a$', etc., are *not* formulas).[2] But this last provision is in effect the choice of Option II for the case of apparent identity statements.

**3. Option II.** Statement (1) is not of the form correctly represented by formula (2). Why? We may try adopting the view that only those apparent logical subjects which are *not* vacuous are *genuine* logical subjects, and so that only these are to be represented by individual constants in our system of logic. This is the most frequently adopted solution, probably because it keeps the formal development of logic simple by limiting its application to statements devoid of vacuous apparent logical subjects. But this approach also is problematic, for we may feel that limiting the application of logic is unwelcome. We may also feel that the policy constitutes an unwelcome intrusion of factual knowledge into logic, since to be able to determine the logical form of some statements we would need to know certain facts about which things exist. Thus, it seems that we cannot (without special provisions) always use the standard logical techniques to evaluate reasoning about fictional entities (e.g., characters in literature), or about entities whose existence is controversial or in doubt (such as abstract entities or entities in a scientific theory which has not yet been established). It must be noted, though, that this limitation excludes *only* those lines of reasoning in which apparent *logical subjects* are used to talk about such entities. We are still free to adopt logical *predicates* applying to the controversial entities, for example:

① is a quark

Even so, the treatment of some of these non-excluded reasonings may strike us as unsatisfactory.

**4. Option III.** The conclusion is true. Why? We might try accepting the thesis that we should distinguish between saying 'Something is $F$' and saying 'There is (or, exists) an $F$'. In such a case, we can truly affirm that

---

[2] Note that if we allowed '$p \neq a$' (to avoid inferring $\exists x\ p = x$'), we might still have to infer '$\exists x (Fx\ \&\ x \neq a)$', even though $a$ might be the *only* thing which in fact is $F$.

something is a flying horse (namely, Pegasus), while truly denying that there is a flying horse (for Pegasus does not exist). And '∃xFx' is to be understood as representing 'Something is F' rather than 'There is an F'. To represent the latter statement, we would need to use the additional predicate:

$$A \; : \; \text{①} \text{ is actual (or existent)}$$

in which case the statement is represented as:

$$\exists x (Ax \; \& \; Fx)$$

This carries with it a systematic complication in symbolization, illustrated as follows:

| | |
|---|---|
| No horses fly. | $\forall x (Ax \supset (Hx \supset {\sim}Fx))$ |
| San Francisco is a city. | $Cs \; \& \; As$ |
| There are cities. | $\exists x (Cx \; \& \; Ax)$ |

But of course we can eliminate this complication in discourse *solely* about actual entities by specifying the sense of the quantifiers in a way with which we are already familiar:

$$\forall \exists :: \; \text{①} \text{ is actual}$$

We should note that Options I, II, and III do not require any modifications in our rules of inference. Options II and III involve modifications in how we symbolize, the former by prohibiting the symbolization of certain statements, the latter by requiring the use of the predicate 'A' in most cases (or a specification of the sense of the quantifiers). Option I may be regarded either as a non-intuitive assignation of truth-values, or as a prohibition on symbolization in some cases (if, for example, we insist on regarding 'Pegasus flies' as *true*).[3] Option IV requires a modification of the rules, but no modification in how we symbolize.

**5. Option IV.** The argument is not valid. Why? We may try to accept the view that logical subjects may be vacuous and that an existential

---

[3] Note that we could get by in this case if we chose:

$$F : \; \text{①} \text{ does not fly}$$

but this wouldn't work if in the same line of reasoning we wanted to be able to regard 'Zeus does not fly' as *true*.

generalization is tantamount to saying that there *is* (or *exists*) such-and-such. In consequence of this, the inference from a statement containing a logical subject to an appropriately related existential generalization requires a *further* given line to the effect that the logical subject is not vacuous. We may pick the formula:

$$\exists x \; x = a$$

to represent the statement that Alfred exists, if '*a*' is the constant we have chosen to represent 'Alfred'. Thus the rule $\exists$I is modified accordingly. For example:

| | | | |
|---|---|---|---|
| 1,2,5 | 13 | *Fab* & *Gba* | |
| 1,3 | 14 | $\exists x \; x = a$ | |
| 1,6 | 15 | $\exists x \; x = b$ | |
| 1,2,3,5 | 16 | $\exists u(Fub \; \& \; Gba)$ | 13,14 $\exists$I(FL) |
| 1,2,3,5,6 | 17 | $\exists v \exists u(Fuv \; \& \; Gva)$ | 16,15 $\exists$I(FL) |

And reflecting on rule $\forall$E shows that it too is best modified in the same way. For example:

| | | | |
|---|---|---|---|
| 1 | 5 | $\forall x \forall y Fxy$ | |
| 2 | 6 | $\exists x \; x = c$ | |
| 1,2 | 7 | $\forall y Fcy$ | 5,6 $\forall$E(FL) |
| 1,2 | 8 | *Fcc* | 7,6 $\forall$E(FL) |

The annotation '(FL)' is a reminder of the modification of the rules; the system of rules with these new versions of $\exists$I and $\forall$E is called *free logic* (because the individual constants are free of any existential import). The other rules remain unchanged.

**6. Application to functors.** If we attempt to represent complex (apparent) logical subjects as functors, we shall admit a large (indeed infinite) collection of terms which fail to denote. For example, '$f^1 m$' is supposed to represent 'the first person who confessed to the marquis', but it will fail to denote something if no one ever confesses to the marquis, or if two (or more) people confess to the marquis simultaneously before anyone else does. As a result, each of the infinite collection of terms '$f^1 f^1 m$', '$f^1 f^1 f^1 m$', etc., as well as others such as '$g^1 f^1 m$', will fail to denote. Furthermore, a term with a variable in it, such as '$f^1 x$', will denote for some values of '*x*' and will fail to denote for others. So we are faced with the problem of what truth-value the formula '$M f^1 x$' has for values of '*x*' for which the term '$f^1 x$' fails to denote. Since we can prove the formula:

$$\forall x(Mf^1x \lor \sim Mf^1x)$$

as a theorem, we must suppose that for every value of '$x$' either the left disjunct of the embedded disjunction or the right disjunct must be true. And this is the same problem as that of 'Pegasus is a flying horse' all over again. To get around this difficulty, we may adopt one of the four options discussed earlier.

**Exercises**

---

1 It is interesting to observe that neither under Option III nor under Option IV can the existence of something be derived as a theorem. Can you figure out a way to prove either of these facts?

---

# Chapter 25

# Definite Descriptions

**1. Complex Logical Subjects Reconsidered.** In light of the problems we have uncovered regarding the introduction of functors, we might be tempted to try another way of getting at the logical form of statements involving complex logical subjects, that of *definite descriptions.* This way of dealing with complex (apparent) logical subjects may be regarded as starting with the observation that at least in many cases (and with special provisions, perhaps in most or even all cases) a complex (apparent) logical subject can be regarded as tantamount to:

the object such that $\cdots$ it $\cdots$

or:

the object $x$ such that $\cdots x \cdots$

where what is represented by the dots is a *statement-like* expression containing (perhaps several occurrences of) a pronoun or variable. For example:

what the marquis said to the abbé and the latter repeated to all he knew

is tantamount to:

the object $x$ such that the marquis said $x$ to the abbé and the abbé repeated $x$ to all he knew

Since all the complexity of the complex (apparent) logical subject is reflected in the statement-like expression (which henceforth we shall call the *description-proper* of the complex logical subject in question), the resources for representing complex statements with which we are already familiar suffice for representing complex logical subjects. This means that we do not need to expand our phrase-books, as we did in the case of functors. But we do need a new symbol to represent the phrase:

the object $x$ such that

For this, let us use variable-binding prefixes such as '$\iota x$' (a Greek iota followed by a variable). And let us use expressions of the form:

$$\iota x [ \cdots x \cdots ]$$

to represent phrases of the form 'the $x$' occurring in logical-subject positions.[1] Thus, given the phrase-book:

$$
\begin{array}{rl}
P : & \text{①  is a person} \\
S : & \text{①  said  ②  to  ③} \\
R : & \text{①  repeated  ②  to  ③} \\
K : & \text{①  knew  ②} \\
m : & \text{the marquis} \\
a : & \text{the abbé}
\end{array}
$$

we may represent the example above as:

$$\iota z [Smza \ \& \ \forall x (Px \supset (Kax \supset Razx))]$$

And, if we add to our phrase-book the logical predicates:

$$
\begin{array}{rl}
A : & \text{①  is an abbé} \\
S : & \text{①  was shocked}
\end{array}
$$

we may represent the complex logical subject:

the abbé who repeated to the marquis what some person told him

with the expression:

$$\iota x [Ax \ \& \ Rx \iota y [\exists z (Pz \ \& \ Szyx)]m]$$

Occasionally there are problems in representing definite descriptions in this way. We might on reflection see that 'the abbé' should be regarded as "complex", on the grounds that we want to be able to infer from:

---

[1] Here we depart from our standing rule for parentheses in requiring that "descriptions-proper" be *always* enclosed in square brackets to avoid ambiguities such as '$G\iota xFxa$'. Would this say that $\iota xFxa$ is $G$, or that $\iota xFx$ is $G$ to $a$? The square brackets remove this ambiguity. Another way to remove the ambiguity would be to require that a predicate letter *always* be written with a superscript indicating its degree.

the abbé was shocked

to:

some abbé was shocked

But we can hardly represent 'the abbé' as '$\iota x[Ax]$'. The reason is that there may be more than one abbé, even if there is not more than one abbé in question. A rough-and-ready solution is to introduce into the phrase-book the predicate:

$$Q \ : \quad ① \text{ is in question}$$

so that the argument becomes:

$$S\iota x[Ax \ \& \ Qx]$$
$$\exists x(Ax \ \& \ Sx)$$

which we *will* be able to show to be valid once we introduce several new inference rules.

**Exercises**

---

1   Represent each of the following *complex logical subjects* using the phrase-book provided:

$$
\begin{array}{ll}
B \ : & ① \text{ is a book} \\
I \ : & ① \text{ intrigued } ② \\
L \ : & ① \text{ loaned } ② \text{ to } ③ \\
P \ : & ① \text{ is a person} \\
R \ : & ① \text{ read } ② \\
W \ : & ① \text{ wrote } ② \\
\\
a \ : & \text{Alfred} \\
b \ : & \text{Bertha} \\
c \ : & \text{Conan Doyle}
\end{array}
$$

(a) the book that Conan Doyle wrote

(b) the book that intrigued Alfred

(c) the book that intrigued Alfred and that he loaned to Bertha

(d) the person who wrote the book that Alfred read

(e) the book that intrigued the person who loaned it to Alfred

(f) the person who wrote the book that intrigued the person who loaned it to Alfred

2 Using the same phrase-book, represent the logical form of each of the following *statements*.

(a) Alfred loaned Bertha the book that intrigued him.

(b) If the book that Alfred loaned Bertha was written by Conan Doyle, then Bertha read the book that Alfred loaned her.

(c) Conan Doyle wrote the book that intrigued Alfred and that he loaned to Bertha.

(d) No one loaned Alfred the book that Bertha was loaned and read.

(e) Conan Doyle was the person who wrote the book that intrigued the person who loaned it to Alfred.

---

**2. Uniqueness.** Let us now consider how our rules of derivation may be adapted to deal with formulas containing definite descriptions in *logical subject* positions. Two rules suggest themselves as obvious enough and we shall adopt them as additional rules of inference. On a certain hypothesis (to be discussed), adding these two rules and extending our previous rules to the new formulas suffice to exhibit as formally valid all formally valid arguments involving definite descriptions in logical-subject positions (of the forms so far recognized). But extending our previous rules to the new formulas, in the presence of the two new rules, generates certain difficulties. The hypothesis just mentioned provides one means of explaining and solving these difficulties. The solution is to put certain *restrictions* on some of our previous rules when we extend them to the new formulas.

An alternative approach leads to regarding definite descriptions as occupying quantifier-like positions. Here, too, the two new rules (suitably altered) suffice to show formal validity, and no restrictions on the previous rules are necessary. The two approaches can be, and are here, combined. Each seems to be appropriate for certain cases.

The first of these two rules depends on the fact that, roughly speaking, in every possible case it is true that *the F thing is G* only if there is such a thing as *the F thing* (i.e., *there is exactly one thing which is F*) and *that thing is G*, whatever *F* and *G* may be. So the first rule will sanction inferences from such statements as:

$$\text{the } F \text{ thing is } G$$

to such statements as:

there is exactly one thing which is $F$ and it is $G$

The second rule depends on the fact that, conversely, in every possible situation if it is true that *there is exactly one F thing and that F thing is G*, it is also true that *the F thing is G*. So the second rule will sanction inferences from such statements as:

there is exactly one $F$ thing and that $F$ thing is $G$

to statements such as:

the $F$ thing is $G$

We now have to consider how to represent statements such as:

there is exactly one thing which is $F$ and it is $G$

We must capture both that something is both $F$ and $G$ and that exactly one thing is $F$, that is (so to speak), the something that is both $F$ and $G$ is *the only* thing which is $F$. A concise way is:

something is both $F$ *uniquely* and also $G$

that is:

$$\exists x(x \text{ is } F \text{ uniquely } \& Gx)$$

How shall we represent the fact that $x$ is $F$ *uniquely*? Here is a compact way:

$$\forall y(Fy \equiv y = x)$$

For ("looking from left to right") this ensures that whatever is $F$ is identical with $x$. So there are *no* things *other* than $x$ that are $F$. But also ("looking from right to left") whatever is identical with $x$ is $F$. So $x$ (which is identical with $x$) is $F$. In short, $x$ is $F$ and nothing other than $x$ is $F$. That is, $x$ is $F$ *uniquely*. So the compact representation of 'exactly one thing is $F$ and it is also $G$' is:

$$\exists x(\forall y(Fy \equiv y = x) \& Gx)$$

We want now to remove our talk of $F$ and $G$, thus allowing a totally general expression of definite descriptions. As a transitional example, consider the statement:

there is exactly one thing which is both $A$ and $B$, and it is either $R$ to something or $S$ to everything.

A representation of the logical form of such a statement is this:

$$\exists x (\forall y ((Ay \ \& \ By) \equiv y = x) \ \& \ (\exists z Rxz \ v \ \forall u Sxu))$$

It may be useful for fixing the pattern in mind to consider a sort of "diagram":

$$\exists x (\forall y (\ \cdots \ y \ \cdots \ \equiv y = x) \ \& \ \text{---} x \ \text{---})$$

Employing this sort of diagram, we can exhibit the general pattern of the first rule as follows.  Given:

$$\exists x (\forall y (\ \cdots \ y \ \cdots \ \equiv y = x) \ \& \ \text{---} x \ \text{---})$$

Infer:

$$\text{---} \iota x [\ \cdots \ x \ \cdots \ ] \text{---}$$

And we can exhibit the general pattern of the second rule thus.  Given:

$$\text{---} \iota x [\ \cdots \ x \ \cdots \ ] \text{---}$$

Infer:

$$\exists x (\forall y (\ \cdots \ y \ \cdots \ \equiv y = x) \ \& \ \text{---} x \ \text{---})$$

Note that the dots play the role of the '$F$' in our earlier discussion and the dashes the role of the '$G$'.

3. **Russellian Expansions**.  To be able to state these rules with complete precision (but without too much cumbersomeness), we need some technical terminology.  We have noted that a definite description will have the pattern:

$$\iota x [\ \cdots \ x \ \cdots \ ]$$

That is, a definite description will consist of the Greek letter iota followed by a variable, followed by a formula enclosed in square brackets (the formula containing one or more occurrences of the variable that follows the iota).[2]  We call the formula which is enclosed in square brackets the

---

[2] We add the requirement that none of the occurrences of this variable *within* this formula is to be within a quantifier expression or following an iota. For example, the strings of symbols:

*description-proper* of the definite description in question. The variable following the iota is the *variable of the definite description*, or the *definite description's variable*. A definite description is *closed* when every occurrence within it of every variable is part of an occurrence within it of either a universal or an existential generalization with respect to that variable, or is a definite description whose variable that variable is.[3] We shall say that a formula is a *uniqueness clause* of a closed definite description when that definite description and the formula exhibit the following pattern:

$$\iota x[\ \cdots\ x\ \cdots\ ]$$

$$\forall y(\ \cdots\ y\ \cdots\ \equiv y = x)$$

*provided* that the new variable ('*y*' in this case) does not occur in the definite description. Note that the new variable *replaces* the variable of the definite description in the description-proper, and the two variables combine in the identity formula.

More precisely, a formula is a *uniqueness clause* of a definite description if and only if the definite description is closed and the formula is a universal generalization (with respect to some variable not occurring in the definite description) of a biconditional (a) whose left side is the result of replacing in the description-proper all occurrences of the variable of the definite description by the first-mentioned variable (adding outermost parentheses if the description-proper is binary), and (b) whose right side is an identity formula containing the two variables.

$$\iota x[\exists xFx]$$
$$\iota x[Fx\ \&\ \forall xGx]$$
$$\iota x[Hx\iota x[Gx]]$$

are *not* definite descriptions. But the following are definite descriptions:

$$\iota x[Fx\ \&\ \forall yGy]$$
$$\iota x[Hx\iota y[Gy]]$$

[3] Thus, for example, the strings:

$$\iota x[Fx]$$
$$\iota x[Fx\ \&\ \exists yGy]$$
$$\iota x[\exists y(Fy\ \&\ Gxy]$$
$$\iota x[\forall yHxy]$$
$$\iota x[H\iota y[Fya]x]$$

are closed, but the following are not:

$$\iota x[Fxy]$$
$$\iota x[Fxy\ \&\ \exists yGy]$$
$$\iota x[\exists y(Fy\ \&\ Gxyz]$$
$$\iota x[\forall yHxy\ \&\ Gy]$$
$$\iota x[H\iota y[Fyz]x]$$

We are now ready to describe a relationship between formulas in terms of which we can concisely state the two rules. Let us say that a formula is a *Russellian expansion* of another formula when the former bears to the latter a relationship whose pattern is suggested by the following diagram:

$$\exists x (\forall y ( \cdots y \cdots \equiv y = x) \ \& \ \text{---}\, x\, \text{---})$$

$$\text{---}\, \iota x [ \cdots x \cdots ]\,\text{---}$$

*provided* that the description is closed.[4] Loosely speaking:

(1)    a uniqueness clause of some closed definite description occurring in the original formula has been taken as the left conjunct

(2)    the definite description has been replaced at all occurrences[5] in the original formula by the variable of the definite description, and the result has been taken as the right conjunct

(3)    the existential generalization with respect to the variable of the definite description has been formed of the conjunction.

More precisely: a formula is a *Russellian expansion* of a second if and only if, for some *closed* definite description occurring in the second formula, the first formula is an existential generalization with respect to the variable of that definite description of a conjunction (a) whose left conjunct is a uniqueness clause of the definite description, and (b) whose right conjunct is the result of replacing all occurrences of the definite description in the second formula by the definite description's variable (adding outermost parentheses, if the second formula is binary).

---

[4] The importance of the definite description's being *closed* can be seen if we attempt to form a Russellian expansion of a formula with respect to a definite description which is not closed:

$$\forall y F \iota x [Gxy]$$

$$\exists x (\forall z (Gzy \equiv z = x) \ \& \ \forall y Fx)$$

While the former represents a complete sentence, capable of being true or false, the latter does not, since the first occurrence of '$y$' lacks a "cross-reference" to a quantifier expression (or an iota expression) containing that variable.

[5] To avoid misunderstanding, we require that two occurrences count as occurrences of the same definite description only if they are alike in *all* their symbols, *including* the variable of the definite description. So the formula:

$$F \iota x [Gx] \iota u [Gu]$$

does *not* contain two occurrences of one definite description but, rather, one occurrence of each of two different definite descriptions.

**4. Two New Rules.** We can now state the two rules. The first is called 'DDI' (for Definite Description Introduction):

---

DDI      Given a Russellian expansion of a formula, infer that formula. As supposition numerals of the inferred line, take all those of the given line.

---

Examples of the application of rule DDI:

$$
\begin{array}{ll|ll}
1,2 & & 5 & \exists u (\forall w (Fw \equiv w = u) \,\&\, Gu) \\
1,2 & & 6 & G\iota u [Fu] \qquad\qquad\qquad\qquad\qquad\qquad\qquad 5\ \text{DDI}
\end{array}
$$

$$
\begin{array}{ll|ll}
9 & & 9 & \exists x (\forall z (Gz \iota y [Hy] \equiv z = x) \,\&\, Fx) \qquad\qquad \text{S}\\
9 & & 10 & F\iota x [Gx \iota y [Hy]] \qquad\qquad\qquad\qquad\qquad\qquad 9\ \text{DDI}
\end{array}
$$

$$
\begin{array}{ll|ll}
1 & & 7 & \exists y (\forall z (Hy \equiv z = y) \,\&\, F\iota x [Gxy]) \\
1 & & 8 & F\iota x [Gx \iota y [Hy]] \qquad\qquad\qquad\qquad\qquad\qquad 7\ \text{DDI}
\end{array}
$$

The second rule is called 'DDE' (for Definite Description Elimination):

---

DDE      Given a formula, infer a Russellian expansion of that formula (if there is one). As supposition numerals of the inferred line, take all those of the given line.

---

Examples of the application of rule DDE:

$$
\begin{array}{ll|ll}
2,6 & & 11 & G\iota x [Fx] \supset H\iota x [Fx] \\
2,6 & & 12 & \exists x (\forall y (Fy \equiv x = y) \,\&\, (Gx \supset Hx)) \qquad 11\ \text{DDE}
\end{array}
$$

$$\begin{array}{ll} 1,3,6 & \quad 9 \quad \exists uG\iota x[Fx]\iota w[Fw]u \\ 1,3,6 & \quad 10 \quad \exists w(\forall v(Fv \equiv v = w) \ \& \ \exists uG\iota x[Fx]wu) \qquad \text{9 DDE} \end{array}$$

$$\begin{array}{ll} 2,3 & \quad 7 \quad F\iota x[G\iota y[Hy]x] \\ 2,3 & \quad 8 \quad \exists y(\forall z(Hz \equiv z = y) \ \& \ F\iota x[Gyx]) \qquad \text{7 DDE}^7 \end{array}$$

$$\begin{array}{ll} 2,3 & \quad 7 \quad F\iota x[G\iota y[Hy]x] \\ 2,3 & \quad 8 \quad \exists x(\forall z(G\iota y[Hy]z \equiv z = x) \ \& \ Fx) \\ 2,3 & \quad 9 \quad \exists y(\forall u(Hu \equiv u = y) \ \& \ \exists x(\forall z(Gyz \equiv z = x) \ \& \ Fx)) \end{array}$$

## Exercises

3   These last two examples should suggest a strategic moral. What is it?

4   Give a Russellian expansion of each of the following formulas:

(a) $S\iota x[Ax \ \& \ Bx]$

(b) $La\iota x[Bx \ \& \ Ixa]b$

(c) $\exists v(Bv \ \& \ Lav\iota z[\sim Fz])$

(d) $\forall xF\iota z[Gbz] \supset H\iota y[Gbx]$

5   Construct a derivation from the first formula to the second:

$$S\iota x[Ax \ \& \ Qx]$$
$$\exists x(Ax \ \& \ Sx)$$

6   Show that the following argument is valid:

There is at least one king of France.
There is at most one king of France.
Everything which is a king of France is bald.

The king of France is bald.

---

⁷ Notice that rule DDE cannot be applied to line (8), because '$\iota x[Gyx]$' is not closed. Line (8) *has no* Russellian expansion.

7    Conversely, show that each of the premises of the argument in the pre-
     vious exercise follows from the conclusion alone. (You will need to pro-
     vide three derivations to do this.)

---

**5. Problems With Previous Rules.** We should now consider extending our
previous (basic) rules to apply to definite descriptions in logical subject
positions. At first, one might be tempted simply to allow definite descriptions in logical subject positions to be treated in the same way in which
we have so far treated individual constants, the first representation of logical subjects we adopted. The complications we considered with regard to
vacuous logical subjects (both with respect to individual constants and
with respect to functors) should, however, lead us to exercise caution.
Indeed, the inference from:

$$\forall x Gx$$

to:

$$G\iota y[Fy]$$

already seems wrong; there may not be anything which is $F$, or there may
be more than one thing which is $F$. In either case, there is no such thing
as *the thing which is F*, and so it doesn't seem true that the $F$ is $G$ (even
if everything is $G$).

But we have a worse difficulty on our hands! If we adopt the two new
rules and extend just the *truth-functional* rules to allow inferences involving these new formulas, we can produce a "derivation" from:

$$\sim\exists x (\forall y (Fy \equiv y = x) \,\&\, Gx)$$

to:

$$\sim G\iota x[Fx]$$

and thence to:

$$\exists x (\forall y (Fy \equiv y = x) \,\&\, \sim Gx)$$

which is patently invalid reasoning. For, surely, from the fact that *there
isn't* anything which is both $F$ uniquely and $G$, it doesn't follow that *there
is* something which is both $F$ uniquely and *not G*!

**Exercises**

---

8    Construct the "derivation" mentioned just above. Then construct a
semantical assignment to show that that line of reasoning is in fact formally invalid.

---

**6. An Explanation**. What has gone wrong? An explanation is forthcom-
ing on a hypothesis championed by the philosopher and logician Sir Peter
Strawson. In extending our truth-functional rules unamended to formulas
containing definite descriptions in logical subject positions, we have, in
effect, assumed that what is represented by these formulas is either true or
false in every possible case. This has led us to regard, for instance,

$$G \iota x[Fx]$$

as *false* in every possible case in which it *isn't true* that both there is
exactly one thing which is $F$ and this thing is $G$. That is, we regard this
formula as false not only in a case in which there is exactly one thing
which is $F$ and that thing is not $G$, but also in a case in which there isn't
exactly one thing which is $F$ at all. This is tantamount to counting the
formula:

$$\sim G \iota x[Fx]$$

as true when:

$$\exists x(\forall y(Fy \equiv y = x) \ \& \ \sim Gx)$$

is true, *and* when:

$$\sim \exists x(\forall y(Fy \equiv y = x) \ \& \ Gx)$$

is true. This would do no harm if the formula:

$$\sim G \iota x[Fx]$$

could be viewed as the *disjunction* of the two cases. But taking '$\iota x[Fx]$' to
be *in a logical subject position* forces us to regard this formula as having
the logical predicate:

$$\sim G \text{①}$$

and so as tantamount to, and true in *just* those cases in which:

$$\exists x(\forall y(Fy \equiv y = x) \,\&\, {\sim}Gx)$$

is true. Thus a conflict arises between our truth-functional rules and our new rules. The former rules treat:

$$\sim G\iota x[Fx]$$

as if it were true in those cases in which *one or the other* of the formulas:

$$\exists x(\forall y(Fy \equiv y = x) \,\&\, {\sim}Gx)$$
$$\sim\exists x(\forall y(Fy \equiv y = x) \,\&\, Gx)$$

is true, while our new rules treat it as if it were true in *just* the cases in which:

$$\exists x(\forall y(Fy \equiv y = x) \,\&\, {\sim}Gx)$$

is true.

One may feel that what is at fault is our *new* rules. But they are correct enough, as long as we adhere to the view that the definite descriptions with which they deal occur in *logical subject positions*. To consider alternatives to the new rules is to consider definite descriptions as *not* occupying logical subject positions. One suggestion is to consider them as occurring in quantifier-like positions. We shall investigate this option shortly.

If we stick to our new rules, we see that they carry with them an assumption that formulas (or sentences) containing definite descriptions in logical subject positions are *neither true nor false* in certain possible cases. This can be seen as follows. According to the new rules,

$$G\iota x[Fx]$$

is true just in those cases in which:

$$\exists x(\forall y(Fy \equiv y = x) \,\&\, Gx)$$

is true, and:

$$\sim G\iota x[Fx]$$

is true in just those cases in which:

$$\exists x(\forall y(Fy \equiv y = x) \,\&\, {\sim}Gx)$$

is true. But there are possible cases in which neither of these two longer formulas is true. So there are possible cases in which neither of the two shorter formulas is true. But we regard one of them as the *negation* of the other! Further, as long as we hold that a negation is false if and only if its negatum is true (and *vice versa*), we must conclude that in those possible cases, neither of the shorter formulas is false either.

This is precisely the hypothesis championed by Strawson with respect to ordinary expressions which we represent by definite descriptions in logical subject positions. When such expressions are vacuous, the sentences containing them do not express statements which have a truth-value.

7. **Restricting the Previous Rules**. Let us now consider how our previously-adopted rules of inference may be adapted to deal with formulas containing definite descriptions in *logical-subject positions*. The following proposal is believed (by us) to be very close to mirroring the logical behavior of complex logical subjects in ordinary language and thinking. We shall explain the proposal partly in full generality and partly by illustration.

(1)  The "supposition-reducing" (or complex) rules CP, $\equiv$I, and RAA, and the rule $\vee$I are modified as follows: we impose the *restriction* that a formula may be inferred by one of these rules only if for *every* definite description:

$$\iota x\,[\,\cdots\,x\,\cdots\,]$$

occurring in the *inferred* line, there is a *given* line of the form:

$$\exists y\ y = \iota x[\,\cdots\,x\,\cdots\,]$$

all of whose suppositions are among the suppositions of the inferred line.

(2)  Rule SI is modified to include the provision that a line of the form:

$$\iota x[\,\cdots\,x\,\cdots\,] = \iota x[\,\cdots\,x\,\cdots\,]$$

may be inferred only from a *given* line of the form:

$$\exists y\ y = \iota x[\,\cdots\,x\,\cdots\,]$$

(the *inferred* line having the supposition numerals of the *given* line).

(3)  Rule $\forall$E is modified as illustrated to require an additional *given* line; given:

$$\forall x ( \cdots x \cdots )$$

and:

$$\exists u \; u = \iota y [\text{---} y \text{---}]$$

you may infer:

$$\cdots \iota y [\text{---} y \text{---}] \cdots$$

For example:

$$
\begin{array}{lll}
3 \mid & 4 & \exists x \; x = \iota y [Fya] \\
\\
1,2 \mid & 7 & \forall x (Px \supset Gx) \\
\\
1,2,3 \mid & 9 & P\iota y [Fya] \supset G\iota y [Fya] \qquad\qquad 4,7 \; \forall E^*
\end{array}
$$

where the asterisk is used to indicate that a *modified* version of the rule is being invoked.

(4)   Rule $\exists$I is *expanded* to allow for replacement of a definite description by a variable.  For example:

$$
\begin{array}{lll}
1 \mid & 3 & G\iota x [Fxa]\iota x [Fxa] \\
1 \mid & 4 & \exists y Gy\iota x [Fxa] \qquad\qquad 3 \; \exists I^*
\end{array}
$$

(5)   The other rules remain unaltered, except of course that they may be applied to formulas containing definite descriptions.  This is not, however, to be understood as allowing the use of a definite description in the place of a variable in applying rules $\forall$I or $\exists$E.

**8.  Three More New Rules.**  The two rules that we have adopted so far allow us to introduce or eliminate a definite description in the appropriate circumstances, and our revised rules allow us to treat a definite description as we treat almost any logical subject.  We now add three further rules, designed to exploit the special properties of definite descriptions:

SR          Given a line of the form:

$$--- \iota x[\cdots x \cdots]---$$

Infer the line of the form:

$$\exists u\ u = \iota x[\cdots x \cdots]$$

As supposition numerals of the inferred line, take all those of the given line.

For example:

$$
\begin{array}{lll}
\phantom{1,2}\ \vdots & \phantom{5}\ \vdots \\
1,2 & 5 & Sm\,\iota x[Ax\ \&\ Qx] \\
1,2 & 6 & \exists y\ y = \iota x[Ax\ \&\ Qx] \qquad\qquad 5\ \text{SR} \\
\phantom{1,2}\ \vdots & \phantom{5}\ \vdots
\end{array}
$$

$\exists$D          Given a line of the form:

$$\exists y\ y = \iota x[\cdots x \cdots]$$

Infer the line of the form:

$$\exists u\, \forall v(\cdots v \cdots \ \equiv u = v)$$

And *vice versa*. As supposition numerals of the inferred line, take all those of the given line.

For example:

$$
\begin{array}{lll}
\phantom{1,3}\ \vdots & \phantom{8}\ \vdots \\
1,3 & 8 & \exists y\ y = \iota x[Ax\ \&\ Qx] \\
1,3 & 9 & \exists y\, \forall x((Ax\ \&\ Qx) \equiv x = y) \qquad 8\ \exists\text{D} \\
\phantom{1,3}\ \vdots & \phantom{8}\ \vdots
\end{array}
$$

$$
\begin{array}{lll}
\phantom{1,3}\ \vdots & \phantom{8}\ \vdots \\
1,3 & 8 & \exists y\, \forall x((Ax\ \&\ Qx) \equiv x = y) \\
1,3 & 9 & \exists y\ y = \iota x[Ax\ \&\ Qx] \qquad\qquad 8\ \exists\text{D}
\end{array}
$$

As illustrated in these examples, parentheses may have to be added or dropped according to our standing rule for parentheses.

---

$\forall$D      Given a line of the form:

$$--- \iota x[ \cdots x \cdots ]---$$

Infer the line of the form:

$$\forall x( \cdots x \cdots \supset ---x---)$$

As supposition numerals of the inferred line, take all those of the given line.

---

For example:

$$
\begin{array}{c}
\vdots \qquad \vdots \\
4 \mid \quad 12 \quad G\iota x[Qx \ \& \ Ax] \ \& \ Hm\iota x[Qx \ \& \ Ax] \\
\vdots \qquad \vdots \\
4 \mid \quad 15 \quad \forall x((Qx \ \& \ Ax) \supset (Gx \ \& \ Hm\iota x[Qx \ \& \ Ax])) \quad 12 \ \forall D \\
\vdots \qquad \vdots
\end{array}
$$

*Derived* quantificational rules, if any have been adopted, must not be used in this connection, since the modifications which we have introduced carry over only in various complicated ways to them.

**9. An Alternative Approach.** The above proposal is intended for cases in which statements containing a definite description "presuppose" the existence of the object denoted by the definite description. For cases in which there is no such "presupposition", we introduce a different way of symbolizing. For example, in:

If John has any children, then the eldest is a musician

it is plausible that the entire *conditional* does *not* "presuppose" the existence of John's eldest child, though the *consequent* does. To represent this, we use definite descriptions *in quantifier-like positions*:

$$\exists x Cxj \supset \iota y[Eyj]{:}z \ Mz$$

And for such constructions we add the rule:

---

RR          Either of the two following formulas may be inferred from the
            other:

$$\iota y [ \cdots y \cdots ]{:}x (---x---)$$

$$\exists x (\forall y ((\cdots y \cdots) \equiv x = y) \& ---x---)$$

As supposition numerals of the inferred line, take all those of
the given line.

---

For example:

$$
\begin{array}{llll}
\vdots & \vdots & & \\
1,2 \mid & 3 & \iota u [Au \& Qu]{:}x\ Smx & \\
\vdots & \vdots & & \\
1,2 \mid & 8 & \exists x (\forall u ((Au \& Qu) \equiv u = x) \& Smx) & \quad 3\ RR \\
\vdots & \vdots & &
\end{array}
$$

**10. Rule SDD.** Finally, we could achieve the same effect by taking over
our rules for predicate logic with identity and simply *prohibiting* their use
(other than for rule S) in connection with any formula containing a
definite description in *logical-subject position*, and *adding* rule RR and
the rule:

---

SDD         Either of the two following formulas may be inferred from the
            other:

$$\iota x [ \cdots x \cdots ]{:}y (---y---)$$

$$---\iota x [ \cdots x \cdots ]---$$

As supposition numerals of the inferred line, take all those of
the given line.

---

**11. Definite Descriptions and Functors.** Neither functors nor the definite
description operator are absolutely necessary for our project of classifying
lines of reasoning as valid or invalid. It is easy to see that we can
dispense with functors in favor of definite descriptions. For, suppose we
were inclined to introduce a functor in the representation of some

statement.  For instance:

The present king of France is bald

Instead of adding the following functor to our phrase-book:

$$k^1 : \quad \text{the present king of } ①$$

and representing the logical form as:

$$Bk^1f$$

we could represent the statement in question as:

$$B \iota x [Kxf]$$

Further, we know that this formula is equivalent to any one of its Russellian expansions, for instance:

$$\exists x (\forall y (Kyf \equiv x = y) \ \& \ Bx)$$

So this purely quantificational formula can be taken as a representation of the logical form of the statement, 'the present king of France is bald'. So, apparently, we could get by without all the recent revision of our rules of derivation, and without either functors or the definite description operator.

**Exercises**

9    Construct a derivation from the first formula to the second:

$$\exists x (\forall y (Kyf \equiv x = y) \ \& \ Bx)$$
$$\exists x (Kxf \ \& \ Bx) \equiv {\sim}\exists x (Kxf \ \& \ {\sim}Bx)$$

# PART V

## Metalogic

So far, our aim has been to develop various systems of logic and to use them to determine the logical properties of statements and arguments. Now our goal is to study these systems more methodically and abstractly. We do this by giving precise definitions of the fundamental notions involved in these systems. This will make clear exactly what a system of logic is; it will also help reveal the relationships among different systems of logic and highlight what would be involved in developing other systems of logic. Furthermore, characterizing systems of logic precisely enables us to prove certain facts about them.

# Chapter 26

## Syntax

**1. Metalogic and Metavariables.** We have developed a variety of logical "tools" (such as formulas, semantical assignments, and derivations) and we have used these tools to establish, for example, that one formula follows from another, or that a set of formulas is consistent. In Part V, we turn our attention to these tools, characterize them precisely, and study their abstract properties. This endeavor is called *metalogic*.

Proofs in metalogic need themselves to be easily recognizable as (formally) valid or not (formally) valid. So it is convenient to exhibit their form as much as possible in stating the proofs. The forms exhibited are in fact those that have been studied: those of quantificational logic with identity and functors. We exhibit these forms by using certain symbols as variables, others as functors. For ease of reading, logical predicates tend to be left in ordinary English.

Because the statements and proofs in metalogic are (in part) *about* symbols (formulas, etc.), it is important to distinguish symbols being talked about (said to be *mentioned*) from the symbols used to talk about them (said to be *used*). When we mention a symbol or string of symbols, we will either set the symbol(s) off from the text by displaying it, e.g.:

$$\&$$

or, in the text, we will use the *quotation-name* of the symbol (or string of symbols), e.g.: '&'. Furthermore, Greek letters are used as variables in metalogic (metavariables) and the symbols '∼', '&', '⊃', 'v', and '≡' are used as symbols for the functors 'the negation of ...', 'the conjunction of ... and ...', and so forth—except that these symbols carry no superscripts and, when binary, are written *between* the arguments of the functors rather than in front of them. For example, consider the claim, here stated in English, that from any conjunction, either conjunct follows. We could state this claim more explicitly, thus:

for any two statements, the conjunction of one with the other implies the first and implies the second.

Using the techniques studied up through Part IV, we may construct the following phrase-book:

$$\forall\exists \;::\quad \textcircled{1} \text{ is a statement}$$
$$I \;:\quad \textcircled{1} \text{ implies } \textcircled{2}$$
$$c^2 \;:\quad \text{the conjunction of } \textcircled{1} \text{ and } \textcircled{2}$$

and exhibit the form of this statement as:

$$\forall x \,\forall y \,(Ic^2xyx \;\&\; Ic^2xyy)$$

When doing metalogic, we would write this statement as:[1]

$$\phi \;\&\; \psi \text{ implies } \phi, \text{ and } \phi \;\&\; \psi \text{ implies } \psi$$

It is customary to interpret the functors '&', etc., *purely syntactically*.[2] On this interpretation, what is meant (e.g.) by:

$$\phi \;\&\; \psi$$

is just this:

the result of writing $\phi$ followed by '&' followed by $\psi$

Remember that the Greek letters here are *variables*. Or, in writing a string of metavariables, such as this:

$$\theta\alpha_1\alpha_2 \cdots \alpha_n$$

---

[1] Actually, as we shall see at the end of this chapter, this statement is written slightly differently, as follows: $*\phi \;\&\; *\psi$ implies $\phi$, and $*\phi \;\&\; *\psi$ implies $\psi$. The '*' notation is explained later.

[2] In light of this, we can view this symbolization as involving just *one* "invisible" functor meaning 'the result of writing $\phi$ followed by $\psi$'. If we make this functor visible by prepending an underlined space, then '$\phi \;\&\; \psi$' could be rendered as: $\_\_\phi \;\&\; \psi$, or as: $\_\phi\_ \;\&\; \psi$ (which denote the same thing).

Incidentally, it is possible to interpret the syntactic functors '&', '≡', etc., more abstractly, in such a way that $\phi \;\&\; \psi$ is the conjunction of $\phi$ and $\psi$ *irrespective* of what symbols are used to represent this conjunction, i.e., no matter how conjunctions are rendered orthographically. We will follow the less abstract and more perspicuous route.

we mean the corresponding string of symbols:[3]

> the result of writing $\theta$ followed by $\alpha_1$ followed by $\alpha_2$ $\cdots$ followed by $\alpha_n$

**2. Primitive Symbols in Formulas.** Our first main goal is to define the syntactic notion of a formula. We shall define what a formula is in terms of the components out of which formulas are composed. This involves two stages, really. First, we shall delimit the primitive symbols out of which formulas can be constructed; we do this by giving definitions of various expressions ('is a logical constant', 'is a primitive symbol', etc.) which apply to the selected symbols. These primitive symbols can be viewed as the vocabulary of a special language that we use to abbreviate statements. Next, we will specify which combinations of those primitive symbols count as formulas. This can be viewed as a formulation of the rules of "grammar" for the language.

The list of primitive types of symbols in formulas is short:

$\phi$ is a *logical constant* iff[4] $\phi$ is one of the following symbols:

$$\sim \qquad \& \qquad \vee \qquad \supset \qquad \equiv \qquad = \qquad \forall \qquad \exists \qquad ( \qquad )$$

$\phi$ is a *propositional constant* iff $\phi$ is an English capital letter with or without a numerical subscript. Examples: $A$, $B$, $P$, $Q$, $Z$, $A_1$, $B_1$, $Z_1$, $A_{17}$, $H_{334}$. *Not* examples: $A^{31}$, $A'$, $W_4^{22}$, $A_{IV}$, $a$, $b$, $z$, $\alpha$, $\alpha_7$, $\phi$, $\Gamma$, $*\phi$, $\phi^{\alpha/\beta}$.

$\phi$ is a *predicate constant* iff $\phi$ is an English capital letter with or without a numerical subscript.[5] Examples: the same as for propositional constants.

---

[3] We make one exception to this policy in those cases in which $\theta$ is what we call a *general predicate (in symbolism) of degree n.* See below.

[4] We shall henceforth occasionally use the abbreviation 'iff' to stand for 'if and only if'.

[5] Note that $\phi$ is a predicate constant iff $\phi$ is a propositional constant. It is customary to refer to the number of logical constants that immediately follow the predicate constant in atomic sentences formed using that predicate as the *degree* of the predicate. Logicians usually adopt the official policy of indicating the degree of a predicate constant with a *superscript* of some sort; in this way, predicate constants are usually distinguished from propositional constants (because propositional constants have no degree-indicating superscript). However, logicians customarily also follow the practice of omitting those degree-indicating subscripts when predicate constants are used in formulas. We have chosen to let our own official policy square with the customary practice, so our predicate constants have no degree-indicating superscripts. No syntactic ambiguity results from omitting these superscripts because, in any context in which a predicate constant is used, the degree of the predicate constant is simply the number of individual symbols that immediately follow it. In the next chapter we point out that no *semantic* ambiguity arises from our policy.

$\phi$ is an *individual constant* iff $\phi$ is an English lower-case letter from '$a$' to '$t$', with or without a numerical subscript. Examples: $a$, $b$, $c$, $r$, $s$, $t$, $a_1$, $t_1$, $a_{48}$. *Not* examples: $u$, $v$, $y$, $z$, $A$, $a'$, $a^6$, $\alpha$, $\beta$.

$\phi$ is an *individual variable* iff $\phi$ is an English lower-case letter from '$u$' to '$z$', with or without a numerical subscript.[6] Examples: $u$, $v$, $y$, $z$, $u_1$, $v_1$, $u_{39}$. *Not* examples: $a$, $b$, $t$, $U$, $V$, $u'$, $u^1$, $\alpha$, $\omega$.

Now we can define what it means, in general, to be a primitive symbol:

$\phi$ is an *individual symbol* iff $\phi$ is either an individual constant or an individual variable.

$\phi$ is a *constant* iff $\phi$ is either a logical constant, a propositional constant, a predicate constant, or an individual constant.

$\phi$ is a *primitive symbol* iff $\phi$ is either a constant or an individual variable.

The following diagram illustrates these relationships:

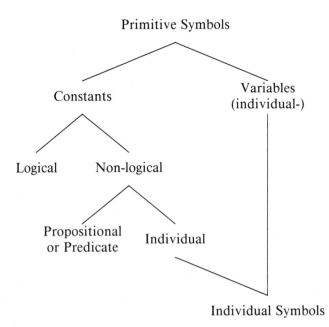

<hr />

    [6] In this book we are concerned only with individual variables, so we will sometimes refer to these simply as variables.

## Exercises

1  Which of the following are propositional constants? Predicate constants? Individual constants? Individual variables? Which are individual symbols, and which are constants? Are any logical constants?

$\Lambda_{12}$ $\quad$ $V_6$ $\quad$ $z_{32}^{10}$ $\quad$ $P_{10}$ $\quad$ $t_{12}$ $\quad$ $\beta_{12}$ $\quad$ $\equiv$ $\quad$ $Q_3^{13}$ $\quad$ ( $\quad$ $N$ $\quad$ $q_{14235}$

2  In each of the following parts, make your examples as different from one another as possible.

(a) Give two examples of two kinds of individual symbols.

(b) Give four examples of constants.

3  Following the example set in the text, define: $\phi$ is a non-logical constant.

4  Suppose the list of definitions in the previous section were to include the following two definitions:

$\phi$ is a *super-propositional constant* iff $\phi$ is an English capital letter with *both* a numerical subscript *and* a numerical superscript.

$\phi$ is a *super-individual variable* iff $\phi$ is an English lower-case letter from '$u$' to '$z$', with *both* a numerical subscript *and* a numerical superscript.

(a) Give five examples of super-propositional constants, and five examples of super-individual variables.

(b) Provide a new definition of *individual symbol* so that the definition applies to super-individual variables as well as all the previous types of individual symbols. Also provide a new definition of *constant* which covers super-propositional constants as well as all the previous types of constants.

5  The primitive symbols described in this chapter include all those that occur in the formulas studied up through Part III. In Part IV, however, additional primitive symbols are used.

(a) Describe in detail how the specifications of primitive symbols given in this chapter would have to be modified in order to include formulas containing functors.

(b) Explain what would be involved in doing the same for formulas containing definite descriptions in logical subject positions.

6  Since the expanded English alphabet contains infinitely many propositional constants, there are an infinite number of different propositional constants out of which formulas can be composed. Our definition of the expression '$\phi$ is a propositional constant' made reference to *numerical subscripts* without defining what numerical subscripts are. A numerical subscript is a subscript that is a numeral. It is possible to give a

purely syntactic and finite definition of what it means to be a subscript. However, is it possible to give a *purely syntactic* and *finite* definition of: $\phi$ is a numeral? (One can define a numeral as a symbol used to *stand for* a number—that is, one can define it in terms of its semantic function. But a definition in terms of semantic function is not a purely syntactic definition; it is not given in terms of purely geometric shapes and patterns. One can give a purely syntactic definition of a numeral by listing them all. However, the list would be infinite.)

---

**3. Compositional Definition.** Many of the notions that we seek to define in metalogic have an *infinite* number of ever *more complex* instances. For example, there are an infinite number of ever longer formulas and derivations. If we tried to define these types of items by *listing* all of their instances, the definition would be infinitely long. Still, these types of items can be characterized in a finite definition by referring to their *composition*, because the items are composed out of a precise list of primitive items by a precise series of methods. Definitions of this kind are called *compositional*. The main focus of this chapter is to define what it means to be a formula using a compositional definition of this type.

A compositional definition of a type of item has three stages. First, the primitive items are characterized (perhaps by listing them, if they are finite in number); this is the *basis* of the definition. Second, each method by which compound items can be composed out of component items is characterized; this stage of the definition is the *induction*. Third, anything not satisfying the basis or the induction is explicitly excluded from the type; this is the definition's *restriction*.

Seeing some examples should clarify these ideas. To simplify our examples, we will first explicitly define what it means to be a digit:

$\alpha$ is a *digit* iff ($\alpha$ = '0' v $\alpha$ = '1' v $\cdots$ v $\alpha$ = '9')

Now, consider *finite strings of digits*, that is, any string of symbols in the following series of strings:

0, 1, 2, $\cdots$ 9, 00, 01, $\cdots$ 99, 000, 001, $\cdots$ 999, $\cdots$

We will give a compositional definition of what it means to be a finite string of digits. We describe each primitive finite string of digits, and each way in which compound strings are composed out of component strings. The definition consists of three stages: the basis, induction, and restriction given below.

BASIS If $\alpha$ is a digit, then $\alpha$ is a *finite string of digits*.

INDUCTION

> If $\alpha$ is a *digit* and $\beta$ is a *finite string of digits*, then $\alpha\beta$ is a *finite string of digits* (i.e., the result of writing $\alpha$ followed by $\beta$ is a finite string of digits).

RESTRICTION

> Nothing else is a *finite string of digits*.

Notice first that the basis is just a list of all the primitive finite strings of digits. All finite strings of digits that are composed out of other finite strings of digits are covered in the induction of the definition.

Second, notice that the expression being defined ('finite string of digits') occurs in the basis of the definition. This might make the definition look circular or self-defeating, but this threat is only apparent. The basis simply allows us to recognize certain instances of the term being defined.

Third, the induction part of the definition consists of a conditional, both the consequent and the antecedent of which contain the expression 'finite string of digits'. In the consequent, the use of this expression does not threaten circularity any more than it did in the basis. However, using this expression in the antecedent of the induction is another matter. Here the threat is more realistic, because the induction part of the definition makes no sense, and is of no use, without some prior understanding of what it means to be a finite string of digits. The induction states that, *if* one thing is a digit and a second is a finite string of digits, *then* the result of writing the one next to the other is a finite string of digits. Before one can apply this conditional, one must *first* be able to recognize some finite strings of digits. The basis allows us to do just this. The induction then allows us to recognize more finite strings of digits, so there are more finite strings of digits to which the induction applies again. The basis and the induction serve to define what it means to be a finite string of digits because *each finite string of digits will eventually be generated by some finite number of applications of the basis and the induction,* and *nothing that is not a finite string of digits will ever be generated.*

Consider any string of symbols $\sigma$ about which both the basis and the induction are "silent", that is, any string $\sigma$ that is not generated in some finite number of applications of the basis and the induction. Notice that neither the basis nor the induction *restrict* $\sigma$ from being a finite string of symbols. To ensure that the definition excludes strings of symbols like $\sigma$, we must add the restriction to the definition.[7]

---

[7] The exact formulation of the restriction seems to raise a philosophical question, for it appears to require surprisingly substantial ontological presuppositions. Formulations of the

As compositional definitions go, the definition of finite string of digits is extremely simple. Still, it illustrates many of the characteristic features of compositional definitions. There is one special feature of some compositional definitions that the definition of a finite string of digits does *not* illustrate: the feature of being a *simultaneous* compositional definition of more than one expression. A simultaneous compositional definition is just what you would expect: two (or more) expressions are defined compositionally with a shared basis, induction, and restriction. The basis part of the definition contains instances of *each* of the expressions being defined, and the conditionals in the inductive part of the definition can contain either expression in both their antecedents and their consequents. The main definition in the next section is a simultaneous compositional definition of the expressions 'unary formula' and 'binary formula'.

There is a different but closely related type of compositional definition that we will encounter in metalogic. We seek to characterize certain notions that *apply to* types of items that have an infinite number of ever more complex instances. For example, being true and being derivable are notions that apply to an infinite number of ever more complex sentences. In this case, a compositional definition of the notion refers to the composition of the items to which the notion applies. First, one explains how the notion applies to primitive items of the type (the *basis* step). Then, one explains how the notion applies to items composed in each of the permissible ways out of components of the type (the *induction* step). The next chapter contains many examples of this second type of compositional definition.

An example should make this second kind of compositional definition clearer. We will define a notion that applies to finite strings of digits. This example is just an illustration of a form of compositional definition, so we will fabricate a notion (which we will express by the term 'balanced') that applies to finite strings of digits. The following compositional definition captures what it means for a finite string of digits to be balanced.

If *f* is a finite string of digits, then:

BASIS

---

restriction fall into two basic types: (1) explicitly referring to the other parts of the definition, in which case a hierarchy of languages is required, or (2) taking the set-theoretic intersection of all those sets that satisfy the basis and the induction, in which case the ontology of set theory is required. This sort of issue is explored in the philosophy of logic. (In practice, the restriction is usually left implicit, and in this book we usually do this, too.)

if $f$ is a digit, then $f$ is *balanced* iff $f$ is not '0';

INDUCTION

if $f$ is $\alpha\beta$, for some digit $\alpha$ and some finite string of digits $\beta$, then $f$ is *balanced* iff either $\alpha$ is not '0' and $\beta$ is *balanced*, or $\alpha$ is '0' and $\beta$ is not *balanced*.

RESTRICTION

No other finite strings of digits are *balanced*.

Using this definition, we can begin classifying finite strings of digits into those that are balanced and those that are not. Here is the beginning of one classification:

Balanced: 1, 00, 100, 101000, 0000, $\cdots$

Not Balanced: 0, 10, 1000, 000, 101, $\cdots$

The four points noted about the first form of compositional definition apply equally to this second form of compositional definition.

## Exercises

---

7    In the following exercises, modify the definition of finite string of digits so that certain other finite strings of digits are defined.

(a) The definition of finite string of digits counts any string of digits preceded by a string of '0's as a finite string of digits, including '0000431' and '00000'. Give a compositional definition of finite string of digits that *excludes* these strings of digits preceded by strings of zeros (but allows the digit '0'), and includes everything else included by the definition in the text. These strings are *Arabic numerals for non-negative whole numbers, without commas or any other punctuation.*

(b) In the previous exercise, the notion of being an Arabic numeral for a non-negative whole number (without commas or any other punctuation) was defined. Modify the definition from the previous exercise so that it includes numerals for negative numbers (and otherwise includes exactly what the previous definition includes). These strings are *Arabic numerals for whole numbers, without commas or any other punctuation.*

(c) Modify the definition from the previous exercise so that it *requires* the strings to have the standard punctuation for Arabic numerals; i.e., a comma must separate the hundreds from the thousands, the hundred thousands from the millions, etc. These strings are *Arabic numerals for whole numbers.*

(d) Modify the definition from the previous exercise so that it includes numerals for fractions (written with a numerator and a denominator). These strings are *Arabic numerals.*

---

**4. Formulas.** We can now specify exactly which combinations of primitive symbols are formulas. First we define two specific types of formulas, unary formulas and binary formulas. Then we define a formula as something which is either a unary formula or a binary formula.

Unary formula and binary formula are defined together in a simultaneous compositional definition. In fact, these two notions *must* be defined simultaneously. For convenience, at the same time we also define three familiar types of formulas: atomic, molecular, and general.

BASIS

If $\phi$ is a propositional constant, then $\phi$ is a *unary formula* (and *atomic*).

If $\phi$ is $\theta\alpha_1...\alpha_n$, where $\theta$ is some predicate constant and $\alpha_1, \ldots, \alpha_n$ are $n$ individual symbols, for some positive number $n$, then $\phi$ is a *unary formula* (and *atomic*).

If $\phi$ is $\alpha = \beta$, for some individual symbols $\alpha$ and $\beta$ (not necessarily distinct), then $\phi$ is a *unary formula* (and *atomic*).

INDUCTION

If $\phi$ is a unary formula, then $\sim\phi$ is a *unary formula* (and *molecular*).

If $\phi$ is a binary formula, then $\sim(\phi)$ is a *unary formula* (and *molecular*).

If $\phi$ and $\psi$ are unary formulas, then $\phi \mathbin{\&} \psi$, $\phi \vee \psi$, $\phi \supset \psi$, and $\phi \equiv \psi$ are *binary formulas* (and *molecular*).

If $\phi$ is a binary formula and $\psi$ is a unary formula, then $(\phi) \mathbin{\&} \psi$, $(\phi) \vee \psi$, $(\phi) \supset \psi$, $(\phi) \equiv \psi$, $\psi \mathbin{\&} (\phi)$, $\psi \vee (\phi)$, $\psi \supset (\phi)$, and $\psi \equiv (\phi)$ are *binary formulas* (and *molecular*).

If $\phi$ and $\psi$ are both binary formulas, then $(\phi) \mathbin{\&} (\psi)$, $(\phi) \vee (\psi)$, $(\phi) \supset (\psi)$, and $(\phi) \equiv (\psi)$ are *binary formulas* (and *molecular*).

If $\phi$ is a unary formula in which the variable $\alpha$ occurs but neither $\forall\alpha$ nor $\exists\alpha$ occurs, then $\forall\alpha\phi$ and $\exists\alpha\phi$ are *unary formulas* (and *general*).

If $\phi$ is a binary formula in which the variable $\alpha$ occurs but in which neither $\forall\alpha$ nor $\exists\alpha$ occurs, then $\forall\alpha(\phi)$ and $\exists\alpha(\phi)$ are *unary formulas* (and *general*).

Much of the complexity of the induction of this definition is to ensure that parentheses surround all binary component formulas. In the next section, we introduce a notation that allows us to avoid this sort of complexity in the future.

In terms of the notions of a unary formula and a binary formula, it is easy to define what it means to be a formula, in general.

$\phi$ is a *formula* iff $\phi$ is either a unary formula or a binary formula.[8]

The following diagram represents the relationships between these various types of formulas.

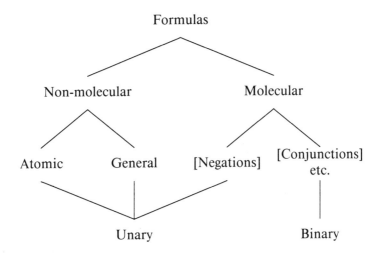

**Exercises**

8   Which of the following strings of symbols are formulas, and which are not? For those that are not, describe *each* reason why they are not.

(a)  ≡

(b)  ∀($P ≡ Q_7$)

(c)  $P ≡ Q$ & $R$

---

[8] We could just as well define a formula as either an atomic formula, a molecular formula, or a general formula.

(d)  $\sim P$ & $Q$

(e)  $(\sim P)$ and $Q$

(f)  $\Lambda = (\forall x Fx \supset Fa)$

(g)  $Tu_{12}n_{13}t_3$

(h)  $(\exists x)(Fx$ & $Gx)$

(i)  $(\exists x)(Fy$ & $Gy)$

9   Which of the following formulas are unary, and which are binary? Which are atomic, which molecular, and which general?

(a)  $Lxz$ & $Iy$

(b)  $Bxypqz$

(c)  $\exists y(By$ & $Dyy)$

(d)  $Y_{12}$

(e)  $\forall x Px \supset \exists y(Py \supset Lsy)$

(f)  $x = a$

(g)  $\sim((\sim A \lor \sim B) \equiv \sim(A$ & $B))$

(h)  $\sim(P \supset Q) \equiv \sim(Q \supset P)$

10  Consider all those formulas that could be composed by starting with propositional constants (only) and building new formulas using (only) negation or conjunction; one might call these *negation-conjunction* formulas (or *NC* formulas, for short).

(a)  Give three examples of NC formulas, making them as different from each other as possible.

(b)  Give a compositional definition of: $\phi$ is an NC formula. (Hint: devise a simultaneous compositional definition of unary NC formula and binary NC formula. Pattern your definition after the one given in the text.)

11  The definition of formula given in the text can be modified to produce definitions of various other types of formulas.

(a)  In Part II we represented *only* the propositional form of statements; it would be natural to call such formulas *propositional formulas*. Construct a precise and complete definition of: $\phi$ is a propositional formula. Do this by producing a simultaneous compositional definition of unary *propositional* formula and binary *propositional* formula.

(b)  In Chapters 14-16, we did not represent the quantificational form of statements. We represented only logical subjects and predicates, identity, and propositional form. It would be natural to call such formulas *identity-logic formulas*. By giving a simultaneous compositional definition of unary identity-logic formula and binary identity-logic formula, construct a precise and complete definition of: $\phi$ is an identity-logic formula.

12  How would the definition of a formula have to be modified in order to allow formulas that contain:

(a)  functors?

(b)  vacuous logical subjects?

(c)  definite descriptions?

---

**5. Sentences and Other Syntactic Types.** With the notion of a formula defined, we can now define a few other syntactic types. First, there is a very convenient syntactic type that appears repeatedly in Part V. One can see the value of this syntactic type by considering how one would refer to the conjunction of two arbitrary formulas $\phi$ and $\psi$.[9]

One might think that $\phi$ & $\psi$ is the conjunction of $\phi$ and $\psi$, but in general it is not. If both $\phi$ and $\psi$ are *unary* then $\phi$ & $\psi$ *is* their conjunction. But if one of them is *binary* (or both are), then $\phi$ & $\psi$ is not even a formula. For example, if $\phi$ is '$P \supset Q$' and $\psi$ is '$\sim Q$ v $P$', then $\phi$ & $\psi$ is '$P \supset Q$ & $\sim Q$ v $P$', and this string of symbols is not a formula (it is missing parentheses). Since binary conjuncts must be surrounded by parentheses, one might think that ($\phi$) & ($\psi$) is the conjunction of two arbitrary formulas $\phi$ and $\psi$. But this also does not hold if either $\phi$ or $\psi$ is unary (or both are). For example, if $\phi$ is '$P$' and $\psi$ is '$Q$', then ($\phi$) & ($\psi$) is '($P$) & ($Q$)', and this is not a formula because it contains two sets of "illegal" parentheses.

One way to deal with this predicament is to use an explicitly disjunctive definition such as this: the conjunction of $\phi$ and $\psi$ is, *either* $\phi$ & $\psi$ if $\phi$ and $\psi$ are both unary, *or* $\phi$ & ($\psi$) if $\phi$ is unary and $\psi$ is binary, *or* ($\phi$) & $\psi$ if $\phi$ is binary and $\psi$ is unary, *or* ($\phi$) & ($\psi$) if $\phi$ and $\psi$ are both binary. As one can imagine, using this sort of explicitly disjunctive definition would quickly get quite tedious.

---

[9] Our need for this notation stems from our practice of using in formulas only those parentheses that are absolutely necessary. Many logic books avoid the need for our special notation because they require all molecular formulas to be surrounded with an outermost set of parentheses in all contexts—whether or not the parentheses are superfluous in that context. (In general, this is done to simplify metalogic and metalogical proofs. Usually, while the official definitions in metalogic require these parentheses, the practical expedient of omitting superfluous parentheses is adopted.) Since we believe it is natural not to use superfluous parentheses in logical practice, we have our metalogic match our logical practice. As a result, we (willingly) pay the price of slightly complicating metalogic and metalogical proofs.

One could refer to the conjunction of $\phi$ and $\psi$ much more simply if one had a notation that referred to $\phi$ if $\phi$ is unary and to ($\phi$) if $\phi$ is binary. The following simple definition accomplishes this:

$$*\phi = \begin{cases} \phi & \text{if } \phi \text{ is a unary formula} \\ (\phi) & \text{if } \phi \text{ is a binary formula} \end{cases}$$

Notice that '*' is, in effect, a functor that applies to formulas. Using this functor, it is easy to express the conjunction of two arbitrary formulas $\phi$ and $\psi$, regardless of whether the formulas are unary or binary: $*\phi$ & $*\psi$. The beauty of the '*' functor is that it allows us to talk about compound formulas without having to worry about whether the component formulas are binary and, thus, in need of parentheses. We do not know whether there are any parentheses in $*\phi$ & $*\psi$, but we are sure that it contains parentheses *if and only if* they are needed to make it a formula.

Notice also that $*\phi$ is *undefined* if $\phi$ is *not* a formula, so we must make sure to use '*' only when $\phi$ is a formula;[10] otherwise, we would be using a vacuous logical subject.

We also need to define a notation for describing two formulas that are alike except for all occurrences of a symbol in one being replaced by occurrences of another symbol in the other.

$\phi^{\alpha/\beta}$ = the result of replacing all occurrences of $\alpha$ in $\phi$ by $\beta$.

In other words, $\phi^{\alpha/\beta}$ is just like $\phi$ except that $\phi^{\alpha/\beta}$ contains an occurrence of $\beta$ everywhere that $\phi$ contains an occurrence of $\alpha$. (The $\phi^{\alpha/\beta}$ notation is, in effect, a suggestive way of writing a functor that takes three arguments $\phi$, $\alpha$, and $\beta$.) We will use $\phi^{\alpha/\beta}$ only in cases in which $\alpha$ is an individual variable and $\beta$ is an individual constant.[11] For example, if $\phi$ is 'Fxy & Gxb', $\alpha$ is 'x', and $\beta$ is 'a', then $\phi^{\alpha/\beta}$ is 'Fay & Gab'.

*Sentences* are formulas which have no "dangling", unquantified variables. In order to define what it means to be a sentence, we first define what it

---

[10] $*\phi$ *could* be characterized so that it would be defined even if $\phi$ were not a formula, as follows: $*\phi = (\phi)$ if $\phi$ is a binary formula, and $*\phi = \phi$ if $\phi$ is *not* a binary formula. In this case, all '*' does is put outermost parentheses around binary formulas, and leave everything else unchanged. However, it is not uncommon in metalogic to employ functors that are not defined for all arguments. For example, typically the syntactic negation functor, '~', is defined only for arguments that are formulas (or, at least, strings of symbols).

[11] One could define a more general substitution function that applies to arbitrary symbols $\alpha$ and $\beta$ by slightly altering the definition given in the text: replace '$\beta$' with '$*\beta$' (and to accommodate this, '*' should be defined for symbols besides formulas, as described above).

means to be a "dangling", unquantified variable (which we shall call a *free* variable).

> $\alpha$ is *free* in $\phi$ iff some result of replacing in $\phi$ an occurrence of a formula $\psi$ by $\forall\alpha\psi$ or $\forall\alpha(\psi)$ is a formula.

In other words, $\alpha$ is free in $\phi$ iff $\alpha$ would be bound if the quantifier $\forall\alpha$ (and a pair of parentheses, if needed) were inserted in $\phi$ at the appropriate spot.[12] For example, if $\phi$ is '$\forall x(Fy \supset Lyx)$', '$y$' is free in $\phi$ because there are formulas that are the result of adding a quantifier to $\phi$, such as the formula '$\forall x\forall y(Fy \supset Lyx)$'. Now, we can define what it means to be a formula with no "dangling", unquantified variables.

> $\phi$ is a *sentence* iff $\phi$ is a formula in which no variable is free.

## Exercises

---

13   For each of the following formulas $\phi$, write down the string $*\phi$.

(a)  $P$

(b)  $P \equiv (R \supset Q)$

(c)  $\sim(A \supset (B \supset (A \supset B)))$

(d)  $\forall xAx \supset P$

(e)  $\exists x\exists y((Dx \ \& \ Dy) \supset \forall z((Lzx \ v \ Lzy) \supset \sim Lxy))$

14   The string of symbols '$P \supset Q \ \& \ \sim Q \ v \ P$' is not a formula, because it is missing sets of parentheses. List all the different formulas that can be formed if parentheses are inserted into this string of symbols.

15   '$\forall y(Fy \supset Lyx)$' is not a sentence, because '$x$' is free in it. (It still is a formula, of course.) List all the different sentences that result from inserting the quantifier '$\forall x$' (and, if necessary, a set of parentheses) into '$\forall y(Fy \supset Lyx)$'.

16   Assume that $\phi$ = '$P$' and $\psi$ = '$Q \ v \ R$'. Exactly what formula is $\chi$?

(a)  $\chi = \ *\sim*\phi \ \& \ *\psi$

(b)  $\chi = \ \sim**\phi \ \& \ *\psi$

17   In the text it was pointed out that $*\phi$ and $\phi^{\alpha/\beta}$ are really just suggestive ways of writing functors.

---

[12] Note that $\phi$ may be the same formula as $\psi$. By the way, the quantifier $\exists\alpha$ would work just as well as $\forall\alpha$.

(a) Using only English and circled numerals, express the functor '$\alpha/\beta$'. (Hint: it will be a functor of degree three that takes the arguments $\phi$, $\alpha$, and $\beta$.)

(b) Using only English and circled numerals, express the functor '*'. (Hint: it will be a one-place functor, taking the argument $\phi$.)

18  Using the '*' notation, simplify the definition of: $\alpha$ is free in $\phi$.

19  In Part II we talked about *non-molecular sentences*. In this exercise you will give two different definitions of this notion. (Recall the definition of a sentence.)

(a) Give a non-compositional definition of: $\phi$ is a non-molecular sentence. You may use *only* terms defined in the previous section of the text.

(b) Give a compositional definition of: $\phi$ is a non-molecular sentence. You should use '*' but you cannot use the notions of atomic, molecular, or general sentences.

20  In the following exercises, use '*' to construct definitions of the following syntactic notions.

(a) The idea of the *main connective* of a molecular or general formula is quite natural and useful in metalogic. The following examples illustrate this idea: '&' is the main connective of '$P$ & $Q$'; '$\supset$' is the main connective of '$\exists x(Fx$ & $Gx) \supset \forall y(P \equiv Hyy)$'; '~' is the main connective of '$\sim\exists x(x = a)$'; '$\forall z$' is the main connective of the formula '$\forall z \forall y \exists x Lxyz$'. Give a compositional definition of: $\xi$ is the main connective of $\phi$.

(b) The idea of an *immediate component formula* of a general or molecular formula is quite natural and useful in metalogic. The following examples illustrate this idea. '$P$' is the immediate component formula of '$\sim P$'; '$\sim P$' is the immediate component formula of '$\sim\sim P$'; '$P$' and '$Q$' are the immediate component formulas of '$P$ & $Q$'; finally, '$\forall y \exists x Lxyz$' is the immediate component formula of the formula '$\forall z \forall y \exists x Lxyz$'. Furthermore, no formula is an immediate component formula of itself. Give a compositional definition of: $\psi$ is an immediate component formula of $\phi$.

21  The idea of one formula being a *subformula* of another formula is quite natural and useful in metalogic. Intuitively, $\psi$ is a subformula of $\phi$ just in case $\psi$ is one of the formulas out of which $\phi$ is composed; i.e., either $\psi$ is an immediate component formula of $\phi$, or $\psi$ is an immediate component formula of an immediate component formula of $\phi$, or $\psi$ is an immediate component formula of an immediate component formula of an immediate component formula of $\phi$, etc. Furthermore, no formula is a subformula of itself. Give a compositional definition of: $\psi$ is a subformula of $\phi$. You should use the notion (defined in the previous exercise) of an immediate component formula. You should not need to use '*'.

22  The idea of an *instantiation* of a quantified formula is quite natural and useful in metalogic. An instantiation of a general formula is a formula that results by removing the outermost quantifier (the main connective) and its associated variable (and, if necessary, a set of parentheses), and replacing each occurrence of the variable that was quantified by the quantifier by some constant; the same constant must replace each of the variables made free by the removal of the quantifier. Using the '$\alpha/\beta$' notation and '*', give a definition of: $\phi$ is an instantiation of $\psi$.

23  The stages in the definition of formula would be much simplified if the '*' notation were used. However, the '*' notation is defined in terms of the distinction between unary and binary formulas, so it would be circular to use the '*' notation in the definition of unary and binary formula. Is it possible to avoid this circularity and define '*' without using the notions of a formula (in general), a unary formula, or a binary formula?

# Chapter 27

# Semantics

**1. Introduction.** Throughout this book we have used a variety of semantic notions. In this chapter, we will explain these in detail. Our primary goal is to define what it means for a sentence to be true with respect to a semantical structure (such as a truth-value assignment or a semantical assignment).[1] Once we have done this, it is straightforward to define other important semantic notions.

We have focussed on three semantic structures: truth-value assignments, truncated semantical assignments, and (full) semantical assignments. These three semantic structures are used as *precise simulations* of the intuitive notion of "possible case" or "possible situation" which we have been using all along in logic. For example, intuitively a sentence $\phi$ follows from a set $\Gamma$ of sentences just in case

> there is no *possible situation* in which all the sentences in $\Gamma$ are true and $\phi$ is not true.

Now, using semantical assignments, we construe this intuitive remark as:

> there is no *semantical assignment* in which all the sentences in $\Gamma$ are true and $\phi$ is not true.

There are two advantages of using these precise semantic simulations: the notion of truth relative to a precise simulation is itself quite explicit and precise, and thinking in terms of precise simulations helps us to focus on only the logically significant features of possible situations.

---

[1] We should emphasize that we define truth only in a *relative* sense: we define truth *with respect to* (or *in*) certain semantical structures. Whether there is a non-relative account of sentence truth, and what such a non-relative account could be—these questions are left to be addressed in the philosophy of logic.

In this chapter we will characterize these three semantic structures. Along the way we will also illustrate how simpler semantic structures are modified and extended to form more complex structures. Through the exercises, we aim to teach the reader how to define many different sorts of semantic structures.

**2. Set-Theoretic Semantics.** It is quite natural to regard semantical structures as sets, and it is in part because of set theory that metalogic enjoys a high degree of precision. Accordingly, a brief and highly selective review of elementary set theory is in order. A set is a collection of objects, said to be the *members* of the set. We indicate that some object $x$ is a member of some set $s$ by writing:

$$x \in s$$

The members of a set may be any kinds of objects at all, so they might well be sets themselves, or sets of sets, or sets of sets of sets, and so on *ad infinitum*. Two sets are identical if and only if they have exactly the same members. This is called the *Principle of Extensionality,* and it can be represented formally as follows: for any sets $x$ and $y$,

$$x = y \; \textit{iff} \; \forall z (z \in x \equiv z \in y)$$

A standard way of referring to the set whose members are the objects $o_1, o_2, \ldots, o_n$, for some number $n$, is to list its members within braces (curly brackets):

$$\{o_1, o_2, \ldots, o_n\}$$

When using this *brace notation*, the order in which the members of a set are listed is immaterial, so:

$$\{o_1, o_2\} = \{o_2, o_1\}$$

and, in general:

$$\{o_1, \cdots, o_n\} = \{o_1, \cdots, o_{n-2}, o_n, o_{n-1}\} = \cdots = \{o_n, o_{n-1}, \cdots, o_1\}$$

Also, the number of times a member is listed is immaterial, so $\{o\} = \{o, o\} = \{o, o, o\}$, etc. All of these facts about the brace notation follow from the Principle of Extensionality.

There is a special set with *no* members, the *empty set* (or the *null set*). We have already introduced the symbol '$\Lambda$' to designate this set; using the brace notation, it is designated by '$\{\}$'.

A set containing a single member $x$ is the *unit* set of $x$. For example, the unit set of the null set is $\{\Lambda\}$, that is, $\{\{\}\}$. The set consisting of all the objects that are members of *either* the set $s_1$ *or* the set $s_2$ is the *union* of $s_1$ and $s_2$, and we designate this set as '$s_1 \cup s_2$'. In other words,

$$x \in s_1 \cup s_2 \textit{ iff } (x \in s_1 \lor x \in s_2)$$

In semantics we will talk about ordered $n$-tuples. As we have seen, an ordered $n$-tuple whose members are the objects (in the order) $o_1, o_2, \ldots, o_n$ is designated by writing its members within angle brackets *in the order given*, like this:

$$<o_1, o_2, \cdots, o_n>$$

Ordered $n$-tuples, like sets, are collections of objects, but they differ from sets in that two ordered $n$-tuples are identical only if their members are in exactly the same order. So, if $o_1 \neq o_2$, then $<o_1, o_2> \neq <o_2, o_1>$. Because two *different* ordered $n$-tuples can contain exactly the same members, the analogue of the Principle of Extensionality does not hold for ordered $n$-tuples. One can express the conditions under which two ordered $n$-tuples are identical in this way:

$$<x_1, x_2, \cdots, x_n> = <y_1, y_2, \cdots, y_n> \textit{ iff } x_1 = y_1 \ \& \ x_2 = y_2 \ \& \ \cdots \ \& \ x_n = y_n$$

Since the members of ordered $n$-tuples are ordered, it makes sense to refer to them in terms of their position in the $n$-tuple. So, $o_1$ is the *first* component of $<o_1, o_2>$, and $o_2$ is its *second* component.

It is possible to simulate ordered $n$-tuples by certain special sets. Two things make this possible. First, an ordered pair can be simulated by a certain kind of set, as follows:

$$<x, y> = \{x, \{x, y\}\}$$

Second, an ordered $n$-tuple can be simulated by a special ordered pair (the first component of which is an ordered $(n-1)$-tuple). To illustrate an ordered triple first:

$$<x, y, z> = <<x, y>, z> = \{\{x, \{x, y\}\}, \{\{x, \{x, y\}\}, z\}\}$$

and, in general:

$$<x_1, \ldots, x_n> = <<x_1, \ldots, x_{n-1}>, x_n>$$

By combining these two simulations, any ordered $n$-tuple can be simulated by a set. It turns out that it is convenient to simulate an ordered 1-tuple *not* with a special set but with its single component,[2] thus:

$$<x> = x$$

Ordered $n$-tuples can be used to simulate a wide variety of other things. For example, a string or list of $n$ items can be simulated by an ordered $n$-tuple of those items, and, as we shall see next, functions can be simulated by sets of ordered pairs.

In semantics we will want to talk about certain functions. Intuitively, a function is a mapping that associates each object in a certain set with a *unique* object in a (possibly different) set. For example, consider the *mother of* relation. This relation is a function, which associates each person in the set of all persons with that person's unique mother in the set of all mothers. It is a function because each person has *exactly one* mother.

Functions are simulated in set theory by special sets of ordered pairs. In particular, a *function* is a set $f$ of ordered pairs that is *single-valued*—that is, $f$ is such that, for any members $<x_1,x_2>$ and $<y_1,y_2>$ of $f$, if $x_1 = y_1$ then $x_2 = y_2$. Such a set simulates a function in that membership of $<x,y>$ in $f$ is tantamount to $y$ being the *value* of $f$ with respect to $x$. That is, $y$ is the value of $f$ with respect to $x$ iff $<x,y> \in f$. The following two sets are examples of functions:

$$\{<1,5>, <2,6>, <3,7>, <4,8>\}$$

---

[2] When we study semantics (in the following sections) we will find it convenient to be able to say that the semantical correlates of logical predicates of degree $n$, for any number $n$, are sets of ordered $n$-tuples. But, in fact, up to now we have said that the semantical correlates of logical predicates of degree *one* are sets of *ordinary objects*, such as $\{1, 2, 3\}$, rather than sets of 1-tuples, such as $\{<1>, <2>, <3>\}$. In order to be able to have our cake and eat it too, we follow the usual procedure of having $<x> = x$.

We should note that our procedure for representing ordered $n$-tuples involves a certain risk. Our procedure will run aground if we envision predicates that apply to ordered $n$-tuples of ordered $n$-tuples. (The logical predicate '① loves ②' applies to ordered pairs of *persons*. Optional Exercise 1: give three examples of predicates that apply to ordered pairs of *ordered n-tuples*. Optional Exercise 2: explain and illustrate the problem for semantics if we allow predicates to apply to ordered $n$-tuples.) To get around this problem and allow domains to include ordered $n$-tuples, we could give up the usual procedure of having $<x> = x$ and having $<x,y,z> = <<x,y>,z>$, and instead adopt a procedure that would not allow an entity to be both an ordered $n$-tuple and an ordered $(n+1)$-tuple. For example, we could have:

$<x> = \{x\}$,
$<x,y> = \{x,\{x,y\}\}$ (as is usual),
$<x,y,z> = \{<<x,y>,z>,\{\{<<x,y>,z>\}\}\}$,
$<x,y,z,w> = \{<<x,y,z>,w>,\{\{\{<<x,y,z>,w>\}\}\}\}$, etc.

$$\{<\{h,b\},c>, <\{q,p\},d>, <e,f>\}$$

You can easily verify that both these sets of ordered pairs are single-valued.

It will be useful to introduce some standard terminology concerning functions. Consider the following function $f$:

$$f = \{<\{1,2\},6>, <\{1,3\},7>, <3,5>, <4,8>\}$$

An *argument* of a function is a first component of a member of the function.[3] Since $<\{1,2\},6> \in f$, the first component of $<\{1,2\},6>$ is an argument of $f$; that is, $\{1,2\}$ is an argument of $f$. Similarly, $\{1,3\}$, 3, and 4 are arguments of $f$, because each is a first component of a member of $f$. For any function, the *set* of all its arguments is the *domain* of the function. Thus, the domain of $f$ is the set $\{\{1,2\}, \{1,3\}, 3, 4\}$. A *value* of a function is a second component of a member of the function. Since $<\{1,2\},6> \in f$, 6 is a value of $f$. Similarly, 5, 7, and 8 are values of $f$. For any function, the *set* of all its values is the *range* of the function. Thus, the range of $f$ is $\{5, 6, 7, 8\}$. A function is said to be *from* its domain *to* its range.

Combining these ideas, it is clear that $f$ is a function from $\{\{1,2\}, \{1,3\}, 3, 4\}$ to $\{5, 6, 7, 8\}$, that $\{1,2\}$ is a member of $f$'s domain, that 6 is a member of $f$'s range, and that 6 is the value of $f$ for the argument $\{1,2\}$.

## Exercises

---

1    List all the members of the following sets.

(a)  $\{\Lambda, \{0\}, \{1\}, \{0,1\}\}$

(b)  $\{\{\Lambda\}, \{3, 5, 7, \{2, 6, 8, 10\}, T, Fx\}\}$

(c)  $\{x_1, \ldots, x_n\}$

(d)  $\{\{0,1\}, \{1,0\}\}$

2    List the members of the following sets:

---

[3] In this chapter, and in the rest of Part V, we consider only functions that have one argument. However, functions may have more than one argument. A function may map *two* objects onto a third object (the *addition* function maps two numbers onto their sum). In general, for *any* natural number $n$, a function may have $n$ arguments. Functions of more than one argument have already been described in Chapter 23.

Functions of $n$ arguments (for $n > 1$) may be simulated by functions of one argument, in just the manner in which ordered $n$-tuples are simulated with ordered pairs. So, $\{<1,1,1>, <0,1,0>, <1,0,1>\}$ is a function, but $\{<1,1,1>, <1,1,0>\}$ is not a function.

    (a) $\{\Lambda\} \cup \{\{\{\Lambda\}\}\}$

    (b) $<x,y> \cup <y,x>$

3    Write down *all* the ordered triples that have exactly the members 1, 2, and 3.

4    How many empty sets are there? Why are there exactly that number?

5    Using the Principle of Extensionality, determine whether the following statements are true or false:

    (a) $\{a,\{b,a\},\{c,b,a\}\} = \{a,\{a,b\},\{a,b,c\}\}$

    (b) $\{x,\{x\},\{x,y\}\}=\{\{x\},\{x,y\},x\}$

    (c) $\{x,\{x,\{x,\{x\}\}\}\} = \{\{\{x\},x\},x\}$

    (d) $\{<x,y>\} = \{\{\{y,x\},x\}\}$

    (e) $\{<x,y>\} = \{<y,x>\}$

    (f) $\{\frac{1}{2}\} = \{\frac{1}{4} + \frac{1}{4}\}$

    (g) $\{`\frac{1}{2}'\} = \{`\frac{1}{4} + \frac{1}{4}'\}$

    (h) $\{\frac{1}{2}\} = \{\frac{1}{4}, \frac{1}{4}\}$

6    What *ordered pair* simulates the ordered quadruple $<1,2,3,4>$?

7    What *set* simulates the ordered quadruple $<1,2,3,4>$?

8    In general, what set simulates the ordered *n*-tuple $<x_1, \ldots, x_n>$?

9    When, if ever, is $<x>$ a set?

10  Using only primitive logical symbols, the brace notation, and the predicate '∈' expressing set membership, formulate these claims:

    (a) $x$ is the null set.

    (b) $x$ is the unit set of $y$.

    (c) $x$ is the unit set of the unit set of $y$.

    (d) $x$ is the ordered quadruple $<u,v,w,z>$.

    (e) $x$ is a member of the unit set of $x$.

    (f) $x$ is the unit set of $<x,y>$.

    (g) $x$ is the unit set of $<y,z> \cup <z,y>$.

    (h) $x$ is a member of the unit set of the unit set of $<y,z> \cup <z,y>$.

11  Using only primitive logical symbols, the brace notation, and the predicate '∈' expressing set membership, formulate these claims:

(a)  the unit set of $x$ is a member of the unit set of the unit set of $x$.

(b)  the unit set of $x$ is a member of the union of the unit set of $x$ and the unit set of the unit set of $x$.

(c)  the unit set of $<x,y>$ is a member of the unit set of the unit set of $<x,y>$.

(d)  nothing is a member of the null set (i.e., there is no member of the null set).

(e)  the unit set of some member of $x$ is a member of $x$.

(f)  $x$ is the *only* member of the unit set of $x$.

12  It is possible to formulate every claim within pure set theory using a language that contains *no braces* (and no angle brackets), but only *primitive logical symbols* and *one non-logical constant*, the predicate '$\in$' expressing set membership. For example, we may formulate the claim that $z = \{x_1, \ldots, x_n\}$ as follows:

$$\forall w (w \in z \equiv (w = x_1 \ \lor \ \cdots \ \lor \ w = x_n))$$

Using this restricted language, state the following claims:

(a)  $z \in \{x_1, \ldots, x_n\}$

(b)  $z \in \{1,2,3\}$

(c)  $z = \{1,2,3\}$

(d)  $z = \{x,\{y\}\}$

(e)  $z = <x,y>$

(f)  $z \in <x,y>$

(g)  $z = x \cup y$

(h)  $z \in x \cup y$

13  Which of the following sets of ordered pairs are functions?

(a)  $\{<A,h>,<B,q>,<C,t>,<J,a>,<T,Bxa>\}$

(b)  $\{<1,3>,<1,1+1+1>\}$

(c)  $\{<\{x,x\},x>,<x,x>,<\{x,x,x\},x>\}$

(d)  Give the domain and range of each function in (a)-(c) above.

14  Let $A$ be the set of all persons who are parents (each person in $A$ has at least one child) and let $B$ be the set of all children (each person in $B$ is a child of some person in $A$).

(a)  Explain why the *parent of* relation is not a function from $A$ to $B$.

(b)  Explain why the *child of* relation is not a function from $B$ to $A$.

    (c) Is there *any* function from *A* to *B*? In other words, is there any function with domain *A* and range *B*? If there is one, what is it? If not, explain why not. (Hint: remember that a function is *any* single-valued set of ordered pairs.)

---

**3. Truth-Functional Semantics.** We shall develop the semantics for truth-functional logic in three stages. First, we define a semantic structure that simulates the intuitive notion of a possible situation or possible case—the familiar *truth-value assignment*. Then, we define what it means for a sentence to be true relative to a truth-value assignment. Finally, using the notion of truth relative to a truth-value assignment, we show how to define basic semantic notions of truth-functional logic.

Truth-value assignments simulate only the *truth-functional* aspects of possible situations. Intuitively, a possible situation corresponds to a collection of true and false statements. A truth-value assignment simulates a collection of true and false statements with a collection of 'T's and 'F's matched with non-molecular sentences. The following definition specifies what a truth-value assignment is:

    $\tau$ is a *truth-value assignment* iff $\tau$ is a function from non-molecular sentences to either 'T' or 'F'.[4]

So, by our previous definition of a function, a truth-value assignment $\tau$ is a single-valued set of ordered pairs, whose first components are non-molecular sentences, and whose second components are either 'T' or 'F'. Since $\tau$ is single-valued, for every non-molecular sentence $\phi$ and truth-values $x$ and $y$, if $<\phi,x> \in \tau$ and $<\phi,y> \in \tau$, then $x = y$. Earlier we would have described a truth-value assignment in this way:

$$
\begin{array}{ccc}
A & - & T \\
B & - & T \\
C & - & F
\end{array}
$$

---

[4] The domain of $\tau$ consists of *only* non-molecular sentences, and the range has just two members: the letters 'T' and 'F'. In other words, neither the domain nor the range of $\tau$ contain any "extraneous", "non-semantic" elements. For example, $\tau$ cannot pair the Statue of Liberty with 'T', or with anything else, for that matter. (The analogous statement applies to truncated semantical assignments and semantical assignments.)

    The domain of $\tau$ need not contain *all* non-molecular sentences; it is sufficient if it contains *some* non-molecular sentences. (In fact, the domain of $\tau$ *may* be empty, although such a truth-value assignment is of no practical significance.)

Using the definition above, we can describe the same truth-value assignment as the following single-valued set of ordered pairs (which we will call $V$):

$$V = \begin{Bmatrix} <A,T> \\ <B,T> \\ <C,F> \end{Bmatrix}$$

or, listing the members in the usual fashion:

$$V = \{<A,T>, <B,T>, <C,F>\}$$

Earlier, in Part II, truth-value assignments assigned truth values only to *atomic sentences* (propositional constants), whereas we have now defined truth-value assignments as functions from *non-molecular sentences* to truth values. This difference is easy to explain. In Part II, we represented all non-molecular sentences with propositional constants; it was not until Part III that we devised techniques for representing the different aspects of logical form that might be found within non-molecular sentences. Now that we have such techniques, we must be sure to allow a truth-value assignment to assign a truth value to *any* non-molecular sentence, including those with logical subjects and predicates, including identity, as well as those with quantifiers.[5] For example, we want to allow the following sort of truth-value assignment:

$$
\begin{array}{rcl}
A & - & T \\
Fabc & - & T \\
\forall x Hxx & - & F \\
\exists x (\forall y Fyx \supset Gxaa) & - & T
\end{array}
$$

We can describe this truth-value assignment as a set (which we will call $V^+$):

$$V^+ = \begin{Bmatrix} <A, T> \\ <Fabc,T> \\ <\forall x Hxx,F> \\ <\exists x (\forall y Fyx \supset Gxaa),T> \end{Bmatrix}$$

---

[5] We saw earlier that an argument can be truth-functionally invalid but valid in identity logic. This is (in part) because atomic sentences and non-molecular sentences are treated alike in truth-functional semantics.

or, listing $V^+$'s members in the usual way:

$$V^+ = \{<A,T>,<Fabc,T>,<\forall xHxx,F>,<\exists x(\forall yFyx \supset Gxaa),T>\}$$

In general, a truth-value assignment will not determine truth values for all sentences, because a given truth-value assignment need not assign 'T's and 'F's to *every* non-molecular sentence. Roughly, a truth-value assignment determines the truth-value of a sentence (or, as we shall say, *valuates* the sentence) if and only if that sentence can be truth-functionally composed solely out of non-molecular sentences, each of which is assigned either a 'T' or an 'F' by that truth-value assignment. The notion of being valuated by a truth-value assignment can be captured exactly in the following compositional definition:

If $\tau$ is a truth-value assignment, then:

**BASIS**

> if $\phi$ is a non-molecular sentence, then $\phi$ is *valuated by* $\tau$ iff either $<\phi,T> \in \tau$ or $<\phi,F> \in \tau$;

**INDUCTION**

> if $\phi$ is $\sim^*\psi$, for some non-molecular sentence $\psi$, then $\phi$ is *valuated by* $\tau$ iff $\psi$ is valuated by $\tau$;
>
> if $\phi$ is $^*\psi$ & $^*\chi$, $^*\psi$ v $^*\chi$, $^*\psi \supset ^*\chi$, or $^*\psi \equiv ^*\chi$, for some non-molecular sentences $\psi$ and $\chi$, then $\phi$ is *valuated by* $\tau$ iff both $\psi$ and $\chi$ are valuated by $\tau$.

The two truth-value assignments $V$ and $V^+$ can be used to illustrate what it means for a truth-value assignment to valuate a sentence:

- Both $V$ and $V^+$ valuate '$A$', '$A \supset A$', and '$\sim(A \supset A)$'.

- $V$ but not $V^+$ valuates '$B$' and '$A \equiv B$'.

- $V^+$ but not $V$ valuates '$\forall xHxx$' and '$A \supset \forall xHxx$'.

- Neither $V$ nor $V^+$ valuates '$B$ & $\forall xHxx$' and '$A$ & $D$'.

Now we can define compositionally what it means for a sentence to be true *relative to* a given truth-value assignment that valuates the sentence. We break the definition down according to the logical form of the sentence— that is, according to the way the sentence is composed. The main idea is simple. Given a truth-value assignment that valuates a non-molecular sentence (i.e., a non-compound sentence), the sentence is true if and only if 'T' is assigned to it by the truth-value assignment. The basis covers this case. If a sentence is molecular (i.e., it is a compound sentence), then whether the sentence is true or not is determined by two things: the main connective of the sentence, and the truth value(s) of its immediate component sentence(s). Both of these cases are covered in the induction. The induction has a clause corresponding to each type of main connective. These clauses are related to the truth-table of the main connective; it describes how the truth-value of any sentence with that main connective is a function of the truth-value of the immediate components of that sentence.

If $\tau$ is a truth-value assignment and $\phi$ is valuated by $\tau$, then:

BASIS

> if $\phi$ is a non-molecular sentence, then $\phi$ is *true with respect to $\tau$* iff $<\phi,\text{T}> \in \tau$;

INDUCTION

> if $\phi$ is $\sim^*\psi$, for some sentence $\psi$, then $\phi$ is *true with respect to $\tau$* iff $\psi$ is not true with respect to $\tau$;

> if $\phi$ is $^*\psi$ & $^*\chi$, for some sentences $\psi$ and $\chi$, then $\phi$ is *true with respect to $\tau$* iff both $\psi$ and $\chi$ are true with respect to $\tau$;

> if $\phi$ is $^*\psi$ v $^*\chi$, for some sentences $\psi$ and $\chi$, then $\phi$ is *true with respect to $\tau$* iff either $\psi$ or $\chi$ is true with respect to $\tau$ (or both are);

> if $\phi$ is $^*\psi$ v $^*\chi$, for some sentences $\psi$ and $\chi$, then $\phi$ is *true with respect to $\tau$* iff either $\psi$ is not true with respect to $\tau$ or $\chi$ is true with respect to $\tau$ (or both);

> if $\phi$ is $^*\psi \equiv {}^*\chi$, for some sentences $\psi$ and $\chi$, then $\phi$ is *true with respect to $\tau$* iff either both $\psi$ and $\chi$ are true with respect to $\tau$, or both $\psi$ and $\chi$ are not true with respect to $\tau$.

Consider how this definition determines truth-values with respect to the truth-value assignments $V$ and $V^+$:

- With respect to $V$, '$A$', '$\sim C$', and '$(A$ & $B)$ v $C$' are true.

- With respect to $V$, '$\sim A$', '$(A$ & $B)$ & $C$', and '$\forall x H x x$' are not true.

Note that the reason '$\forall x H x x$' is not true with respect to $V$ is that the sentence is not even *valuated* by $V$.

- With respect to $V^+$, '$A$', '$\sim\forall x H x x$', and '$\sim A$ v $Fabc$' are true.

●    With respect to $V^+$, '$\forall x Hxx$' and '$Haa$' are not true.

Notice that '$Haa$' is not true with respect to $V^+$ even though $V^+$ assigns 'T' to '$\forall x Hxx$'.

Having defined what a truth-value assignment is, and what it means for a sentence to be true relative to a truth-value assignment, we can now define the basic notion of truth-functional semantics.

> $\phi$ is a *truth-functional consequence* of $\Gamma$ iff $\phi$ and all the members of $\Gamma$ are sentences and there is **no** truth-value assignment $\tau$ such that $\phi$ and all the members of $\Gamma$ are valuated by $\tau$, all the members of $\Gamma$ are true with respect to $\tau$, and $\phi$ is not true with respect to $\tau$.

It will be convenient to have a brief way to refer to truth-functional consequences, so we adopt the following definition:

> $\Gamma \vDash_T \phi$ iff $\phi$ is a truth-functional consequence of $\Gamma$.

We can go on and define other basic notions of truth-functional semantics. For example:

> $\phi$ is a *truth-functional truth* (or a *tautology*) iff $\phi$ is a sentence and there is **no** truth-value assignment $\tau$ such that $\phi$ is valuated by $\tau$ but $\phi$ is not true with respect to $\tau$.

It is convenient to have a brief way to refer to truth-functional truths:

> $\vDash_T \phi$ iff $\phi$ is a truth-functional truth.

Additional basic notions of truth-functional semantics are defined in the exercises.

**Exercises**

---

15  State the following semantic claims in English (you may use Greek letters):

   (a)  $\Gamma \vDash_T \phi$

   (b)  $\Gamma \cup \Delta \vDash_T \phi$

   (c)  $\Gamma \cup \{\psi\} \vDash_T \phi$

   (d)  $\Gamma \vDash_T {}^*\phi \supset {}^*\psi$

   (e)  $\Lambda \vDash_T \phi$

(f) $\vDash_T \phi$

16 Express the following truth-value assignment as a function (i.e., as a single-valued set of ordered pairs):

$$
\begin{array}{lcc}
A_{16} & - & F \\
\forall x \, \forall y Pxyy & - & T \\
Babc & - & F \\
a = c & - & T
\end{array}
$$

17 Let $\phi$ and $\psi$ be any non-molecular formulas. Are the following claims true or false?

(a) $\{\phi\} \vDash_T \phi$

(b) $\{\sim^*\phi\} \vDash_T \phi$

(c) $\{^*\phi \text{ v } ^*\psi\} \vDash_T \phi$

(d) $\{^*\phi \text{ \& } ^*\psi\} \vDash_T \phi$

(e) $\{\phi, ^*\phi \supset ^*\psi\} \vDash_T \psi$

(f) $\{\phi, \sim^*\phi\} \vDash_T \psi$

(g) $\vDash_T \psi$

(h) $\vDash_T ^*\phi \text{ v } ^*\psi$

(i) $\vDash_T ^*\phi \text{ v } \sim^*\phi$

18 Consider the following truth-value assignment $\tau$:

$$\tau = \{<A,F>, <\forall xPx,F>, <C,F>, <\exists yFy,T>, <Fabc,F>\}$$

Determine which of the following formulas are valuated by $\tau$ and which are not valuated by $\tau$. For those that are *not* valuated by $\tau$, explain why not.

(a) $C_{12}$

(b) $\exists yFy$

(c) $\exists xFx$

(d) $\sim\forall xPx$

(e) $A \equiv (C \supset A)$

(f) $Pa$

(g) $\forall xPx \supset (\exists yFy \supset (\sim C))$

(h) $((A \equiv \exists yFy) \equiv (Fabc \text{ \& } C)) \supset (\forall xPx \text{ \& } A)$

19 Explain why the sentence '$\sim\forall xFxx$' is *not true* with respect to each of the following truth-value assignments:

(a) $\{<\forall xFxx,T>\}$

(b) $\{<A,F>, <B,F>\}$

20  Indicate whether the following sets of ordered pairs are truth-value assignments:

(a) $\{<A,T>, <A,F>\}$

(b) $\{<\exists xFx,F>, <Fa,T>\}$

(c) $\{<a = a,F>\}$

(d) $\{<\forall xFx,F>\}$

(e) $\{<A,T>, <B \ \& \ C,T>\}$

(f) $\{<A,T>, <Aa,F>, <Abc,T>\}$

(g) $\{<A_{12},F>, <Fabc,T>, <\sim\forall xFx,T>\}$

(h) $\{<T,F>, <F,T>\}$

21  Indicate whether the following sentences are true with respect to the following truth-value assignment:

$$\{<A_{12},F>, <C,T>, <Pabc,T>, <Pcba,F>, <\forall zHz,F>\}$$

(a) $A_{13}$

(b) $(C \equiv Pabc) \ v \ A_{12}$

(c) $(\forall zHz \equiv Pacb) \ v \ A_{12}$

(d) $Ha$

(e) $\exists yPybc$

22  Suppose that $\tau$ is a truth-value assignment which valuates $\phi$, $\psi$, and all the members of $\Gamma$. Suppose also that all of the members of $\Gamma$ are true with respect to $\tau$. In each of the following five exercises, also suppose that the claim stated is true. In each case, if it is possible to determine whether $\phi$ is true or not true with respect to $\tau$, state whether $\phi$ is true or not true with respect to $\tau$. If it is *not* possible to determine whether or not $\phi$ is true with respect to $\tau$, explain why not.

(a) $\Gamma \vDash_\tau \phi$

(b) $\Gamma \vDash_\tau {}^*\phi \ v \ {}^*\psi$

(c) $\Gamma \vDash_\tau {}^*\phi \ \& \ {}^*\psi$

(d) $\Gamma \vDash_\tau {}^*\phi \equiv {}^*\phi$

(e) $\Gamma \vDash_\tau {}^*\phi \supset {}^*\phi$

23  In terms of being valuated by truth-value assignments and being true relative to truth-value assignments, explain why the following are truth-functional truths:

(a)  $A \vee \sim A$

(b)  $C \vee ((\sim C \vee B) \& (\sim C \vee D))$

24  Define the following semantic notions (follow the pattern set in the definitions of truth-functional consequence and truth-functional truth):

(a)  $\phi_1$ and $\phi_2$ are *truth-functionally equivalent* sentences.

(b)  $\phi$ is a *truth-functional falsehood*.

(c)  $\Gamma$ is a *truth-functionally consistent* set of sentences.

(d)  $\Gamma$ is a *truth-functionally inconsistent* set of sentences.

(e)  $\Gamma_1$ and $\Gamma_2$ are *truth-functionally equivalent* sets of sentences.

25  You may have noticed that we have not defined what it means for a sentence to be *false* with respect to a truth-value assignment. Such a definition could take one of two forms.

(a)  Using the notion of a sentence being true with respect to a truth-value assignment, define what it means for a sentence to be false with respect to a truth-value assignment.

(b)  If the notion of truth with respect to a truth-value assignment is used in the definition of falsity with respect to a truth-value assignment, then the notion of falsity with respect to a truth-value assignment cannot be used in the definition of truth with respect to a truth-value assignment. Give a simultaneous compositional definition of what it means for a sentence to be true with respect to a truth-value assignment and of what it means for a sentence to be false with respect to a truth-value assignment.

26  Prove the following semantic claims:

(a)  For any sentence $\phi$ and set $\Gamma$ of sentences, if $\Gamma \vDash_T \phi$ then, for any set $\Delta$ of sentences, $\Gamma \cup \Delta \vDash_T \phi$.

(b)  For any sentence $\phi$ and set $\Gamma$ of sentences, if $\Gamma \vDash_T \phi$ and $\Gamma \vDash_T \sim^*\phi$, then $\Gamma$ is truth-functionally inconsistent.

(c)  For any sentences $\phi$ and $\psi$ and set $\Gamma$ of sentences, $\Gamma \vDash_T {}^*\phi \supset {}^*\psi$ if and only if $\Gamma \cup \{\phi\} \vDash_T \psi$.

---

**4. Identity Semantics.** Truth-value assignments determine truth-values for all non-molecular sentences in a similar manner: a truth-value is simply assigned to the sentence. In Part III, we began to devise techniques for representing details of logical form found within non-molecular sentences. We first isolated logical subjects and predicates, including the identity predicate. Since the goal of semantics is to show how the truth-conditions of a sentence are affected by the sentence's logical form, we now need to specify how logical subjects and predicates affect the truth-conditions of sentences containing them. Truth-value assignments do not do this; we need a way to simulate possible situations in more detail, so that we can take into account logical subjects and logical predicates. Truncated semantical assignments achieve this by containing semantical correlates for logical subjects and predicates.

The first step is to define the notion of a truncated semantical assignment. Roughly, a truncated semantical assignment is a truth-value assignment with two types of additions: objects are associated with individual constants, and sets of ordered $n$-tuples are associated with predicates. To describe truncated semantical assignments more exactly is somewhat more involved.

Truth-value assignments may assign truth-values to any non-molecular sentence. Some non-molecular sentences consist of a predicate constant followed by some number of individual constants, and truncated semantical assignments may not assign truth-values to these sentences. Rather, truncated semantical assignments assign semantical correlates to the predicate constant and the individual constants, and the truth-value of any atomic sentence composed out of them is determined by the relationship between these semantical correlates.

May truncated semantical assignments assign truth-values to general sentences?[6] The answer to this question depends on whether or not the general sentence contains any individual constants. If the general sentence does not contain any individual constants, then it may be assigned a truth-value by a truncated semantical assignment. On the other hand, if it *does* contain individual constants, then it is treated as if it were a sentence formed out of a logical predicate and logical subjects. The individual constants in the sentence are assigned objects, as is the case with other individual constants. The logical predicate in the sentence is assigned a set of ordered $n$-tuples, as is the case with other predicates. But what is the *logical predicate* in a general sentence containing individual constants? It is a special kind of predicate, which we will call a *general predicate (in symbolism)*. A general predicate (in symbolism) of degree $n$ is the result of replacing, in a general sentence with exactly $n$ distinct individual constants $\beta_1, \ldots, \beta_n$, each occurrence of the constant $\beta_i$ with the circled numeral $i$, for each $i$, $1 \leq i \leq n$. For example, '$\exists x Faxb$' is a general sentence with two individual constants. '$\exists x F①x②$' is a general predicate (of degree 2) formed by replacing '$a$' with '①' and '$b$' with '②' in the sentence; '$\exists x F②x①$' is a different general predicate formed from the same sentence. Another example:

---

6 General sentences are simply formulas that both are general (i.e., the main connective of which is either '∀' or '∃') and are sentences (i.e., contain no free variables).

$$\forall x (\exists y (Lxyx \ \& \ Lyxy) \supset Laax)$$

is a general sentence containing one individual constant, and:

$$\forall x (\exists y (Lxyx \ \& \ Lyxy) \supset L \textcircled{1}\textcircled{1}x)$$

is a general predicate (of degree 1) formed by replacing '$a$' with '$\textcircled{1}$' in that sentence. There was no need to mention general predicates when we considered truncated semantical assignments in Chapter 16, because in that chapter all general predicates were represented simply by predicate constants. Once we have isolated quantifiers, however, we must be sure to allow truncated semantical assignments to assign semantical correlates to general predicates.

There is one more difference between truth-value assignments and truncated semantical assignments that we should mention here. Truth-value assignments are functions, but, although truncated semantical assignments are *in effect* functions, they are not *really* functions. It would be more appropriate to call truncated semantical assignments something like *semi-functions*. We allow a given predicate constant to represent any number of different logical predicates, *provided* that the logical predicates are of different degrees.[7] Because of this, a truncated semantical assignment can pair a predicate constant with any number of different sets of $n$-tuples—provided that the predicate constant is not paired with two sets of ordered $n$-tuples *for the same number n*. (And since predicate constants double as propositional constants, a truncated semantical assignment might also assign a truth-value to the same symbol to which it assigns sets of ordered $n$-tuples.) Therefore, a truncated semantical assignment need not be single-valued; a single argument (a predicate constant) can have *different* values (different sets of $n$-tuples). Nevertheless, as we have stressed, a truncated semantical assignment must be *like* a function. In particular, any truncated semantical assignment $\rho$ must be *semantically single-valued* (to coin a term): for any members $<x_1,x_2>$ and $<y_1,y_2>$ of $\rho$, if $x_1 = y_1$ and $x_2$ and $y_2$ both are the *same type of semantical correlate* (i.e, both are truth-values, or both are sets of ordered $n$-tuples for the same number $n$), then $x_2 = y_2$.[8] If we define a *semantic semi-function* as any set of ordered

---

[7] Remember that, just as we are using the same symbols to represent statements and logical predicates, so, likewise, we are using the same symbols to represent predicates of different degrees. So, a given truncated semantical assignment might pair the *same* non-molecular predicate with *many* sets of ordered $n$-tuples—provided that no two are distinct (non-empty) sets of ordered $n$-tuples for the *same n*. This possibility is the result (in semantics) of our policy (in syntax) of not using degree-indicating superscripts. No semantical ambiguity is engendered because at most one (non-empty) set of ordered $n$-tuples, for any given $n$, is matched with a single non-molecular predicate.

[8] In other words, $\rho$ is semantically single-valued iff $\rho = \rho_1 \cup \cdots \cup \rho_n$, where each $\rho_i$ $(1 \leq i \leq n)$ is a *strict* function from propositional or predicate constants to a set of the *same*

pairs that is semantically single-valued, then a truncated semantical assignment is a semantic semi-function.

Taking into account these qualifications, the following definition specifies what a truncated semantical assignment is:

$\rho$ is a *truncated semantical assignment* iff $\rho$ is a semantic semi-function

(a)   from propositional constants or general sentences not containing any individual constants to 'T' or 'F',

(b)   from predicate constants or general predicates (in symbolism) of degree $n$ to **sets** of ordered $n$-tuples of objects, and

(c)   from individual constants to objects.

Truncated semantical assignments, then, are certain sets of ordered pairs of linguistic items and their semantical correlates.

In Part III we would have characterized a truncated semantical assignment as follows:

$$
\begin{array}{lcl}
L & - & \{1,2,3\} \\
L & - & \{<3,1>, <3,2>, <3,3>\} \\
G & - & \{<1,2,3>, <1,2,2>, <2,2,2>\} \\
a & - & 1 \\
b & - & 2
\end{array}
$$

(Note that '$L$' represents two different logical predicates *of different degrees* in this truncated semantical assignment.) Now we can write this truncated semantical assignment as a set (which we will call $I$):

$$
I = \begin{cases}
<L,\{1,2,3\}> \\
<L,\{<3,1>,<3,2>,<3,3>\}> \\
<G,\{<1,2,3>,<1,2,2>,<2,2,2>\}> \\
<a,1> \\
<b,2>
\end{cases}
$$

Since we now allow general predicates (in symbolism) to be paired with sets of ordered $n$-tuples, the following is also a truncated semantical assignment (written in the earlier fashion):

---

*type of semantical correlate.*

$$
\begin{array}{rcl}
L & - & \{1,2,3\} \\
L & - & \{<1,2>, <2,2>, <2,1>\} \\
\exists x(Lx① \& L①x) & - & \{1,2,3\} \\
\forall x\forall y(Gxy① \supset Gyx②) & - & \{<1,1>, <2,2>, <3,3>\} \\
a & - & 1 \\
b & - & 2
\end{array}
$$

and written as a semantic semi-function (which we will call $I^+$):

$$
I^+ = \left\{
\begin{array}{l}
<L, \{1,2,3\}> \\
<L, \{<1,2>,<2,2>,<2,1>\}> \\
<\exists x(Lx① \& L①x), \{1,2,3\}> \\
<\forall x\forall y(Gxy① \supset Gyx②), \{<1,1>,<2,2>,<3,3>\}> \\
<a, 1> \\
<b, 2>
\end{array}
\right\}
$$

The next step is to define the conditions under which a given truncated semantical assignment valuates a given sentence. To do this, all we need to add to the definition of being valuated by a truth-value assignment are clauses describing under what conditions atomic sentences with individual constants and predicate constants (including '=') are valuated. This is handled by adding two new clauses to the basis (and keeping, but slightly changing, the previous basis). The rest of the definition is carried over exactly from the earlier definition.

If $\rho$ is a truncated semantical assignment, then:

**BASIS**

> if $\phi$ is **a propositional constant or a general sentence not containing any individual constants,** then $\phi$ is *valuated by* $\rho$ iff either $<\phi,T> \in \rho$ or $<\phi,F> \in \rho$;
>
> **if, for some number** $n$, $\phi$ **is** $\theta\beta_1...\beta_n$, **for some predicate constant or general predicate (in symbols)** $\theta$ **of degree** $n$ **and for some** $n$ **individual constants** $\beta_1, \ldots, \beta_n$,[9] **then** $\phi$ **is** *valuated by* $\rho$ **iff**
>
> (i)    for every $i$, $1 \le i \le n$, there is some object $x$ such that $<\beta_i,x> \in \rho$, and

---

[9] If $\theta$ is a general predicate (in symbols) of degree $n$, then we write '$\theta\beta_1...\beta_n$' to refer to, for every $i$, $1 \le i \le n$, the result of substituting $\beta_i$ for the circled numeral $i$ in $\theta$. For example, if $\theta$ is '$\exists xF②x①$', $\alpha$ is '$a$', and $\beta$ is '$b$', then $\theta\alpha\beta$ is '$\exists xFbxa$'.

(ii)   for some set $\sigma$ (possibly empty) of ordered $n$-tuples of objects,[10] $<\theta,\sigma> \in \rho$;

if $\phi$ is $\beta_1 = \beta_2$, for some individual constants $\beta_1$ and $\beta_2$, then $\phi$ is *valuated by* $\rho$ iff, for some objects $x$ and $y$, $<\beta_1,x> \in \rho$ and $<\beta_2,y> \in \rho$;

INDUCTION

if $\phi$ is $\sim\!\!^*\psi$, for some sentence $\psi$, then $\phi$ is *valuated by* $\rho$ iff $\psi$ is valuated by $\rho$;

if $\phi$ is $^*\psi$ & $^*\chi$, $^*\psi$ v $^*\chi$, $^*\psi \supset {}^*\chi$, or $^*\psi \equiv {}^*\chi$, for some sentences $\psi$ and $\chi$, then $\phi$ is *valuated by* $\rho$ iff both $\psi$ and $\chi$ are valuated by $\rho$.

We can use $I$ and $I^+$ to illustrate what it means for a truncated semantical assignment to valuate sentences.

By studying $I$ and $I^+$, you can verify the following:

- Both $I$ and $I^+$ valuate '$(La$ v $Lab) \supset a = b$'.

- $I$ but not $I^+$ valuates '$(La$ v $Lab) \supset Lbbb$'.

- $I^+$ but not $I$ valuates '$\exists x(Lxa$ & $Lax)$'.

- Neither $I$ nor $I^+$ valuates '$L$'.

Now we can define what it means for a sentence to be true relative to a truncated semantical assignment that valuates the sentence. This definition is an extension of the definition of truth relative to a truth-value assignment. Two clauses are added to the basis (and the previous basis, slightly modified, is retained, to handle predicate constants and individual constants). The rest of the definition is just as before.

If $\rho$ is a truncated semantical assignment and $\phi$ is valuated by $\rho$, then:

BASIS

if $\phi$ is **a propositional constant or a general sentence not containing any individual constants**, then $\phi$ is *true with respect to* $\rho$ iff $<\phi,T> \in \rho$;

---

[10] Remember that $\{<x>,<y>,<z>\} = \{x,y,z\}$.

if, for some number $n$, $\phi$ is $\theta\beta_1...\beta_n$, for some predicate constant or general predicate $\theta$ of degree $n$ and for some $n$ individual constants $\beta_1, \ldots, \beta_n$, then $\phi$ is *true with respect to* $\rho$ iff there is an ordered $n$-tuple $<x_1, \ldots, x_n>$ such that

(i)     for all $i$, $1 \le i \le n$, $<\beta_i, x_i> \in \rho$, and

(ii)    $<x_1, \ldots, x_n>$ is a member of some set $\sigma$ of ordered $n$-tuples such that $<\theta, \sigma> \in \rho$;

if $\phi$ is $\beta_1=\beta_2$, for some individual constants $\beta_1$ and $\beta_2$, then $\phi$ is *true with respect to* $\rho$ iff there is some object $x$ such that $<\beta_1, x> \in \rho$ and $<\beta_2, x> \in \rho$;

INDUCTION

if $\phi$ is $\sim^*\psi$, for some sentence $\psi$, then $\phi$ is *true with respect to* $\rho$ iff $\psi$ is not true with respect to $\rho$;

if $\phi$ is $^*\psi$ & $^*\chi$, for some sentences $\psi$ and $\chi$, then $\phi$ is *true with respect to* $\rho$ iff both $\psi$ and $\chi$ are true with respect to $\rho$;

if $\phi$ is $^*\psi$ v $^*\chi$, for some sentences $\psi$ and $\chi$, then $\phi$ is *true with respect to* $\rho$ iff one or both of $\psi$ and $\chi$ are true with respect to $\rho$;

if $\phi$ is $^*\psi \supset ^*\chi$, for some sentences $\psi$ and $\chi$, then $\phi$ is *true with respect to* $\rho$ iff either $\psi$ is not true with respect to $\rho$, or $\chi$ is true with respect to $\rho$ (or both);

if $\phi$ is $^*\psi \equiv ^*\chi$, for some sentences $\psi$ and $\chi$, then $\phi$ is *true with respect to* $\rho$ iff either both $\psi$ and $\chi$ are true with respect to $\rho$, or both $\psi$ and $\chi$ are not true with respect to $\rho$.

Consider our examples $I$ and $I^+$ once again.

- With respect to both $I$ and $I^+$, '$La$ & $Lb$' is true.

- With respect to both $I$ and $I^+$, '$\forall x Lx$' is not true.

- With respect to $I$ but not $I^+$, '$\sim Lbb$' is true.

- With respect to $I^+$ but not $I$, '$\exists x(Lxb$ & $Lbx)$' is true.

Finally, parallel to the two basic semantic notions of truth-functional semantics defined previously, we define two basic semantic notions of identity semantics.

$\phi$ is an *identity consequence* of $\Gamma$ iff $\phi$ and all the members of $\Gamma$ are sentences and there is **no** truncated semantical assignment $\rho$ such that $\phi$ and all the members of $\Gamma$ are valuated by $\rho$, all the members of $\Gamma$ are true with respect to $\rho$, and $\phi$ is not true with respect to $\rho$.

$\phi$ is an *identity truth* iff $\phi$ is a sentence and there is **no** truncated semantical assignment $\rho$ such that $\phi$ is valuated by $\rho$ but $\phi$ is not true with respect $\rho$.

Again, we introduce abbreviations for these two notions.

$\Gamma \vDash_I \phi$ iff $\phi$ is an identity consequence of $\Gamma$.

$\vDash_I \phi$ iff $\phi$ is an identity truth.

## Exercises

27 Write out $I^+$ as a set.

28 Which of the following are truncated semantical assignments? For those that are not truncated semantical assignments, explain why not.

   (a) { <P,T>, <Fab,T>, <∀xFx,F>, <L, {<1,2>, <2,1>}> }

   (b) { <F,{1,2}>, <F,{<1,1>, <2,2>}> }

   (c) { <∃x(Lx① & L②x),{1,2,3}> }

   (d) { <∃x(Lx① & L②x),{<1,2>, <2,2>}> }

29 Is a truth-value assignment ever a truncated semantical assignment? Why or why not?

30 Is a truncated semantical assignment ever a truth-value assignment? Why or why not?

31 Construct a set $\Gamma$ of sentences and sentences $\phi$ and $\psi$ such that the following hold: $\Gamma \vDash_I \phi$ and $\{\phi\} \vDash_I \psi$.

32 Are the following claims true or false? Explain why or why not.

   (a) $\{a \neq a\} \vDash_T Fa$.

   (b) $\{a \neq a\} \vDash_I Fa$.

   (c) $\vDash_I \forall x(Fx \lor {\sim}Fx)$.

33 Which of the following sentences are valuated by $I^+$ and which are not? For those that are *not* valuated by $I^+$, explain why not.

   (a) *Laaa*

   (b) *Lab*

(c)  *Lc*

(d)  ∀*xLxy*

(e)  ∃*x*(*Lx*① & *L*①*x*)

(f)  ∃*x*(*Lxa* & *Lax*)

(g)  ∃*x*(*Lxa* & *Lbx*)

(h)  ∃*x*(*Lxa* & *Lxa*)

(i)  ∀*x*∀*y*(*Lxya* ⊃ *Lyxa*)

(j)  *c* = *c*

(k)  *a* = *a*

(l)  *L*

34  Which of the following are true with respect to $I^+$?

(a)  *a* = *b*

(b)  ∃*xLx*

(c)  *a* = *b* ⊃ ~∃*xLx*

(d)  *Laa* ≡ *a* = *b*

(e)  ∀*x*∀*y*(*Lxya* ⊃ *Lyxb*)

(f)  ∀*x*∀*y*(*Lxyb* ⊃ *Lyxb*)

35  Define the following semantic notions (follow the pattern set in the definitions of identity consequence and identity truth):

(a)  $\phi_1$ and $\phi_2$ are *identity equivalent* sentences.

(b)  $\phi$ is a *identity falsehood*.

(c)  Γ is a *identity consistent* set of sentences.

(d)  Γ is a *identity inconsistent* set of sentences.

(e)  $\Gamma_1$ and $\Gamma_2$ are *identity equivalent* sets of sentences.

36  If $\phi_1$ and $\phi_2$ are truth-functionally equivalent sentences, does it follow that $\phi_1$ and $\phi_2$ are identity equivalent sentences?

37  If $\phi_1$ and $\phi_2$ are identity equivalent sentences, does it follow that $\phi_1$ and $\phi_2$ are truth-functionally equivalent sentences?

38  If $\phi$ is $\beta_1 = \beta_2$, for some individual constants $\beta_1$ and $\beta_2$, is it possible for the following to hold: $\vDash_I \phi$? Explain.

39  Prove the following semantic claims:

(a)  $\vDash_I$ *a* = *a*.

(b)  For any set $\Gamma$ of sentences, if $\Gamma \vDash_I a = a \supset P$, then $\Gamma \vDash_I P$.

(c)  For any sentence $\phi$ and set $\Gamma$ of sentences, $\Gamma \cup \{a \neq a\} \vDash_I \phi$.

(d)  For any set $\Gamma$ of sentences, if $\Gamma \vDash_I a \neq a$, then $\Gamma$ is identity inconsistent.

---

**5. Quantificational Semantics.** We shall now define the notions needed in the semantic treatment of quantificational logic, including identity. Our work in this section will parallel our work in truth-functional semantics and identity semantics, and we will focus on those changes that must be made in order to handle quantified sentences.

The main difference between a truncated semantical assignment and a (full) semantical assignment is the addition of a domain. The only other differences are certain simplifications that follow from the fact that semantical assignments deal explicitly with the semantical significance of general sentences and general predicates. The following is the definition of a semantical assignment:

$\mu$ is a *semantical assignment* iff $\mu = \{\{\delta\}\} \cup f$, where $\delta$ is a non-empty set (the "domain" of $\mu$), and $f$ is a semantic semi-function[11]

(a)  from propositional constants to 'T' or 'F', and

(b)  from predicate constants of degree $n$ to **sets** of ordered $n$-tuples of objects from $\delta$, and

(c)  from individual constants to objects from $\delta$.

In Part III we indicated semantical assignments in the following manner:

$$
\begin{array}{lll}
\mathbf{D} & - & \{1,2,3\} \\
F & - & \{1,2,3\} \\
J & - & \{<1,2>, <2,2>, <3,2>\} \\
a & - & 2 \\
b & - & 2
\end{array}
$$

We would now write this as the following set (which we will call $S$):

$$
S = \left\{
\begin{array}{l}
\{\{1,2,3\}\} \\
<F,\{1,2,3\}> \\
<J,\{<1,2>,<2,2>,<3,2>\}> \\
<a,2> \\
<b,2>
\end{array}
\right\}
$$

---

[11] Recall the discussion of semantic semi-functions above. Recall, also, that a function

Recall that the domain of a semantical assignment is just the member of the semantical assignment that is a unit set of a set.

We should specify officially what a domain is:[12] $\delta$ is the domain of $\mu$ just in case the unit set of $\delta$ is the unique unit set contained in $\mu$; that is,

$$\delta \text{ is the } \textit{domain} \text{ of } \mu \text{ iff } \forall \delta_1 (\{\delta_1\} \in \mu \equiv \delta_1 = \delta)$$

What must be added to truncated semantical assignments to construct a semantical structure that provides truth-conditions for quantified sentences? The quantified sentence '$\exists xFx$' is true under a semantical assignment just in case there is some object in its domain such that, if that object were assigned to the variable '$x$', then the formula '$Fx$' would be true. Similarly, the quantified sentence '$\forall xFx$' is true under a semantical assignment just in case, for every object in the domain, if that object were assigned to the variable '$x$', then the formula '$Fx$' would be true. But semantical assignments do not assign objects to variables, so a formula containing free variables, like '$Fx$', is not given a truth-value by a semantical assignment. To provide truth-conditions for these formulas, we will define another semantical structure—called a *valuation*—which is just like a semantical assignment except that it may assign objects to individual variables.

BASIS

If $\mu$ is a semantical assignment, then $\mu$ is a *valuation*.

INDUCTION

If $\mu$ is a valuation, $\delta$ is the domain of $\mu$, $\alpha$ is a variable, and, for all $y$, $\mu$ does not contain $<\alpha,y>$, then, for all $x \in \delta$, $\mu \cup \{<\alpha,x>\}$ is an *$\alpha$-valuation* of $\mu$.

If $\mu_1$ is an $\alpha$-valuation, for some $\alpha$, of some valuation $\mu_2$, then $\mu_1$ is a *valuation*.

An $\alpha$-valuation of $\mu$ is just like $\mu$ except that, in addition, it maps the individual *variable* $\alpha$ onto some object from the domain of $\mu$. For example, the following is not a semantical assignment, because it maps an individual variable onto a member of the domain **D**. However, it is an '$x$'-valuation of a semantical assignment, so it is a valuation.

---

unit set.

[12] Strictly speaking, according to this definition, there is no requirement that $\mu$ be a semantic structure if it has a domain; *any set at all* that contains exactly one unit set will have the member of that unit set as its domain. However, we are interested in domains only of semantic structures.

$$
\begin{array}{lll}
\mathbf{D} & - & \{1,2,3\} \\
F & - & \{1,2,3\} \\
J & - & \{<1,2>, <2,2>, <3,2>\} \\
a & - & 2 \\
x & - & 2
\end{array}
$$

Now, as before, we need to specify how semantical assignments determine the truth-conditions of quantificational sentences. To do this, we simply change the definition of being valuated by a truncated semantical assignment by adding a clause in the induction to handle quantified sentences (we also make slight changes in the basis, so that, among other things, *non*-sentences like '*Fx*' or '*x* = *y*' are valuated with respect to an '*x*'-valuation).

If $\mu$ is a valuation, then:

BASIS

if $\phi$ is a **propositional constant**, then $\phi$ is *valuated by* $\mu$ iff either $<\phi,\mathrm{T}> \in \mu$ or $<\phi,\mathrm{F}> \in \mu$;

if $\phi$ is $\theta\gamma_1...\gamma_n$, for some **predicate constant** $\theta$ and some number $n$ of **individual symbols** $\gamma_1,..,\gamma_n$, then $\phi$ is *valuated by* $\mu$ iff

(i)     for every $i$, $1 \leq i \leq n$, there is some object $x_i$ such that $<\gamma_i,x_i> \in \mu$, and

(ii)    for some set $\sigma$ (possibly empty) of ordered $n$-tuples, $<\theta,\sigma> \in \mu$;

if $\phi$ is $\gamma_1 = \gamma_2$, for some **individual symbols** $\gamma_1$ and $\gamma_2$, then $\phi$ is *valuated by* $\mu$ iff, for some $x$ and $y$, $<\gamma_1,x> \in \mu$ and $<\gamma_2,y> \in \mu$;

INDUCTION

if $\phi$ is $\sim^*\psi$, for some sentence $\psi$, then $\phi$ is *valuated by* $\mu$ iff $\psi$ is valuated by $\mu$;

if $\phi$ is $^*\psi \ \& \ ^*\chi$, $^*\psi \ \mathrm{v} \ ^*\chi$, $^*\psi \supset ^*\chi$, or $^*\psi \equiv ^*\chi$, for some sentences $\psi$ and $\chi$, then $\phi$ is *valuated by* $\mu$ iff both $\psi$ and $\chi$ are valuated by $\mu$;

if $\phi$ is $\forall\alpha^*\psi$ or $\phi$ is $\exists\alpha^*\psi$, for some formula $\psi$, then $\phi$ is *valuated* by $\mu$ iff $\psi$ is valuated by some $\alpha$-valuation of $\mu$.

Examples:

- $S$ valuates '$\forall x((x = a \lor x = b) \supset Jxx)$' but not '$Fa \ \& \ Fc$'.

Given the definition of truth relative to a truncated semantical assignment, defining truth relative to a (full) semantical assignment requires only the addition of a clause in the induction for each quantifier (and slight alterations in the basis, as well).

If $\mu$ is a valuation and $\phi$ is valuated by $\mu$, then:

BASIS

> if $\phi$ is a **propositional constant**, then $\phi$ is *true with respect to $\mu$* iff $<\phi,\text{T}> \in \mu$;
>
> if $\phi$ is $\theta\gamma_1...\gamma_n$, for some **predicate constant** $\theta$ and for some $n$ **individual symbols** $\gamma_1, \ldots, \gamma_n$, then $\phi$ is *true with respect to $\mu$* iff there is an ordered $n$-tuple $<x_1, \ldots, x_n>$ such that
>
> (i)   for all $i$, $1 \leq i \leq n$, $<\gamma_i,x_i> \in \mu$, and
>
> (ii)  $<x_1, \ldots, x_n>$ is a member of some set $\sigma$ of ordered $n$-tuples such that $<\theta,\sigma> \in \mu$;
>
> if $\phi$ is $\gamma_1 = \gamma_2$, for some **individual symbols** $\gamma_1$ and $\gamma_2$, then $\phi$ is *true with respect to $\mu$* iff there is some $x$ such that $<\gamma_1,x> \in \mu$ and $<\gamma_2,x> \in \mu$;

INDUCTION

> if $\phi$ is $\sim^*\psi$, for some sentence $\psi$, then $\phi$ is *true with respect to $\mu$* iff $\psi$ is not true with respect to $\mu$;
>
> if $\phi$ is $^*\psi \ \& \ ^*\chi$, for some sentences $\psi$ and $\chi$, then $\phi$ is *true with respect to $\mu$* iff both $\psi$ and $\chi$ are true with respect to $\mu$;
>
> if $\phi$ is $^*\psi \lor \ ^*\chi$, for some sentences $\psi$ and $\chi$, then $\phi$ is *true with respect to $\mu$* iff one or both of $\psi$ and $\chi$ are true with respect to $\mu$;
>
> if $\phi$ is $^*\psi \supset \ ^*\chi$, for some sentences $\psi$ and $\chi$, then $\phi$ is *true with respect to $\mu$* iff either $\psi$ is not true with respect to $\mu$, or $\chi$ is true with respect to $\mu$ (or both);
>
> if $\phi$ is $^*\psi \equiv \ ^*\chi$, for some sentences $\psi$ and $\chi$, then $\phi$ is *true with respect to $\mu$* iff either both $\psi$ and $\chi$ are true with respect to $\mu$, or both $\psi$ and $\chi$ are not true with respect to $\mu$;
>
> if $\phi$ is $\forall\alpha^*\psi$, for some formula $\psi$, then $\phi$ is *true with respect to $\mu$* iff $\psi$ is true with respect to every $\alpha$-valuation of $\mu$;
>
> if $\phi$ is $\exists\alpha^*\psi$, for some formula $\psi$, then $\phi$ is *true with respect to $\mu$* iff $\psi$ is true with respect to at least one $\alpha$-valuation of $\mu$.

Examples:

- With respect to $S$, '$\forall x((x = a \lor x = b) \supset Jxx)$' is true.

- With respect to $S$, '$\forall x \forall y(Jxy \supset Jxx)$' is not true.

We end by defining two basic notions of quantificational semantics.

> $\phi$ is a *quantificational consequence* of $\Gamma$ iff $\phi$ and all the members of $\Gamma$ are sentences and there is **no** semantical assignment $\mu$ such that $\phi$ and all the members of $\Gamma$ are valuated by $\mu$, all the members of $\Gamma$ are true with respect to $\mu$, and $\phi$ is not true with respect to $\mu$.

> $\phi$ is a *quantificational truth* iff $\phi$ is a sentence and there is **no** semantical assignment $\mu$ such that $\phi$ is valuated by $\mu$ but $\phi$ is not true with respect to $\mu$.

As before, we introduce abbreviations for these two notions:

$\Gamma \vDash_Q \phi$ iff $\phi$ is a quantificational consequence of $\Gamma$.

$\vDash_Q \phi$ iff $\phi$ is a quantificational truth.

## Exercises

---

40 Are the following claims true or false?

(a) $\{\forall x Fx\} \vDash_T Fa$.

(b) $\{\forall x Fx\} \vDash_I Fa$.

(c) $\{\forall x Fx\} \vDash_Q Fa$.

(d) $\vDash_T a = a$.

(e) $\vDash_I a = a$.

(f) $\vDash_Q a = a$.

41 Are the following claims true or false?

(a) $\vDash_Q \forall x Fx$.

(b) $\vDash_Q \forall x \; x = x$.

(c) $\vDash_Q \exists x \; x = x$.

(d) $\{\forall x Fx\} \vDash_Q Fa$.

(e) $\{\exists x Fx\} \vDash_Q Fa$.

(f)  $\{\forall x Fx\} \vDash_Q \sim Fa$.

(g)  $\{\exists x Fx\} \vDash_Q \sim Fa$.

(h)  $\vDash_Q \forall x(Fx \vee \sim Fx)$.

42  Are the following sets semantical assignments?  Explain.

(a)  $\{\ \{\{1,2,3\}\}, <F,\{1,2\}>, <a,\{1\}>\ \}$

(b)  $\{\ \{\{1,2,3\}\}, <F,\{1\}>, <F,\{1,2\}>, <F,\{1,2,3\}>\ \}$

(c)  $\{\ \ \{\{1,2,3\}\}, <F,\{1,2,3\}>, <F,\{<1,1>,\ <1,2>\}>, <F,\{<1,2,3>,\ <2,2,3>\}>\ \}$

(d)  $\{\ \{\{1,2,3\}\}, <\forall x Fx,T>, <L,\{<1,2>\}>, <a,2>\ \}$

(e)  $\{\ \{\{1,2,3\}\}, <P,T>, <L,\{<1,2>\}>, <a,4>\ \}$

43  Is a truth-value assignment ever a semantical assignment?  Explain.

44  Is a truncated semantical assignment ever a semantical assignment?  Explain.

45  Write the '$x$'-valuation on p. 291 as a set $\mu \cup \{<\alpha,m>\}$, for the appropriate semantical assignment $\mu$, the appropriate variable $\alpha$, and the appropriate member $m$ of the domain of $\mu$.

46  In this exercise, write valuations as sets.

(a)  Give three different '$x$'-valuations of the semantical assignment S.

(b)  Give two different '$y$'-valuations of an '$x$'-valuation of S.

(c)  Give two different '$z$'-valuations of a '$y$'-valuation of an '$x$'-valuation of S.

47  Is S a valuation?  Why or why not?

48  Is S an $\alpha$-valuation, for some variable $\alpha$?  Why or why not?

49  Which of the following are valuated by the semantical assignment S?  For those that are *not* valuated by S, explain why not.

(a)  $a \neq b$

(b)  $\forall x \sim Fx$

(c)  $\sim Fab$

(d)  $\exists x \sim(Fx \equiv \forall y Jxy)$

50  Which of the following sentences are true with respect to the semantical assignment S?

(a)  $a = b$

(b) $\forall x Fx$

(c) $\forall x (Fx \supset Jxa)$

(d) $\exists x \exists y Jxy$

(e) $\exists x Jxx$

(f) $\exists x \forall y Jxy$

(g) · $\exists x \forall y Jyx$

(h) $\forall x \exists y Jxy$

(i) $\forall x \exists y Jyx$

51 Define the following semantic notions (follow the pattern set in the definitions of quantificational consequence and quantificational truth):

(a) $\phi_1$ and $\phi_2$ are *quantificationally equivalent* sentences.

(b) $\phi$ is a *quantificational falsehood*.

(c) $\Gamma$ is a *quantificationally consistent* set of sentences.

(d) $\Gamma$ is a *quantificationally inconsistent* set of sentences.

(e) $\Gamma_1$ and $\Gamma_2$ are *quantificationally equivalent* sets of sentences.

52 Compare and contrast the definitions of truth-functional equivalence of sentences, identity equivalence of sentences, and quantificational equivalence of sentences. What is similar about the three definitions? What is different about the three definitions?

53 You might wonder why the domain of a semantical assignment $\mu$ is a *unit set* of a non-empty set. The reason is simply this: we need some device to ensure that the domain of $\mu$ can be distinguished formally from other items contained in $\mu$. Since no other member of $\mu$ could possibly be a unit set (all the other members of $\mu$ are ordered pairs), having the domain be the member of a unit set in $\mu$ suffices to distinguish the domain from other items. However, there are other techniques that would work to distinguish the domain. Devise two other such techniques. Make them as different from each other and from the official technique as you can.

54 Prove the following semantic claims:

(a) $\vDash_Q \forall x \ x = x$

(b) $\vDash_Q \exists x \ x = x$

(c) For any sentence $\phi$ and set $\Gamma$ of sentences, $\Gamma \cup \{\exists x \ x \neq x\} \vDash_Q \phi$

55 Is there any set $\Gamma$ such that $\Gamma \vDash_Q \forall x \ x \neq x$? Explain.

56 What sort of additions would have to be made to the previous definitions in order to define the corresponding semantic notions for

quantificational formulas including *functors*?

57  Describe the changes that would need to be made for formulas involving *definite descriptions* in logical subject positions.

58  Do the same for *vacuous logical subjects*.

# Chapter 28

## Three Systems of Logic

**1. Defining Derivations.** A large share of our work in the previous parts of this book has been figuring out which formulas are derivable from which suppositions. In this chapter, we define precisely what it means to be a derivation. This amounts primarily to specifying precisely each inference rule by which derivations are constructed. These definitions are purely formal and syntactic; reference is made only to the syntactic form of the strings of symbols that make up derivations, and no reference is made to what those symbols may semantically signify.

Derivations are constructed through the application of "inference rules" or "transformation rules". A set of rules can be viewed as a calculus for constructing derivations; such a calculus is commonly also called a *system of logic*. We have studied three systems of logic: a system containing rules for truth-functional connectives, a system containing rules for logical subjects and the identity sign, and a system containing rules for quantifiers. Accordingly, we shall define three specific kinds of derivations: propositional-calculus derivations (or, derivations within the system of propositional logic), identity-calculus derivations (or, derivations within the system of identity logic), and quantificational-calculus derivations (or, derivations within the system of quantificational logic). Something is a derivation, then, if it is one of these specific types of derivations.[1]

Because derivations can be indefinitely long, we first define what it means to be a derivation of some fixed number of steps (lines). Based on this definition, it is easy to define what it means to be a derivation of any length.

**2. Primitive Symbols in Derivations.** Derivations are certain types of lists of strings of symbols, the main components of which are formulas and numerals. Therefore, the primitive symbols out of which derivations are constructed are simply those out of which formulas are constructed, in

---

[1] Further types of derivations are defined in the exercises.

addition to a few others: numerals (for numbering lines and indicating suppositions), the comma ',' (for separating supposition numerals), the symbol 'Λ' (for representing the null set), and the bar '⊢' (for separating supposition numerals from line numerals).[2]

**3. Preliminary Definitions.** To define what it means to be a derivation, we need a way to talk about parts and other features of derivations. So, we first define terms that are used to describe derivations. Notice that all these definitions are purely syntactic.[3]

λ is a *line* iff λ consists of either some finite number of numerals (separated by commas) or the symbol Λ', followed by ⊢, followed by a numeral, followed by a sentence.

$\nu$ is a *supposition numeral* of line λ iff $\nu$ is one of the numerals occurring in line λ to the left of ⊢.

$\nu$ is a *line numeral* of line λ iff $\nu$ is the numeral occurring immediately to the right of the bar in line λ.

$\phi$ is a sentence *on* line λ iff $\phi$ is a sentence occurring in line λ and is not a proper part of any formula occurring in line λ.

λ is a line *in* a string $\sigma$ of lines iff λ is a line occurring in $\sigma$ and is not a proper part of any line occurring in $\sigma$.

$\lambda_1$ is a *supposition line* of line $\lambda_2$ relative to a string $\sigma$ of lines iff $\lambda_1$ is a line in a string $\sigma$ of lines and the line numeral of $\lambda_1$ is among the supposition numerals of line $\lambda_2$.

$\phi_1$ is a *supposition* of $\phi_2$ relative to a string $\sigma$ of lines iff $\phi_1$ is a sentence on some line $\lambda_1$ in $\sigma$, $\phi_2$ is a sentence on some line $\lambda_2$ in $\sigma$, and $\lambda_1$ is a supposition line of $\lambda_2$ relative to $\sigma$.

---

[2] Recall that lists of numerals and certain English capital letters may occur in annotations to the right of lines in derivations, when the inference rule which justifies a line is specified. However, these annotations are not part of the derivation itself; rather, they are a commentary on the derivation, written off to its side. Nevertheless, their presence makes the job of providing and checking derivations much easier.

[3] When we refer in these definitions to occurrences of *numerals*, we mean occurrences of numerals that are not proper parts of other occurrences of numerals. Thus, if an occurrence of '12' is a numeral, then the occurrences of '1' and '2' within that numeral are *not* considered to be occurrences of numerals. We could state this in the definitions below, but it is simpler to state it once here.

## Exercises

---

1   Explain how it is possible for a numeral to be part of a formula.

2   Explain how one line can be a proper part of another line. Give an example. Do any lines *not* have any proper subparts that are lines?

3   Assume that $\phi$ and $\psi$ are sentences, and that $\sigma$ is a string of lines. Expand the following statement by substituting definitions for defined terms, until no defined terms (except 'line') occur: $\phi$ is a supposition of $\psi$ relative to $\sigma$.

4   Must a line contain a supposition numeral? Explain.

5   Suppose $\phi$ is a sentence that occurs in line $\lambda$.

   (a)  Is it possible for $\phi$ to be a sentence *on* line $\lambda$?

   (b)  Under what conditions would $\phi$ *not* be a sentence on line $\lambda$?

   (c)  Give an example of a line $\lambda$ and a sentence $\phi$ such that $\phi$ is *not* a sentence on line $\lambda$.

6   Indicate whether each of the following is a line:

   (a)  $| \ 5 \ P \equiv Q$

   (b)  $\Lambda \ | \ 5 \ P \equiv Q$

   (c)  $1 \ | \ 1 \ \sim P \supset Q \qquad$ S

7   Indicate whether '$P$' is a sentence on the following lines:

   (a)  $1, 2, 3 \ | \ 5 \ P \equiv Q$

   (b)  $1 \ | \ 1 \ \sim P \supset Q$

8   Is it possible to have three lines $\lambda_1$, $\lambda_2$, and $\lambda_3$, such that they all occur in a string $\sigma$ of lines, $\lambda_1$ and $\lambda_2$ are supposition lines of $\lambda_3$ relative to $\sigma$, and the sentence on $\lambda_3$ is the sentence on $\lambda_1$? If so, give an example. If not, why not?

9   Is it possible to have three lines $\lambda_1$, $\lambda_2$, and $\lambda_3$, such that they all occur in a string $\sigma$ of lines, $\lambda_1$ is a supposition line of $\lambda_2$ and $\lambda_3$ relative to $\sigma$, and $\lambda_2$ is a supposition line of $\lambda_3$ relative to $\sigma$? If so, give an example. If not, why not?

---

**4. Propositional-Calculus Derivation.** Now we can specify exactly what it means to be a propositional-calculus derivation. Before defining this, however, three preliminary definitions must be stated. First we define what it means to be a propositional-calculus derivation of one step.

λ is a *propositional-calculus derivation* of 1 step if and only if λ is a line with '1' as both its line numeral and its sole supposition numeral [in this case, λ is an application of rule **S**].

For example, the following is a propositional-calculus derivation of one step:

$$1 \mid \quad 1 \quad Fa \ \& \ a = b$$

Next, we define what it means to expand a derivation by adding one more line to an existing derivation by applying a propositional-calculus rule.[4] This definition contains a separate clause for each propositional-calculus rule. Simple rules are grouped according to how many suppositions they require. Complex rules are treated individually.

σ is a *propositional-calculus expansion* by step $n$ of $σ_1$ if and only if σ consists of $σ_1$ followed by some line λ, the line numeral of λ is the numeral for $n$, and one of the following conditions (a)-(g) holds:[5]

(a)  the line numeral of λ is its sole supposition numeral [in this case, λ is an application of rule **S**];

(b)  there is a line $λ_1$ in $σ_1$, such that the supposition numerals of λ are all those which are supposition numerals of $λ_1$ and one of the following conditions (i)-(v) holds:

   (i)  for some sentence $φ$, the sentence on λ is ~~\*$φ$ and $φ$ is the sentence on $λ_1$ [in this case, λ is an application of rule **DNI**];

   (ii)  for some sentence $φ$, the sentence on λ is $φ$ and ~~\*$φ$ is the sentence on $λ_1$ [in this case, λ is an application of rule **DNE**];

   (iii)  for some sentences $φ$ and $ψ$, the sentence on λ is $φ$ and \*$φ$ & \*$ψ$ or \*$ψ$ & \*$φ$ is the sentence on $λ_1$ [in this case, λ is an application of rule **&E**];

   (iv)  for some sentences $φ$ and $ψ$, the sentence on λ is \*$φ$ v \*$ψ$ or \*$ψ$ v \*$φ$, and the sentence on $λ_1$ is $φ$ [in this case, λ is an application of rule **vI**];

---

[4] It is possible to define what it means to be a propositional-calculus derivation without resorting to propositional-calculus expansions; however, to do so would require complicating (lengthening) the definitions of an identity-calculus derivation and a quantificational-calculus derivation, so we have followed the simpler route.

[5] Note: (a)-(c) correspond to simple rules, while (d)-(g) correspond to complex rules. The difference lies in the way supposition numerals are calculated.

(v)  for some sentences $\phi$ and $\psi$, the sentence on $\lambda$ is $*\phi \supset *\psi$, and the sentence on $\lambda_1$ is either $*\phi \equiv *\psi$ or $*\psi \equiv *\phi$ [in this case, $\lambda$ is an application of rule $\equiv$**E**];

(c)  there are lines $\lambda_1$ and $\lambda_2$ in $\sigma_1$, such that the supposition numerals of $\lambda$ are all those which are supposition numerals of either $\lambda_1$ or $\lambda_2$ and one of the following conditions (i)-(iv) holds:

(i)  for some sentences $\phi$ and $\psi$, the sentence on $\lambda$ is $\psi$, $*\phi \supset *\psi$ is the sentence on $\lambda_1$, and $\phi$ is the sentence on $\lambda_2$ [in this case, $\lambda$ is an application of rule **MPP**];

(ii)  for some sentences $\phi$ and $\psi$, the sentence on $\lambda$ is $\sim *\phi$, $*\phi \supset *\psi$ is the sentence on $\lambda_1$, and $\sim *\psi$ is the sentence on $\lambda_2$ [in this case, $\lambda$ is an application of rule **MTT**];

(iii)  for some sentences $\phi$ and $\psi$, the sentence on $\lambda$ is $*\phi \& *\psi$, $\phi$ is the sentence on line $\lambda_1$, and $\psi$ is the sentence on line $\lambda_2$ [in this case, $\lambda$ is an application of rule **&I**];

(iv)  for some sentences $\phi$ and $\psi$, the sentence on $\lambda$ is $\psi$, $*\phi \lor *\psi$ is the sentence on line $\lambda_1$, and $\sim *\phi$ is the sentence on line $\lambda_2$ [in this case, $\lambda$ is an application of rule **DS**];

(d)  there are lines $\lambda_1$, $\lambda_2$, $\lambda_3$, $\lambda_4$, and $\lambda_5$ in $\sigma_1$ such that, for some sentences $\phi$, $\psi$, and $\chi$, the sentence on $\lambda_1$ is $*\phi \lor *\psi$, the sentence on $\lambda_2$ is $\phi$, the sentence on $\lambda_4$ is $\psi$, and $\chi$ is the sentence on $\lambda_3$, $\lambda_5$, and $\lambda$, the line numeral of $\lambda_2$ is its sole supposition numeral and is among the supposition numerals of $\lambda_3$, the line numeral of $\lambda_4$ is its sole supposition numeral and is among the supposition numerals of $\lambda_5$, and the supposition numerals of $\lambda$ are all those which are either among the supposition numerals of $\lambda_1$, or are among the supposition numerals of $\lambda_3$ but not the line numeral of $\lambda_2$, or are among the supposition numerals of $\lambda_5$ but not the line numeral of $\lambda_4$ [in this case, $\lambda$ is an application of the of **vE**];

(e)  there are lines $\lambda_1$ and $\lambda_2$ in $\sigma_1$ such that, for some sentences $\phi$ and $\psi$, $\phi$ is the sentence on $\lambda_1$ and $\psi$ is the sentence on $\lambda_2$, the line numeral of $\lambda_1$ is its sole supposition numeral and is among the supposition numerals of $\lambda_2$, $*\phi \supset *\psi$ is the sentence on line $\lambda$, and the supposition numerals of $\lambda$ are all those of $\lambda_2$ with the exception of the line numeral of $\lambda_1$ [in this case, $\lambda$ is an application of rule **CP**];

(f)  there are lines $\lambda_1$, $\lambda_2$, and $\lambda_3$ in $\sigma_1$ such that, for some sentences $\phi$ and $\psi$, $\sim *\phi$ is the sentence on $\lambda$, $\phi$ is the sentence on $\lambda_1$, $\psi$ is the sentence on $\lambda_2$, $\sim *\psi$ is the sentence on $\lambda_3$, the line numeral of $\lambda_1$ is its sole supposition numeral, the line numeral of $\lambda_1$ is among the supposition numerals of $\lambda_2$ or $\lambda_3$ (or both), and the supposition numerals of $\lambda$ are all those which are either those of $\lambda_2$ or of $\lambda_3$ but not the line numeral of $\lambda_1$ [in this case, $\lambda$ is an application of rule **RAA**];

(g)  there are lines $\lambda_1$, $\lambda_2$, $\lambda_3$, $\lambda_4$ in $\sigma_1$ such that, for some sentences $\phi$ and $\psi$, $*\phi \equiv *\psi$ is the sentence on $\lambda$, $\phi$ is the sentence on $\lambda_1$ and $\lambda_4$, $\psi$ is the sentence on $\lambda_2$ and $\lambda_3$, the line numerals of $\lambda_1$ and $\lambda_3$ are their sole supposition numerals, the line numeral of $\lambda_1$ is among the supposition numerals of $\lambda_2$, the line numeral of $\lambda_3$ is among the supposition numerals of $\lambda_4$, and the supposition numerals of $\lambda$ are all those which are either among the supposition numerals of $\lambda_2$ but not the line numeral of $\lambda_1$ or among the supposition numerals of $\lambda_4$ but not the line numeral of $\lambda_3$ [in this case, $\lambda$ is an application of rule $\equiv$**I**].

Consider a simple example. The following is a propositional-calculus expansion by step two of the one-step derivation displayed above:

$$
\begin{array}{c|cl}
1 & 1 & Fa \;\&\; a = b \\
1 & 2 & Fa
\end{array}
$$

This derivation can be expanded by step three, as follows:

$$
\begin{array}{c|cl}
1 & 1 & Fa \;\&\; a = b \\
1 & 2 & Fa \\
1 & 3 & Fa \;v\; \forall x{\sim}Fx
\end{array}
$$

and this derivation, in turn, can be expanded by step four, as follows:

$$
\begin{array}{c|cl}
1 & 1 & Fa \;\&\; a = b \\
1 & 2 & Fa \\
1 & 3 & Fa \;v\; \forall x{\sim}Fx \\
1 & 4 & a = b
\end{array}
$$

Using this lengthy definition of a propositional-calculus expansion by step $n$, it is easy to define a propositional-calculus derivation of more than one step.

If $\sigma_1$ is a propositional-calculus derivation of $n$ steps and $\sigma$ is a propositional-calculus expansion by step $n+1$ of $\sigma_1$, then $\sigma$ is a *propositional-calculus derivation* of $n+1$ steps.

So, the three previous derivations are propositional-calculus derivations of two, three, and four steps, respectively.

Having specified precisely what it means to be a propositional-calculus derivation of $n+1$ steps, it is straightforward to specify what a propositional-calculus derivation is in general.

> $\sigma$ is a *propositional-calculus derivation* of $\phi$ from $\Gamma$ iff for some $n$, $\sigma$ is a propositional-calculus derivation of $n$ steps such that there is a line $\lambda$ in $\sigma$ whose line numeral is the numeral for $n$, the sentence on $\lambda$ is $\phi$, and the members of $\Gamma$ are all those sentences which are sentences on supposition lines of $\lambda$ relative to $\sigma$.

So, the propositional-calculus derivation of four steps given above is a propositional-calculus derivation of '$a = b$' from $\{Fa \ \& \ a = b\}$.

We are finally in a position to define what it means for a formula to be derivable in the propositional calculus from some assumptions.

> $\phi$ is *derivable in the propositional calculus* from $\Gamma$ iff there is a propositional-calculus derivation of $\phi$ from $\Gamma$.

Note that to say *there is* a certain derivation does not imply that someone *has* constructed that derivation, nor does it imply that someone *will* construct that derivation, nor that someone *could* construct that derivation. All it means is that there is such a derivation to be constructed.[6]

It will be convenient to have an abbreviation for this last notion, so we introduce the following:

> $\Gamma \vdash_{PC} \phi$ iff $\phi$ is derivable in the propositional calculus from $\Gamma$.

**Exercises**

----

10 Define the notion: $\phi$ is a theorem of the propositional calculus. Notation: $\vdash_{PC} \phi$.

11 Which of the following are propositional-calculus derivations of 1 step? For each that is not, explain why not.

----

[6] This gives rise to a philosophical problem concerning logic: what sense can it make to say that derivations that nobody will ever construct *exist*? This problem emerges repeatedly in metalogic. For example, let $\phi$ be the longest formula that anyone will ever construct. There exist an infinite number of formulas that are longer than $\phi$: e.g., the negation of $\phi$, the negation of the negation of $\phi$, etc.

(a)  1 | 1

(b)  1 | 1   P

(c)  3 | 3   P

(d)  1 | 1   P          S

(e)  1 | 1   ∀xFx

(f)  1 | 1   ∀xFx v Gx

(g)  1 | 1 (Fa v Fb) ⊃ ∀xFx

12  Strictly speaking, annotations to the right of lines in a derivation, indi-
    cating which rule has been applied to which line(s), are not considered
    to be *part* of the derivation.

   (a) Describe which preliminary definitions would have to be altered *if*
       annotations to the right *were* considered to be a part of derivations.

   (b) Describe how the clauses in the definitions of propositional-calculus
       derivation of 1 step and propositional-calculus expansion by step *n*
       would have to be altered *if* annotations to the right *were* considered
       to be a part of derivations.

13  Rule vE is one of the "complex" rules. Modify clause (d) concerning vE
    so that it applies to CD (see the exercises of Chapter 8), which is a
    "simple" rule (i.e., {*ϕ v *ψ, *ϕ ⊃ *χ, *ψ ⊃ *χ} ⊢ χ).

14  It is possible to define other systems of logic by altering the clauses in
    the previous definitions. You need to add (or subtract) clauses concern-
    ing other rules of inference to the definition of propositional-calculus
    expansion.

   (a) Construct a clause that could be added to the definition of
       propositional-calculus expansion so that applications of the derived
       rule ~⊃ could be used in propositional-calculus derivations.

   (b) Do the same for the derived rule ~≡.

   (c) Do the same for the derived rule v⊃.

   (d) Do the same for the derived rule ⊃v.

   (e) Do the same for the derived rule DeM. (Hint: the clause should
       have four subclauses corresponding to the four forms of inference
       covered by the rule DeM.)

15  Suppose that σ is a propositional-calculus derivation of 1 step, and that
    the sentence on σ's single line is 'P'. Which rules could be applied to σ
    to form a propositional-calculus expansion by step 2 of σ?

16  Suppose that σ is a propositional-calculus derivation of 1 step, and that
    the sentence on σ's single line is 'P ⊃ Q'. Which rules could be applied
    to σ to form a propositional-calculus expansion by step 2 of σ?

17  Which rules could be used to form a propositional-calculus expansion by step 3 of a two-step propositional-calculus derivation?

18  Is it possible to have a propositional-calculus expansion by step 375 of a derivation? If so, how? If not, why not?

19  Is the following a propositional-calculus derivation? If so, explain why using the notion of a propositional-calculus expansion by step $n$. If not, explain why not?

$$
\begin{array}{c|cc}
1 & 1 & P \\
2 & 2 & Q \\
3 & 3 & R \\
\end{array}
$$

20  Is the above a propositional-calculus derivation of '$R$' from $\{P, Q, R\}$? Why or why not?

21  Prove the following claims:

(a)  For any sentence $\phi$ and sets $\Gamma$ and $\Delta$ of sentences, if $\Gamma \vdash_{PC} \phi$, then $\Gamma \cup \Delta \vdash_{PC} \phi$.

(b)  For any sentences $\phi$ and $\psi$ and sets $\Gamma$ and $\Delta$ of sentences, if $\Gamma \vdash_{PC} \phi$ and $\Delta \vdash_{PC} \psi$, then $\Gamma \cup \Delta \vdash_{PC} {}^*\phi$ & ${}^*\psi$.

(c)  Suppose that $\vdash_{PC} \phi$. For any sentence $\psi$ and set $\Gamma$ of sentences, if $\Gamma \vdash_{PC} \psi$, then $\Gamma \cup \Delta \vdash_{PC} {}^*\phi$ & ${}^*\psi$.

---

**5. Identity-Calculus Derivation.** The definition of what it means to be derivable in the identity calculus builds on the previous definitions. The bulk of the additional work required for giving the identity-calculus definition consists in describing the two identity rules. In addition, one must make sure that propositional-calculus rules can be applied in an identity-calculus derivation.

We begin by defining what it means to be an identity-calculus derivation of one step.

$\lambda$ is an *identity-calculus derivation* of 1 step if and only if one of the following conditions (a) or (b) holds:

(a)  $\lambda$ is a propositional-calculus derivation of 1 step;

(b)  $\lambda$ is a line with '1' as its line numeral, with no supposition numerals, and, for some individual constant $\beta$, $\beta = \beta$ is the sentence on $\lambda$ [in this case, $\lambda$ is an application of rule **SI**].

Next, we define what it means to expand a derivation by adding one more line to an existing derivation by applying an identity-calculus rule.

> $\sigma$ is an *identity-calculus expansion* by step $n$ of $\sigma_1$ if and only if $\sigma$ consists of $\sigma_1$ followed by some line $\lambda$, the line numeral of $\lambda$ is the numeral for $n$, and one of the following conditions (a) or (b) holds:
>
> (a)  $\lambda$ has no supposition numeral and, for some individual constant $\beta$, $\beta = \beta$ is the sentence on $\lambda$ [in this case, $\lambda$ is an application of rule **SI**];
>
> (b)  there are lines $\lambda_1$ and $\lambda_2$ in $\sigma_1$ such that, for some individual constants $\beta_1$ and $\beta_2$ and some sentence $\phi$ containing $\beta_1$, the sentence on line $\lambda_1$ is either $\beta_1 = \beta_2$ or $\beta_2 = \beta_1$, the sentence on $\lambda_2$ is $\phi$, the supposition numerals of $\lambda$ are all those which are supposition numerals of either $\lambda_1$ or $\lambda_2$, and the sentence on $\lambda$ is just like $\phi$ except that any number of occurrences of $\beta_1$ in $\phi$ have been replaced by occurrences of $\beta_2$ [in this case, $\lambda$ is an application of rule **L**];

Recall the four-step derivation from the previous section. The following is an identity-calculus expansion by step five of that derivation:

| 1 | | 1 | $Fa$ & $a = b$ |
|---|---|---|---|
| 1 | | 2 | $Fa$ |
| 1 | | 3 | $Fa \lor \forall x \sim Fx$ |
| 1 | | 4 | $a = b$ |
| 1 | | 5 | $Fb \lor \forall x \sim Fx$ |

We can now define an identity-calculus derivation of more than one step.

> If $\sigma_1$ is an identity-calculus derivation of $n$ steps and $\sigma$ is either a propositional-calculus expansion by step $n+1$ of $\sigma_1$ or an identity-calculus expansion by step $n+1$ of $\sigma_1$, then $\sigma$ is an *identity-calculus derivation* of $n+1$ steps.

So, the identity-calculus expansion by step five given above is an identity-calculus derivation of five steps.

We can now define an identity-calculus derivation in general.

> $\sigma$ is an *identity-calculus derivation* of $\phi$ from $\Gamma$ iff for some $n$, $\sigma$ is an identity-calculus derivation of $n$ steps such that there is a line $\lambda$ in $\sigma$ whose line numeral is the numeral for $n$, the sentence on $\lambda$ is $\phi$, and the members of $\Gamma$ are all those sentences which are sentences on supposition lines of $\lambda$ relative to $\sigma$.

So, the five-step derivation given above is an identity-calculus derivation of '$Fb$ v $\forall x \sim Fx$' from $\{Fa$ & $a = b\}$.

Finally, as before, we can define what it means for a sentence to be derivable in the identity calculus from some assumptions.

> $\phi$ is *derivable in the identity calculus* from $\Gamma$ iff there exists an identity-calculus derivation of $\phi$ from $\Gamma$.

Again, it will be convenient to have a shorthand notation for this last notion, so we introduce the following definition:

> $\Gamma \vdash_{IC} \phi$ iff $\phi$ is derivable in the identity calculus from $\Gamma$.

**Exercises**

---

22  Define the phrase: $\phi$ is a theorem of the identity calculus. Notation: $\vdash_{IC} \phi$.

23  Explain why '$a = a$' is a theorem of the identity calculus.

24  Which of the following are identity-calculus derivations of 1 step? For each line that is not, explain why not.

(a)  $1 \mid 1 \ \ \phi$

(b)  $1 \mid 2 \ \ a = a$

(c)  $1 \mid 1 \ \ a = b$

(d)  $1 \mid 1 \ \ \forall x \forall y Lxy$

(e)  $\Lambda \mid 1 \ \ P \equiv P$

(f)  $\Lambda \mid 1 \ \ b = b$

25  Is it possible for a propositional-calculus derivation of five steps to be an identity-calculus derivation of five steps?  Explain.

26  Is it possible for a propositional-calculus expansion by step 5 to be an identity-calculus expansion by step 5?  Explain.

27  Suppose that $\sigma$ is an identity-calculus derivation of $n$ steps, and that $\sigma$ is *not* a propositional-calculus derivation of $n$ steps.  Is it possible to form a propositional-calculus expansion by step $n+1$ of $\sigma$?

---

**6.  Quantificational-Calculus Derivation.**  To define a derivation in the quantificational calculus, we need to modify the definition of a derivation in the identity calculus by adding clauses covering the quantifier rules.

We must also ensure that propositional-calculus rules and identity-calculus rules can be used in quantificational-calculus derivations.

> $\sigma$ is a *quantificational-calculus derivation* of 1 step if and only if one of the following two conditions (a) or (b) holds:

> (a)   $\sigma$ is a propositional-calculus derivation of 1 step;[7]

> (b)   $\sigma$ is an identity-calculus derivation of 1 step.

> $\sigma$ is a *quantificational-calculus expansion* by step $n$ of $\sigma_1$ if and only if $\sigma$ consists of $\sigma_1$ followed by some line $\lambda$, the line numeral of $\lambda$ is the numeral for $n$, and one of the following conditions (a)-(d) holds:

> (a)   there is a line $\lambda_1$ in $\sigma_1$ such that, for some individual variable $\alpha$, some individual constant $\beta$, and some formula $\phi$, $\forall\alpha^*\phi$ is the sentence on $\lambda_1$, $\phi^{\alpha/\beta}$ is the sentence on $\lambda$, and the supposition numerals of $\lambda$ are all those of $\lambda_1$ [in this case, $\lambda$ is an application of rule $\forall$E];

> (b)   there is a line $\lambda_1$ in $\sigma_1$ such that, for some individual variable $\alpha$, some individual constant $\beta$, and some formula $\phi$, $\phi^{\alpha/\beta}$ is the sentence on $\lambda_1$, $\exists\alpha^*\phi$ is the sentence on $\lambda$, and the supposition numerals of $\lambda$ are all those of $\lambda_1$ [in this case, $\lambda$ is an application of rule $\exists$I];

> (c)   there is a line $\lambda_1$ in $\sigma_1$ such that, for some individual variable $\alpha$, some individual constant $\beta$, and some formula $\phi$, $\phi^{\alpha/\beta}$ is the sentence on $\lambda_1$, $\forall\alpha^*\phi$ is the sentence on $\lambda$, $\beta$ occurs in no supposition line of line $\lambda_1$ relative to $\sigma_1$, and the supposition numerals of $\lambda$ are all those of $\lambda_1$ [in this case, $\lambda$ is an application of rule $\forall$I];

> (d)   there are lines $\lambda_1$, $\lambda_2$, $\lambda_3$, in $\sigma_1$ such that, for some individual variable $\alpha$, some individual constant $\beta$, and some formula $\phi$, the formula $\exists\alpha^*\phi$ is the sentence on $\lambda_1$, $\phi^{\alpha/\beta}$ is the sentence on $\lambda_2$, $\psi$ is the sentence on $\lambda_3$, $\psi$ is the sentence on $\lambda$, the line numeral of $\lambda_2$ is its sole supposition numeral, $\beta$ occurs neither in $\phi$, $\psi$, nor in any supposition line of $\lambda_3$ relative to $\sigma_1$ other than $\lambda_2$, and the supposition numerals of $\lambda$ are all those which are supposition numerals of either $\lambda_1$ or $\lambda_3$ but not the line numeral of $\lambda_2$ [in this case, $\lambda$ is an application of rule $\exists$E].

Recall the five-step derivation from the previous section. The following is a quantificational-calculus expansion by step six of that derivation:

---

[7] Strictly speaking, this clause is redundant because a propositional-calculus derivation of 1 step is an identity-calculus derivation of 1 step.

| 1 | 1 | $Fa$ & $a = b$ |
|---|---|---|
| 1 | 2 | $Fa$ |
| 1 | 3 | $Fa$ v $\forall x{\sim}Fx$ |
| 1 | 4 | $a = b$ |
| 1 | 5 | $Fb$ v $\forall x{\sim}Fx$ |
| 1 | 6 | $\exists y(Fy$ v $\forall x{\sim}Fx)$ |

We can now define a quantificational-calculus derivation of any length.

> If $\sigma_1$ is a quantificational-calculus derivation of $n$ steps, and $\sigma$ is either a propositional-calculus expansion by step $n+1$ of $\sigma_1$, or an identity-calculus expansion by step $n+1$ of $\sigma_1$, or a quantificational-calculus expansion by step $n+1$ of $\sigma_1$, then $\sigma$ is a *quantificational-calculus derivation* of $n+1$ steps.

Now we can define a quantificational-calculus derivation in general:

> $\sigma$ is a *quantificational-calculus derivation* of $\phi$ from $\Gamma$ iff for some $n$, $\sigma$ is a quantificational-calculus derivation of $n$ steps such that there is a line $\lambda$ in $\sigma$ whose line numeral is the numeral for $n$, the sentence on $\lambda$ is $\phi$, and the members of $\Gamma$ are all those sentences which are sentences on supposition lines of $\lambda$ relative to $\sigma$.

So, the six-step derivation above is a quantificational-calculus derivation of '$\exists y(Fy$ v $\forall x{\sim}Fx)$' from $\{Fa$ & $a = b\}$.

We can define what it means for a sentence to be derivable in the quantificational calculus from some assumptions just as we did with the propositional calculus and the identity calculus.

> $\phi$ is *derivable in the quantificational calculus* from $\Gamma$ iff there exists a quantificational-calculus derivation of $\phi$ from $\Gamma$.

We also introduce a shorthand notation for this last notion:

> $\Gamma \vdash_{QC} \phi$ iff $\phi$ is derivable in the quantificational calculus from $\Gamma$.

**Exercises**

---

28  Define the phrase: $\phi$ is a theorem of the quantificational calculus. Notation: $\vdash_{QC} \phi$.

29  Is it possible for there to be a derivation that is a propositional-calculus derivation of 1 step, an identity-calculus derivation of 1 step, and a

quantificational-calculus derivation of 1 step? If it is possible, give an example. If it is not possible, explain why not.

30  Is it possible for there to be a derivation that is an identity-calculus derivation of 1 step and a quantificational-calculus derivation of 1 step but not a propositional-calculus derivation of 1 step? If it is possible, give an example. If it is not possible, explain why not.

31  Is it possible for there to be a derivation that is a quantificational-calculus derivation of 1 step but is neither a propositional-calculus derivation of 1 step nor an identity-calculus derivation of 1 step? If it is possible, give an example. If it is not possible, explain why not.

32  Which rules of inference can be used to form a quantificational-calculus derivation of 1 step?

33  Is it possible for a propositional-calculus derivation to be a quantificational-calculus derivation? Explain.

34  Is *every* identity-calculus derivation a quantificational-calculus derivation?

35  Expand the quantificational calculus so that it includes the rules of inference for sentences with functors described in Chapter 23. End with a definition of: $\sigma$ is a *functor-calculus* derivation of $\phi$ from $\Gamma$.

36  Expand the quantificational calculus so that it includes the rules of inference for sentences containing definite descriptions described in Chapter 25. End with a definition of: $\sigma$ is a *definite-description-calculus* derivation of $\phi$ from $\Gamma$.

37  How would the quantificational calculus have to be modified so that it is a system of free logic? (Recall Option IV for handling vacuous logical subjects.)

# Selected Answers

## Chapter 3

2. (a) The conclusion does follow from the premises. (b) The first premise is true; since there are only 52 weeks in a year, it is impossible for more than 53 different people to have birthdays all in different weeks. The second premise is probably true; its truth-value, of course, varies from year to year. The conclusion is, once again, probably true.

## Chapter 4

1(a). This is a conditional. The antecedent is the statement 'Jones studies' and the consequent is the statement 'Smith studies'. Both of these are non-molecular.

## Chapter 5

2(b). We can take the following phrase-book:

$B$ : Bates will pass his programming assignment
$K$ : Bates uses the famed "Knuth procedure" to write up the answer
$T$ : The T.A. will bother to read Bates' answer

In accordance with this phrase-book, we get the following representation of the logical form:

$$B \equiv K$$
$$(K \supset \sim T) \mathbin{\&} (\sim T \supset B)$$
$$B \supset \sim T$$

The argument as thus symbolized is in fact valid, as we shall show below in the answers to Chapter 13.

## Chapter 6

1(d).

| | | |
|---|---|---|
| 1 | $P \mathrel{\&} {\sim}Q$ | |
| 2 | $P \supset ({\sim}Q \supset R)$ | |
| 3 | $P$ | 1 &E |
| 4 | ${\sim}Q$ | 1 &E |
| 5 | ${\sim}Q \supset R$ | 2,3 MPP |
| 6 | $R$ | 4,5 MPP |

## Chapter 7

1(b).

| | | | |
|---|---|---|---|
| 1 | 1 | ${\sim}{\sim}Q \supset P$ | S |
| 2 | 2 | ${\sim}P$ | S |
| 1,2 | 3 | ${\sim}{\sim}{\sim}Q$ | 1,2 MTT |
| 1,2 | 4 | ${\sim}Q$ | 3 DNE |

## Chapter 8

3(c).

| | | | |
|---|---|---|---|
| 1 | 1 | $P \mathbin{v} (Q \mathbin{v} R)$ | S |
| 2 | 2 | $P \supset S$ | S |
| 3 | 3 | $Q \supset S$ | S |
| 4 | 4 | $R \supset S$ | S |
| 5 | 5 | $Q \mathbin{v} R$ | S (for CP) |
| 3,4,5 | 6 | $S$ | 3,4,5 CD |
| 3,4 | 7 | $(Q \mathbin{v} R) \supset S$ | 5,6 CP |
| 1,2,3,4 | 8 | $S$ | 1,2,7 CD |

## Chapter 9

1(b).

| | | | |
|---|---|---|---|
| 1 | 1 | ${\sim}P \supset P$ | S |
| 2 | 2 | ${\sim}P$ | S (for RAA) |
| 1,2 | 3 | $P$ | 1,2 MPP |
| 1 | 4 | ${\sim}{\sim}P$ | 2,2,3 RAA |
| 1 | 5 | $P$ | 4 DNE |

## Chapter 10

6.

| | | | |
|---|---|---|---|
| 1 | 1 | ~P | S |
| 2 | 2 | P v Q | S |
| 3 | 3 | P | S (for vE) |
| 4 | 4 | ~Q | S (for RAA) |
| 3,4 | 5 | P & ~Q | 3,4 &I |
| 3,4 | 6 | P | 5 &E |
| 1,3 | 7 | ~~Q | 4,1,6 RAA |
| 1,3 | 8 | Q | 7 DNE |
| 9 | 9 | Q | S (for vE) |
| 1,2 | 10 | Q | 2,3,8,9,9 vE |

8.

| | | | |
|---|---|---|---|
| 1 | 1 | ~(P ≡ Q) | S |
| 1 | 2 | P ≡ ~Q | 1 ~≡ |
| 1 | 3 | P ⊃ ~Q | 2 ≡E |
| 1 | 4 | ~Q ⊃ P | 2 ≡E |
| 5 | 5 | ~P | S (for ≡I) |
| 1,5 | 6 | ~~Q | 4,5 MTT |
| 1,5 | 7 | Q | 6 DNE |
| 8 | 8 | Q | S (for ≡I) |
| 8 | 9 | ~~Q | 8 DNI |
| 1,8 | 10 | ~P | 9,3 MTT |
| 1 | 11 | ~P ≡ Q | 5,7,8,10 ≡I |

## Chapter 11

2(f).

| | | |
|---|---|---|
| P | — | F |
| Q | — | T |
| R | — | T |
| S | — | T |

There are also other truth-value assignments that make all the premises true and the conclusion false.

**Chapter 12**

4(h).

$$
\begin{array}{ccc}
P & - & F \\
Q & - & F \\
R & - & F
\end{array}
$$

In this case, there are no other truth-value assignments that make all the premises true and the conclusion false.

**Chapter 13**

11(b). The argument is *valid*. The following derivation shows this:

| | | | |
|---|---|---|---|
| 1 | 1 | $B \equiv K$ | S |
| 2 | 2 | $(K \supset {\sim}T) \, \& \, ({\sim}T \supset B)$ | S |
| 3 | 3 | $B$ | S (for CP) |
| 1 | 4 | $B \supset K$ | 1 $\equiv$E |
| 1,3 | 5 | $K$ | 3,4 MPP |
| 1,2,3 | 6 | $K \supset {\sim}T$ | 2 &E |
| 1,2,3 | 7 | ${\sim}T$ | 5,6 MPP |
| 1,2 | 8 | $B \supset {\sim}T$ | 3,7 CP |

13. No. There are plenty of examples of valid arguments which have consistent premises. For instance, the argument considered in Exercise 10(b) above has consistent premises and is valid.

15. Suppose that a statement is logically false. Hence there is no possible situation in which it is true. Hence there is no possible situation in which it is true *and* some other statement is true. So it is inconsistent with that statement. Conversely, suppose that a given statement is inconsistent with every statement. Then it is inconsistent with itself. So there is no possible situation in which it is true; so it is logically false.

## Chapter 15

2(k).

| | | | |
|---|---|---|---|
| 1 | 1 | $a = b$ | S (for CP) |
| 2 | 2 | $b \neq c$ | S (for CP) |
| 3 | 3 | $c = a$ | S (for RAA) |
| 1,3 | 4 | $c = b$ | 1,3 L |
| 1,3 | 5 | $b = c$ | 4,4 L |
| 1,2 | 6 | $c \neq a$ | 3,2,5 RAA |
| 1 | 7 | $b \neq c \supset c \neq a$ | 2,6 CP |
| $\Lambda$ | 8 | $a = b \supset (b \neq c \supset c \neq a)$ | 1,7 CP |

## Chapter 18

3(a).
$$\exists x((Gx \ \& \ \forall y(By \supset \exists zGxzy)) \ \& \ Nx)$$

3(b).
$$\forall x(Gx \supset (\forall y(By \supset \exists zGxzy) \supset Nx))$$
$$\forall x((Gx \ \& \ \forall y(By \supset \exists zGxzy)) \supset Nx)$$

3(c).
$$\exists x((Gx \ \& \ \exists y(By \ \& \ \exists zGxzy)) \ \& \ Nx)$$

3(d).
$$\forall x(Gx \supset (\exists y(By \ \& \ \exists zGxzy) \supset Nx))$$
$$\forall x((Gx \ \& \ \exists y(By \ \& \ \exists zGxzy)) \supset Nx)$$

3(e).
$$\forall x(Gx \supset (\forall y(By \supset \exists zGxzy) \supset (\exists u(Bu \ \& \ \forall v(Gv \supset \exists wGuwv)) \ \& \ Lxu)))$$
$$\forall x((Gx \ \& \ \forall y(By \supset \exists zGxzy)) \supset \exists u((Bu \ \& \ \forall v(Gv \supset \exists wGuwv)) \ \& \ Lxu))$$

3(f).
$$\exists x(Gx \ \& \ (\exists y((By \ \& \ Lyx) \ \& \ Lxy) \ \& \ Hx))$$

3(g).
$$\forall x(Gx \supset (\exists y((By \ \& \ Lyx) \ \& \ Lxy) \supset Hx))$$
$$\forall x((Gx \ \& \ \exists y((By \ \& \ Lyx) \ \& \ Lxy)) \supset Hx)$$

## Chapter 19

1. All odd-numbered formulas are true, with the following exceptions: (9), (15). Similarly, all even-numbered formulas are false, with the following exceptions: (10), (14), (18), (24).

## Chapter 20

3(g).

| | | | |
|---|---|---|---|
| 1 | 1 | $\forall u \forall v Fuv$ | S |
| 2 | 2 | $\forall u \forall v (Fuv \supset Guv)$ | S |
| 1 | 3 | $\forall v Fav$ | 1 $\forall$E |
| 1 | 4 | $Faa$ | 3 $\forall$E |
| 2 | 5 | $\forall v (Fav \supset Gav)$ | 2 $\forall$E |
| 2 | 6 | $Faa \supset Gaa$ | 5 $\forall$E |
| 1,2 | 7 | $Gaa$ | 4,6 MPP |
| 1,2 | 8 | $Faa \& Gaa$ | 4,7 &I |
| 1,2 | 9 | $\exists v (Faa \& Gav)$ | 8 $\exists$I |
| 1,2 | 10 | $\exists u \exists v (Fuu \& Guv)$ | 9 $\exists$I |

## Chapter 23

2. Let us adopt the following phrase-book:

$$\forall\exists \ :: \quad \textcircled{1} \text{ is a natural number}$$

$$E : \quad \textcircled{1} \text{ is even}$$
$$O : \quad \textcircled{1} \text{ is odd}$$

$$s^2 : \quad \text{the sum of } \textcircled{1} \text{ and } \textcircled{2}$$
$$p^2 : \quad \text{the product of } \textcircled{1} \text{ and } \textcircled{2}$$
$$q^1 : \quad \text{the square of } \textcircled{1}$$

We may then represent these statements as follows:

2(a). If a number is odd, then its square is odd.

$$\forall x (Ox \supset Oq^1x)$$

2(b). The sum of any two odd numbers is even.

$$\forall x \forall y ((Ox \& Oy) \supset Es^2xy)$$

2(c). The sum of the squares of two odd numbers is even.

$$\forall x \forall y ((Ox \& Oy) \supset Es^2q^1xq^1y)$$

2(d). The sum of the three pairwise products of any three odd numbers is not even.

$$\forall x \forall y \forall z (((Ox \& Oy) \& Oz) \supset {\sim}Es^2s^2p^2xyp^2yzp^2xz)$$

# Index